A PEOPLE WITHOUT A STATE

A PEOPLE WITHOUT A STATE

*The Kurds from the Rise of Islam
to the Dawn of Nationalism*

MICHAEL EPPEL

UNIVERSITY OF TEXAS PRESS   Austin

Requests for permission to reproduce material from this work should be sent to:
  Permissions
  University of Texas Press
  PO Box 7819
  Austin, TX 78713-7819
  http://utpress.utexas.edu/index.php/rp-form

♾ The paper used in this book meets the minimum requirements of
ANSI/NISO Z39.48-1992 (R1997) (Permanence of Paper).

LIBRARY OF CONGRESS CATALOGING-IN-PUBLICATION DATA

Names: Eppel, Michael, 1947– author.
Title: A people without a state : the Kurds from the rise of Islam to the dawn of
  nationalism / Michael Eppel.
Description: First edition. Austin : University of Texas Press, 2016. Includes
  bibliographical references and index.
Identifiers: LCCN 2015039589
   ISBN 978-1-4773-0911-7 (cloth : alk. paper)
   ISBN 978-1-4773-1107-3 (pbk : alk. paper)
   ISBN 978-1-4773-0912-4 (library e-book)
   ISBN 978-1-4773-0913-1 (non-library e-book)
Subjects: LCSH: Kurds—History. Kurdistan—History. Nationalism—Kurdistan.
  Kurdistan—Politics and government. Kurds—Ethnic identity. Kurds—Middle
  East—History.
Classification: LCC DS59.K86 E67 2016
   DDC 956.6/7—dc23
   LC record available at http://lccn.loc.gov/2015039589

doi:10.7560/309117

CONTENTS

ACKNOWLEDGMENTS

I AM VERY GRATEFUL TO many people who helped and advised me during the years of writing this book. Of course, all the opinions and errors are my sole responsibility.

I want to thank Ofra Bengio and Amatzia Baram for their valuable advice and encouragement. My short but meaningful meetings with Robert Olson, Michael Gunter, and Amir Hassanpour motivated and inspired me to learn more about Kurdish history and modern-day Kurdistan and to research the issues that became the focus of this book. My gratitude goes to many people for their advice, opinions, and answers to my questions: Butrus Abu Manne, Yuval Ben-Bassat, Joyce Blau, Amnon Cohen, Noga Efrati, Kais Firro, Yehoshua Frenkel, Avner Giladi, Tetyana Karpyuk, Sherko Kirmanj, Uri Kupferschmitd, David Kushnir, Meir Litvak, Liora Lukitz, Ceng Sagnic, Soli Shahvar, Uri Simonsohn, Ehud Toledano, Mahmud Yazbak, Fruma Zachs, and Ronen Zeidel. I am also grateful to Charles G. McDonald and Hussein Tahiri, whose remarks helped me to improve the book.

I have the pleasant duty of thanking Yardena Levinberg of the University of Haifa library, as well as the staff of the library of Oranim College of Education in Tivon, Israel. I want to mention the librarians of the University of Minnesota library, who were very helpful in the first stages of preparing the research. I wish to thank Joyce Blau and the staff of the library of the Institut Kurde de Paris for their kind assistance. Thanks to Marina Bugaev and Sigal Ben Yair from the University of Haifa, who prepared the maps in this book.

Sharon Neeman and Virginia Myers deserve special thanks for the English editing of the book. Copyeditor Cynthia Buck did a great job, and I am grateful to everyone at the University of Texas Press, particularly Senior Editor Jim Burr and Managing Editor Robert Kimzey.

I owe a very special debt to my sons, Amir, Sagi, and Shai, and to my wife, Tali, for their patience, advice, and moral encouragement throughout the long process of studying Kurdish history and writing this book.

A NOTE ON TRANSLITERATION

THE PERSONAL NAMES AND TERMS in this book are written in different styles in different languages: Arabic, Ottoman Turkish, modern Turkish (Latin script), Persian, and Kurdish (Sorani and Kurmanji dialects). The usual form in modern Turkish is not always consistent with the Arabic origins of the words and with the Kurdish dialects. To minimize inconsistencies, in most cases I have chosen to place the Arabic transliteration in parentheses, especially in the chapters dealing with the period before the nineteenth century—for example, "Celebi/Chelebi or Cezire/Chezire (al-Jazira)." The names of Ottoman and Turkish personalities since the nineteenth century are in simplified Turkish transliteration. For example, "Abdulhamid" instead of "'Abd al-Hamid," with the latter placed in parentheses.

A PEOPLE WITHOUT A STATE

THE ORIGINS OF THE KURDS—
MYTHS, HISTORY, AND MODERN POLITICS

FROM ANCIENT TIMES, the large mountainous land mass of Mesopotamia to the north and northeast of the Tigris and Euphrates Valleys was home to a mainly pastoral tribal population whose dialects were related to the northwestern Iranian group of dialects. Over many centuries, the people of this region were caught up in the rivalries and struggles between the strong neighboring powers centered in Mesopotamia, the Iranian plateau, and Anatolia. Although the Kurds have been mentioned in texts since antiquity and throughout the Islamic era, they were always overshadowed by stronger, more cohesive states that enjoyed written cultures. These tribal populations were denoted by signifiers with similar sounds: *Qurtie, Curti, Cartie, Kardu, Karduchi, Kar-da*, and the like. The ethnic origin of the Kurds may well derive from western Iranian populations who arrived at the Zagros and Taurus Mountains from the east and mingled with the indigenous people.[1] Debates on the meaning (especially philological) of the signifier *Kurd* and the relationship between modern Kurdish nationalism and the ancient population of the mountains of Kurdistan have continued among scholars for more than one hundred years.[2]

In Kurdistan, familial, tribal, local, and religious affiliations were the dominant ways in which individuals identified themselves and found solidarity with their group. The signifying term *kurd*, the collective *akrad*, and similar words appear to have been sociologically significant and to have referred to members of pastoral and at least partially nomadic mountain tribes that were characterized by belligerence and the absence of a central government and were a threat to the rural and urban settled populations in adjacent areas. The word *kurd*, or *kord*, originally meant "shepherd," so that it had a social significance as well as a vague socioethnic connotation.[3] If we replace the ecological characteristic "mountainous" with the term "desert," the sociological and cultural characteristics are also appropriate to the definition of "Bedouin" or "Arab."

National movements and nations in the modern sense began to arise in western Europe during the nineteenth century with the onset of modernization, bringing new modes of production and social relations, and especially the spread of capitalism and print capitalism and the concomitant decline of religion and the Church, accompanied by transformations of discourse. Under some conditions, however, collective identities have appeared since ancient times, even if they have not displayed modern national characteristics. In daily life and in social and political activities, the central role in these communities is taken by tribal, familial, regional, or class-related identities, loyalties, and interests. At times, however, broader collective identities—social, cultural, religious, and ethnic-linguistic—have appeared and come to play a role in social discourse and even in political practice.

Although, in the modern sense, no nations or national movements could exist in premodern times, populations were nevertheless culturally and ethnically distinctive and marked by collective identities. Modern national movements gave political significance to these distinctions. That cultural distinctiveness and identity, on the one hand, must be correlated with statehood, on the other, is a concept of modern nationalism. Socioeconomic contrasts between strata, social classes, and groups—such as between pastoral tribes and settled populations—have sometimes developed into cultural identities on which proto-national distinctions and signifiers and, in the modern era, nation-building have been based.

The collective signifiers *kurd* and *akrad* among populations in the Fertile Crescent and the mountains to the north and east and the Kurdish distinctiveness and flashes of Kurdish collective awareness in poetry, medieval history books, and historical memory allow us to examine a continuous history of the speakers of Kurdish dialects who lived in Kurdistan. As with other modern national movements, the narrative of Kurdish history arose from the Kurdish national movement. It did not, however, develop out of thin air. Rather, it was based in the collective signifiers *kurd* and *akrad*; in Kurdish ethnic, linguistic, and social distinctiveness; in sporadic signs of yearning for Kurdish statehood; and in fragments of collective history and myths. Admittedly, tribal and religious identities were stronger and more defined than Kurdish distinctiveness, which was not a focus of supratribal loyalty or identification and, generally speaking, could not serve as a point of origin for any demand for a Kurdish state. Nonetheless, the very existence of Kurdish distinctiveness makes it easier to perceive the continuity in a history that led, under modern conditions, to the growth of a national movement and a national consciousness.

There was no Kurdish nation as such before the twentieth century, when the Kurdish national movement gave the concept of *Kurdayeti* ("Kurdishness") its national significance. However, the "Kurds," whatever the meaning of the term, had long been distinctive in popular discourse and social praxis. Sometimes the consciousness of Kurdish identity was evident among individuals and social groups, and *kurd* and *akrad* acquired social and political meaning. For example, in the sixteenth and seventeenth centuries, Kurdish intellectuals expressed in literature and poetry a collective identity and a longing for the Kurdish king, acknowledged "Kurdishness," and made ethno-political references to Kurds as a community in the context of Iran and the Ottoman Empire.

The purpose of this book is to examine Kurdish distinctiveness and identity from the rise of Islam to the first development of the modern Kurdish national movement after World War I. An additional objective is to describe the historical, social, and political conditions in Kurdistan and Kurdistani society in which the Kurds' ethno-linguistic distinctiveness was manifested, the modern Kurdish national movement emerged, and the developments that might have led to a Kurdish state in the early twentieth century began but then were halted. It is not always possible to determine the exact point in history when certain processes began. Thus, the beginning of the Kurdish national movement may remain disputed by historians, according to their evaluations of nationalism and national consciousness.

I have opted for a flexible approach that reflects historical reality. I describe the geographic boundaries of Kurdistan according to the distribution of Kurdish dialect–speaking groups or of those designated in their day, by themselves or others, as *akrad* without giving that signifier its modern national significance. The common element is the connection of various areas, both over the centuries and in modern times, to a distinctive identity and to the signifiers *Kurd, akrad*, and "Kurdistan."

In tracing the myth and history of the Kurds, Emir Sharaf Khan al-Bitlisi (Bidlisi), in his book *Sharafnama*, or *The History of the Kurdish Nation*, published in 1595, describes the Kurdish dynasty and cites a blood-curdling myth about the origin of the Kurds. A cruel Persian (Iranian) ruler by the name of Dahhak became ill and two snakes grew out of his arms. To ease his pain, Satan advised Dahhak to feed the snakes with two human brains each day. To meet that need, two young men were sacrificed daily. The official responsible for doing this, however, had pity on the young men and sought to save at least some of them. He accordingly killed only one young man and mixed his brain with that of a sheep. He released the second man and allowed him to escape to the mountains. The descendants of the young man who evaded Dahhak's wrath were the Kurds. Bitlisi also alludes to another popular myth, according to which the Kurds were the descendants of King Solomon's mistresses, who mated with devils after his death.[4]

The Kurdish scholar Mehrdad Izady, who favors a Kurdish nationalist approach, has chosen to consider anyone who lived in Kurdistan after the Neolithic era as belonging to the forebears of the Kurds. The populations of Kurdistan—the Kurds and the Armenians—are the descendants of ancient residents of the area who mingled with the waves of conquerors and immigrants who settled there and became part of the population, thereby affecting the development of the Kurdish language. Some of them were denoted by the term *kurd*, which signified the distinctive proto-national (linguistic, sociological, and ethnic) Kurdish identity whose dominant social pattern was one of divisiveness and tribalism.

The concept of the land of Kar-da, near Lake Van, appears as early as the third century BC in Sumerian manuscripts. The Assyrian king Tiglath-Pileser I (1114–1076 BC) fought in the mountains of Kurdistan against the local inhabitants, who were referred to as Qurtie.[5] More unequivocal references to Kurdish tribes may be found in the period preceding Alexander of Macedonia. In 401 BC, 10,000 Greek mercenaries, while passing through the territory later known as Kurdistan on their way back from Iran to Greece, fought against tribes that were described as Carduchians. Xenophon, the ancient Greek philosopher, author, and soldier who was one of the officers in charge of the Greek soldiers and who wrote about their journey, mentions the skirmishes and battles with the Carduchian tribes in his book *Anabasis*.[6] According to Xenophon, the Carduchian country was located south of Armenia and north of the river valleys of Babylon (Mesopotamia), east of the Tigris, and north of its tributary flowing from the east, the Great Zab River.

Xenophon describes the Carduchians as belligerent warriors who were subordinate to neither the rulers of Iran nor the kings of Armenia.[7] A previous attempt by the army of the king of Iran to conquer the area had failed; according to Xenophon, the royal army was utterly defeated. The Carduchians fought the Greeks through a form of guerrilla warfare: staging hit-and-run attacks, blocking the narrow mountain passes, and attacking the rearguard and mounting flank attacks were all tactics characteristic of mountain tribes.

The similarity between the signifiers *Carduchians* and *Kurds* and the geographic location of the Carduchian country have been the bases for the identification of Carduchians as ancient Kurds by scholars writing about the origin of the Kurds since the early nineteenth century. Other scholars have considered the Kurds to be descendants of the ancient Medes. According to this theory, the forebears of the Kurds were those ancient Medes who remained in the mountains of Kurdistan and did not undergo "Iranization" during the time when the Median elite was dominant in Iran under Cyrus, who was himself half-Median, the son of a Median princess. Still other scholars, such as D. N. MacKenzie, primarily on the grounds of a philological analysis, have expressed doubts as to the identification of the Carduchians as forebears of the Kurds and reject the connection between the Kurds and the Medes.[8] MacKenzie, who studied the linguistic relationships between the Kurdish dialects and Iranian languages, was led by his philological analysis to emphasize the connection between the Kurds and the Cyrtii (Kurti), who are mentioned in writings by the Greek historians Polybius and Strabo.[9] An Italian monk and preacher, Riccoldo da Montecroce (1243–1320), who visited Kurdistan in the thirteenth century, also used the signifier *Curti* for the Kurds and briefly discussed their language in his book.[10]

Kurdistan was a source for the militant tribal forces that, from time to time, took over Iran or the Mesopotamian valleys, established dynasties and kingdoms there, and integrated into the local cultures. According to several sources, the Parthian Empire was established by Kurds. The Sassanid dynasty in Iran—the last dynasty before the rise of Islam—was described by its rivals, the Parthians, as Kurdish. They recorded that the first Sassanid ruler, Ardashir I, was "a Kurd, born to the Kurds, raised in the tent of the Kurds."[11] Forced to contend with the Median Kurds, who were apparently vassals of the Parthians, Ardashir I, who conquered the Parthian Empire and established the rule of the Sassanids in the year AD 224, formed a coalition of Kurdish forces from the areas of Hakkari, Shahrizur, and Barazan. The Kurdish dynasties of the emirs of Ardalan and the emirs of Bitlis (Bidlis) (see chapter 2 for their later activity) claimed a blood relationship with the ancient Iranian Sassanid dynasty.[12]

According to the Kurdish national narrative as presented by members of the Bedir Khan family, the Parthians were assimilated into the Persians and Kurds after their state was wiped out by the Sassanids. Thus, the Parthians constituted an additional stratum in the Kurdish population. In the modern era, however, the epic quality of the Parthians and the Medes as forebears of the Kurds became part of the narrative of the modern Kurdish national movement.[13]

A discussion of the origin of the signifier *Kurd* and the historic and mythological forebears of the Kurds would extend beyond the objectives of this book. Nonetheless, it is possible to point out a common denominator for these appellations, the majority of which have referred to members of belligerent pastoral tribes who were not subject to the sovereignty of any state, spoke non-Turkish and non-Arabic dialects from a group of primarily Iranian languages, and pursued a pastoral existence in the extensive mountainous area of the Zagros and eastern Taurus Mountains and the southern Caucasus.

It can be assumed that the Kurds arose from the various population groups that arrived and settled in Kurdistan. They do not have a single ethnic origin—but then, neither does the British nation, which developed from the descendants of the Picts, the Celts, the Bretons, the Anglo-Saxons, the Vikings, and the Normans. From the standpoint of successive Persian-Iranian states, the remote area of Kurdistan and its inhabitants were difficult and even impossible to control. From time to time, tribal forces emerged from that area, took over a state that existed on the heights of Iran or in the valleys of Mesopotamia, and established ruling dynasties that assimilated into the culture and the state. Some similarity may be found in the historical relationship between the Mongol tribes on the steppes north of China and the Chinese state and culture.

The terms *Kurd* and *akrad* appear frequently in Islamic chronicles and history books, starting with the advent of Islam in the seventh century. An in-depth study of various medieval Arabic sources by Boris James points out the various and contradictory meanings of the term—most of them negative.[14] Although the collective signifiers *kurd* and *akrad* have been in use since ancient times, especially since the rise of Islam, and there is long-standing acknowledgment of Kurdish distinctiveness, Kurdistan and the Kurds have remained "in the shadow of history."[15] In premodern and modern Western chronicles and histories of Islam, the active forces in the history of the northern Middle East were the Muslims, the Sunnites, the Shi'ites and their various cults and factions, the Arabs, the Turks, the Persians, the members of various dynasties—the Umayyads, the Abbasids, the Turkish dynasties, the Mameluke houses—and various tribes, as well as these groups' leaders, military commanders, and prominent clergy. The Kurds were mentioned only casually as rebellious, nearly uncontrollable mountain tribes that frightened passersby and harassed settlements. In many cases, Kurdish individuals, tribes, or emirs who participated in specific events were named, but with no reference to their Kurdish identity. The history of the northern Middle East and the regions of Kurdistan has been written, in both premodern and modern times, either from the standpoint of the neighboring states that controlled Kurdistan or from Islamic religious points of view, as well as within the framework of urban cultures, experiences, and discourses. These accounts have consistently described the Kurds as barbaric, violent robbers who threaten the prevailing government, culture, and social order and render economic and commercial life unsafe. In denoting a member of a shepherd tribe, the word *kurd* has also been used to indicate an unrestrained, violent, and at times lawless people.

Modern historians, with their tendency to examine national frameworks and national movements, have focused on the response of the Kurds to the growth of Turkish, Arab, Iranian, and Armenian modern nationalisms. They have also considered the Kurdish revolts in the light of modernizing efforts to construct nation-states or the rebellions against premodern states, both of which, in the discourse of modern national movements, constitute national history. Thus, in the histories written by the surrounding states and cultures, the Kurds have been perceived as peripheral, tribal, anarchical, and possessed of a savage culture.

Kurdistan is indeed a peripheral area, but its geographic fate has been to fall within the spheres of influence of stronger states and more developed cultures with established languages, written alphabets, and a recorded heritage. Throughout most periods from ancient times until the twentieth century, the prevailing culture and languages in the area were Persian, Byzantine Greek, or Arabic after the spread of Islam; Turkish, Ottoman Turkish, and Armenian prevailed after the fall of the Abbasid Empire during the eleventh and twelfth centuries, up until the dawn of the modern era.

There were always Kurdish individuals and groups, whether regional, tribal, or class-related, who became integrated into and at times even founded ruling dynasties in Iran and Mesopotamia. In so doing, however, they became assimilated and lost their Kurdish characteristics. There were also forces originating in Kurdistan that rose to power in neighboring states, especially in Iran but also in the Turkish emirates. There was never, however, a political entity centered in Kurdistan where the language spoken was Kurdish and the conditions could have fostered the development of a high Kurdish language and literature. Although the Kurdish dialects are affiliated with the family of northwestern Iranian languages, their vocabulary has also been influenced by Arabic and Turkish. However, in contrast to Persian, Arabic, Turkish, and Armenian, none of the Kurdish dialects became dominant or acquired the status of a standard Kurdish language, nor did any distinctively Kurdish writing develop. This linguistic weakness was an obstacle to the development of a collective identity and a national narrative in the modern era.

Admittedly, some of the population of Kurdistan was neither tribal nor pastoral. However, tribalism and tribal-emirate frameworks were the most dominant forms of social organization, as reflected in the Kurds' political and social life. Tribal, familial, and local affiliations determined basic loyalties and identities. Nevertheless, the Kurds—that is, the tribal, pastoral, agricultural mountaineers, as well as the speakers of Kurdish dialects in the emirates—maintained a consciousness of their distinctive identity. At times this consciousness accompanied changes in the identity and language of groups and individuals—from a Kurdish to a Turkmenian, Armenian, or Arabic identity, or vice versa—according to changes in social, economic, and political conditions. Generally speaking, however, tribalism and tribal identity were much more relevant and significant than any broad collective distinctiveness such as Kurdish, Arabic, or Turkmenian.[16]

The emirates and the tribal-emirate frameworks that imposed a supertribal sovereignty—especially from the tenth to the twelfth and thirteenth centuries, and again from the fifteenth to the nineteenth centuries—collapsed when confronted by strong external forces: the Mongol and Turkish invasions and the Ottoman and Iranian states. The decline of the emirates before they could give rise to any power strong enough to maintain a lasting supertribal sovereignty or create a stable government, trade, and a significant urban stratum left the stage clear for the reinforcement of tribal frameworks. Because economic conditions remained unchanged, the tribal sociopolitical frameworks were replicated over time in a broad range of combinations.

The growth of the modern Kurdish nation and the Kurdish national movement encountered obstacles from the social, political, and historical developments in Kurdistan as well as from the role of the Kurds relative to nearby Arab, Turkish, Persian, and Armenian national movements. Although not all Kurds were tribal or pastoral, tribal patterns and loyalties determined their political conduct. The identification of the Ottoman state as the legitimate Islamic state, and of Iran as the Shi'ite state during the premodern era, along with the growth of the Arab, Turkish, Armenian, and Iranian national movements and discourses, made the development of a Kurdish national identity and discourse extremely difficult.

KURDISTAN: TOPOGRAPHY AND GEOPOLITICS

The topographical and geopolitical characteristics of Kurdistan were extremely influential in the history of the Kurds and affect socioeconomic and political developments in the region to this day. The central part of Kurdistan extends over the large mountainous mass in the northern Mediterranean, to the north and northeast of the Tigris and Euphrates Valleys. It includes large portions of the southern and northern Zagros Mountains, the western slopes of the Taurus Mountains, and the area to the west and north of Lake Van. Kurds have also lived in extensive areas of the southern Caucasus Mountains.[17] Because Kurdistan is mountainous, it is difficult to control and traverse. It was the topographical isolation of various areas inside Kurdistan and the difficult living conditions that gave rise to a tribal social organization and the tribal-quasi-feudal emirates.

Throughout most of its history, Kurdistan was divided among the strong neighbor states that arose on the plateau of Iran, the kingdoms and empires of Mesopotamia, and the states that developed in Anatolia—Byzantium in the Middle Ages, the Ottoman Empire in the sixteenth century, and Turkey in the twentieth century. This proximity to relatively strong and cohesive political and cultural centers hindered the growth of strong political frameworks and autonomous cultural units in Kurdistan. At the same time, Kurdistan's topography made it difficult for the strong states controlling the area to impose their sovereignty on the rebellious tribal population. The local Kurdish tribes and tribal emirates that periodically acquired status and power also had difficulty developing into political entities that were strong enough to unite Kurdistan and its tribes, or any significant part of them, into a stable state. Continuing splits and struggles within and between the tribes and the emirates were typical of Kurdish society. Economic conditions changed to only a small degree. During relatively peaceful periods, small and medium-sized cities sprang up, but no large, stable urban centers emerged in which a Kurdish bourgeoisie and a written Kurdish culture could have developed over the generations.

Because there was never a proper Kurdish state in the region, and because the boundaries of the areas settled by the Kurdish tribes fluctuated over time, it is difficult to draw the borders of Kurdistan. It is possible, however, to refer to a geographical area on the basis of the spread of various Kurdish dialects throughout history, or according to the successive maps that were drawn by various Kurdish personages and groups during the twentieth century. Referring to Kurdistan as a geographical area in premodern history, however, requires the use of geographical concepts and images that acquired significance only with the growth of the Kurdish national movement, when they were projected onto periods in which there was no national discourse in the modern sense, and when "Kurdistan" either designated only certain parts of the area referred to by that name in modern times or was not used at all.

The Muslim geographer Ibn Hawqal (d. 988) mentions Kurds in his book *Kitab Surat al-Ard* when discussing the regions of Fars and al-Jibal. In his map of the al-Jibal region (the Zagros Mountains northeast of Iraq), he identifies the "summer and winter pastures of the Kurds" (*masaif al-akrad wa shitaifihim*). The first known use of the geographic term *ard al-akrad* ("the land of the Kurds") was in 1057, on a map drawn by Moham-mad Kashgari, a Turkish Muslim geographer, lexicographer, and linguist from Central Asia. In the midtwelfth century, the Seljuk sultan Sinjar (Sul-tan Mu'iz al-Din Ahmad al-Sinjar, 1084–1151) established an administrative district named Kurdistan, which extended over southwestern Iran and re-gions south of where the city of Slemani, or Sulaymaniyya, was founded in the eighteenth century. This district included the cities of Kermanshah, Hulwan, Shahrizur, and Dinavar. In modern times, the Kurds became a mi-nority in a considerable part of this area.[18]

The powers that ruled Kurdistan used "Kurdistan" only to denote the administrative areas in a small territory where the population was Kurdish. Following their conquest of Kurdistan in the early sixteenth century, the Ot-tomans established the province of Kurdistan, which included Kurdish emir-ates and was given the special status of *eyelet* (province). In 1846, as part of administrative reforms, the *eyelet* of Kurdistan was reestablished. It now in-cluded the areas of Diyarbakir, Van, Mush, Chizire (Cizire, al-Jazira in Ara-bic), Botan, and Hakkari, which had been outside the earlier *eyelet*.[19]

After the elimination of the autonomous Kurdish Emirate of Ardalan in 1867, the Iranian authorities established an administrative area called Kurdi-stan south of Lake Urmia. The use of the geographical-administrative sig-nifier had no national significance, but its very usage helped to preserve the reference to Kurdistan as a geographical area. The Ottoman Empire, in spite of its negative attitude toward any Kurdish national consciousness—as well as toward Armenian and Arab ones—had not yet developed the national-ist sensitivity of the post–World War I Turkish nation-state, which sought to eliminate not only Kurdish nationalism but also the geographical concept of Kurdistan.

In *The Sharafnama*, Sharaf al-Din Bitlisi describes the geography of Kurdistan:

> The realm of Kurdistan begins on the coast of the Strait of Hormuz, which borders on the shores of the Indian Ocean. From thence it extends forth on a straight line, terminating with the provinces of Malatya and Mara'sh. To the north of this line are the provinces of Fars, Persian Iraq, Azerbaijan, Ar-menia Minor and Armenia Major. To the southern side lie the Arabian Iraq, Mosul and Diyarbakir.[20]

In this definition, Lorestan (Luristan) was included within Kurdistan, and its residents, the Lur tribes, were considered Kurds. In the modern era, the identification of the Lurs as Kurds is controversial. The question of their ethnic affiliation is important, because the inclusion of Lorestan, in southwestern Iran, would give Kurdistan an outlet to the Persian/Arab Gulf. Kurdish nationalists who are striving for the establishment of Greater Kurdistan include the Lurs and Lorestan within the Kurdish nation.[21]

The modern mapping and description of Kurdistan was carried out in the late nineteenth and early twentieth centuries by a British officer, Francis Richard Maunsell, who conducted expeditions there.[22] His maps and descriptions closely resemble the maps drawn later by Kurdish nationalists, who apparently relied on Maunsell's work. It is evident that the definition of Kurdistan's boundaries depends on the viewpoint and national vision of various Kurdish nationalists.

The difficulty in defining the boundaries is also related to the issue of identity: Who is a Kurd? That is, which population groups consider themselves—or may be considered—Kurds? Throughout history, the signifier *akrad* also referred to the Bakhtyars and Lurs. In the twentieth century, however, the collective consciousness of these population groups leaned toward their inclusion within the Iranian-Persian nationality. Do the boundaries of Kurdistan contain only the areas in which there is currently a Kurdish majority, or do they also include areas that are important to the construction of Kurdish national history but whose Kurdish population in modern times is a minority?

This issue is not unique to the Kurds: elsewhere in the world, demographic changes have led to an incongruity between the nationalistic visions of a fatherland and the demographic and geopolitical reality, with most modern residents having a different national identity and historical narrative. One example is the contentious affiliation of the Kosovo district with the former Yugoslavia. Since 1389, when the great battle between the Christian Kingdom of Serbia and the Muslim Ottoman Empire was fought there, Kosovo has been symbolically important to Serbian national identity. The Muslim Kosovars, however, who constitute an absolute majority there today, view Kosovo as the capital of their own distinctive region.

After World War I, Sharif Pasha, the prominent Kurdish nationalist who was active on the Kurds' behalf at the Versailles Peace Conference, submitted a map of Kurdistan that reflected his nationalist vision. Areas populated by Lurs in southwestern Iran were included in a Kurdistan that extended all the way to the Persian Gulf. Northern Kurdistan embraced areas of the southern Caucasus up to the environs of Yerevan, the present capital of Armenia. These areas were populated by Kurdish tribes in the Middle Ages, but only a few Kurds live there today. Their inclusion, as well as the inclusion of an outlet to the Mediterranean near Alexandretta on the Turkish-Syrian border, is typical of the maximalist maps that were put forward again after World War II. However, the generally realistic core factions within the Kurdish national movement did not consider the Lurs to be Kurds and acknowledged that there was no Kurdish majority near Alexandretta and that Kurdistan was landlocked. Moreover, reducing the area of Kurdistan was the strategy adopted by the majority of the Kurdish political groups, which demanded an autonomous region within the existing states of Iraq, Turkey, and Iran. If they had presented maps of Greater Kurdistan, the suspicions of the states that controlled Kurdistan would have been reinforced and the objections of these states to any manifestation of Kurdish nationalistic ambitions for autonomy would have intensified.

Although it is true that in the past the area populated by Kurds extended from the Mediterranean coastline in the area of Hatay-Alexandretta to the Persian Gulf, the Kurdish population in the Hatay area dwindled during the nineteenth and twentieth centuries. The fact that Kurdistan has had no outlet to the sea throughout decisive periods of history has affected the development of the Kurds as a linguistic-ethnic group. The absence of any direct contact by sea with Europe, and especially with the northern Atlantic area that flourished as a result of the Industrial Revolution and modernization, slowed modernization in Kurdistan by comparison with the Levant cities, Egypt, Istanbul, and the western Ottoman Empire. The effects of the growth of capitalism and modernization in Europe—and later of a global market economy—reached Kurdistan indirectly through the mediation of the Ottoman Empire or via merchants from the Levant or the Gulf.

In the absence of a sea outlet, no commercial cities came into existence in Kurdistan. Because of their entrenched tribal and tribal-emirate social patterns, pastoral-agricultural economy, and limited foreign trade, the Kurds did not develop a stratum of merchant families like those in the nineteenth-century Levant cities. Moreover, the educated Christian merchants in the Levant contributed significantly to the growth of proto-nationalist ideas and to the emergence of Arab and Syrian nationalism.

The small number of urban merchants in Kurdistan were mainly Christians and had an Armenian identity, which became the basis for the Armenian national movement. Only some of a small number of Muslim merchants, craftsmen, and officials began to identify themselves as Kurds, inspired by the strengthening Armenian and Turkish nationalist trends. Overall, however, the few urban Kurds were weak by comparison to the tribes, and the social tension between them and the tribes compelled them to seek support from the Ottoman state. Subsequently, many of them came to identify with either a Turkish or an Iranian nationality. By contrast, Kurdish nationality was perceived as primitive tribalism and not as a collective identity that could constitute the basis for a Kurdish community.

Very little has been written about the premodern history of Kurdistan and the early Kurds, who have remained in the shadow of Islamic, Arabic, Persian, Turkish, and even Armenian history. Both the Kurds' historical vision of themselves and the historical Kurdish discourse developed slowly and belatedly, and the dissemination of their vision and discourse was impeded by the slow pace of modernization in Kurdish society, as well as by the hostile and oppressive attitude of the states that controlled Kurdistan. Because the Kurds had no state of their own that could promote the writing of a national history, and because the prevailing conditions in Kurdistan and Kurdish society hindered the development of a modern educated class, the history of the Kurds has not in fact really been written—a deficiency that this book hopes in some small measure to redress.

CHAPTER I

KURDISH DISTINCTIVENESS UNDER ARAB, PERSIAN, AND TURKISH DOMINANCE

THE KURDS, ISLAM, AND MEDIEVAL MUSLIM STATES

Medieval Muslim chronicles and history books, as well as modern studies devoted to the rise and conquests of Islam in the seventh century, have principally focused on the ways in which the Muslims contended with their most powerful rivals, the Byzantine Empire and the Sassanid Persian Empire, each of which was a fairly cohesive political entity with a strong army and a written culture. The decisive battles against them and the Islamization of the population within the conquered territories occupied the attention of both medieval Muslim chroniclers and modern scholars of Muslim history.

However, in addition to these conflicts with well-organized states, the Muslim conquest of the mountainous areas north and northeast of the Tigris and Euphrates plains and between these and the heights of Iran also had to contend with pastoral tribal population groups that had no central government and engaged in a variety of religious practices. These tribes spoke, not Arabic, but dialects close to Persian, and they were referred to as *al-akrad*—the Kurds.

The terms *kurd* and *akrad* appear in *Futuh al-Buldan* (*The Conquest of the Countries*) by al-Baladhuri (d. 892), the oldest book that cites traditions about the Islamic conquests. According to al-Baladhuri, the Muslims fought against the Kurds during the conquest of Persia and the areas of Mosul and Azerbaijan, and he mentions the Kurdish fortresses (*ma'aqal al-akrad*). The Kurds served—apparently in tribal regiments—in the Sassanid Persian army. During the Muslim Arab conquest, they fought on the Persian side. After the establishment of Muslim rule, the Kurds continued to rebel against their new governors and to launch raids on population centers and roads whenever the central government was weak or beset with internecine strife.[1]

Al-Tabari (Abu Ja'afar Muhammad bin Jarir al-Tabari, 838–932), the greatest of the early Muslim historians, mentions the Kurds in seventeen of the thirty-nine volumes of his monumental *Ta'rikh al-rusul wa-al-muluk* (*History of Prophets and Kings*). Obviously, the reference is to a nomadic, pastoral tribal population group that was difficult to control and that sought to preserve its tribal independence from any central government. Al-Tabari mentions that the Kurds rebelled in the third year of the reign of Caliph 'Othman (644–656), the third of the first four caliphs who were the close associates and successors of the Prophet Muhammad in the area of southern Lorestan near the Karun River.[2] Like al-Baladhuri, he notes that at the time of the Muslim conquest of Iran the Kurds fought on the side of the Persians against the Muslim onslaught in the Fars and Ahwaz areas.[3]

Even before Islam and the Muslim conquest, the terms *kurd* and *akrad* existed in the discourse of the area's residents, who used them to refer to the pastoral or pastoral-agricultural tribal population living in the large mountainous area to the north and northeast of the Tigris and Euphrates Valleys and the Syrian Desert. From a linguistic point of view, that population was also distinct from the Arab tribes, the Armenians, and the Turkmenian tribes in that it spoke Kurdish dialects that were close to Persian. In other words, the relevance of *kurd* and *akrad* was socioeconomic, ecological, and linguistic, or any combination of these—similar to the signifiers *Arab* or *Bedu* (Bedouin) for members of the nomadic pastoral or pastoral-agricultural tribes who spoke Arab dialects in the deserts of the Arabian Peninsula and Syria. In medieval Muslim chronicles and history books, the term *akrad* sometimes appears together with *Arab*, in the sense of pastoral Bedouin tribes. This combination indicates the closeness of the two signifiers and their common characteristics of pastoralism, nomadism, and tribalism.[4]

Whereas the rallying message of Islam spread among the oasis-dwellers and pastoral nomadic tribes of the Arabian Peninsula during the seventh century, creating a source of authority and legitimacy for supratribal leadership, no such distinctive unifying faith or central authority developed among the Kurds. Throughout the Arabian Peninsula, linguistic coalescence had begun even before the rise of Islam and accelerated with its development and that of written Arabic culture, but no parallel linguistic processes took place among the Kurdish tribes, and no written culture or unifying cultural base emerged from any of their dialects. With the development of the Islamic state and culture, Arabic acquired its status as the language of religion, law, and government. Persian, whose growth was linked to the Sassanid Persian state, had formed a written heritage during the pre-Islamic period. Although it adopted the Arabic alphabet, Persian retained its distinctiveness and acquired a special status in Muslim culture and the Muslim world. Poetry continued to be written in the Kurdish dialects, and Kurdish *ulema* who wrote in Arabic contributed to the growth of Islamic culture, but the linguistic dominance of Arabic and Persian (and later of Turkish), along with the absence of a Kurdish alphabet appropriate to the sounds of the Kurdish language, limited the possibilities for a cohesive literary Kurdish language.

The Kurdish tribes entered into the Islamic cultural and religious circle dominated by the Arabic and Persian languages, but their dialects continued to be spoken. The Arab tribes, while retaining their own identities, enjoyed a highly significant advantage over all the tribal groups they encountered: they were imbued with an attractive faith, an organizing principle, and a supratribal leadership endowed with religious legitimacy. The emergence of their religious "community image" gave Muslims power relative to societies that had not undergone a similar process.

From the standpoint of the Muslim state, the Kurds remained a rebellious, anarchical group. Its topography kept Kurdistan a peripheral area that was difficult to control, and its population preserved tribal patterns of organization rooted in the demands of pastoral survival and production. Some historical sources have been found that discuss religious life among the Kurds prior to Islam. Apparently, most of the population was Zoroastrian and Manichaean, with some Christians. One work attesting to Zoroastrianism among the Kurds is a poem by an anonymous poet, apparently dating from the seventh or eighth century. Written in a Kurdish dialect in the Aramaic alphabet, it bewails the destruction of the Zoroastrian temples in Shahrizur by the Arabs in southern Kurdistan.[5]

Most of the Kurds converted to Islam during the Umayyad and Abbasid periods in the seventh and eighth centuries. However, the physical remoteness of Kurdistan and the weak control exerted by the Muslim state helped isolated communities maintain local and pre-Islamic traditions and beliefs, both Zoroastrian and Christian. Heterodox sects developed, some including elements from Shi'ite Islam, Christianity, Zoroastrianism, paganism, and Judaism. The isolated conditions promoted the entrenchment of Sufism in the social and religious patterns of Kurdish society. The preservation of ancient beliefs and sects was also typical of the Christians in Kurdistan—the Assyrians, the Nestorians, and the Armenians. A form of Sufism that included pre-Islamic or extra-Islamic elements led to the rise of heterodox sects such as Ahl al-Haq and the Yazidi.

The Kurdish national movement in the twentieth century constructed its national history—or its view of history from a national perspective—by attributing a modern national meaning to the signifiers *kurd* and *akrad* and creating the concepts of *Kurdayeti* ("Kurdishness" in the sense of identity) and *Kurdavari* (Kurdish way of life). In the same way, the modern Arab national movement retroactively attached national significance to Arabic-speaking tribes that had been designated as "Arabs" by their non-Arab neighbors and ascribed national significance to collective memories and myths relating to real or imagined historical events.

Even ancient population groups with no national consciousness in the modern sense displayed ethnic, linguistic, and social signifiers that fluctuated over time, as well as distinctive expressions in poetry, legends, and narratives. In spite of the absence of a modern national consciousness among the feudal princedoms and medieval tribes of Europe, the historical vision or narratives constructed by modern national movements gave them meaning as initial chapters in the national histories of France, England, Germany, Russia, Poland, and other nations. Neither the Merovingian kings nor Charlemagne had any consciousness of modern French nationalism. Nevertheless, after the French Revolution, when the bourgeoisie gained hegemony and a national discourse developed in the French state, the Franks and Gauls—the Merovingian and Carolingian Dynasties—became constitutive chapters in the national history of France. Since the development of Polish national consciousness, the Piast Dynasty has been considered the founder of the Polish state and the first chapter in Polish national history. German nationalism took a similar approach to the historical events and myths of the Germanic tribes.

In these examples, historical continuity was maintained from the nineteenth century onward in the form of the state, which corresponded—in varying degrees and at times only partially—to the geographical and linguistic region to which the nationalist movements and narratives referred. Historical memory and popular myths, premodern social signifiers, ethnic identification, and proto-national expressions were the "materials" from which the national movements—that is, the groups of modern, educated persons, political movements, and the institutions of modern states—constructed a national historical narrative. At the same time, and in premodern periods as well, the consciousness of French, German, or other distinctiveness varied in intensity and in some cases existed only among certain social strata. It did not serve as a basis for a collective narrative or as a focus for collective loyalty and affinity. Nevertheless, population groups' awareness of their distinctiveness enables us to perceive lines of continuity between such groups that share languages and territory, even if the boundaries are vague.

Until the nineteenth century, the term "Kurds" was generally considered to include the belligerent pastoral tribes and the tribal-clannish emirates. (Nontribal peasants were not included, but were at times referred to as "Kurmanji.") Occasionally, however, identification as "Kurdish" transcended these characteristics. Thus, in a poem written in the late seventeenth century, one of the characters states:

> *I am a peddler, not of noble origins,*
> *Self-grown, not educated.*
> *I am a Kurd from the mountains and distant lands . . .*[6]

Although the tribes and emirates that existed in Kurdistan before the rise of Islam and during the Muslim period were based on tribal and local identities and loyalties, there was still a distinction, which varied from time to time and from one area to another, between Kurds, Turks, Arabs, Georgians, and Armenians. Apparently, Armenian dynasties and tribes sometimes became Kurdish, and vice versa, while groups of tribes that had been considered Kurdish became Persian, Iranian, or Turkmenian. In light of this, the tribal-clannish emir dynasties whose language was one of the many Kurdish dialects may be referred to as Kurdish, just as the European national movements refer to medieval German, Russian, or Polish dynasties as part of their national history. No one can deny the existence of an ethnic-linguistic Kurdish identity, even if that identity does not conform to the criteria of the modernist-nationalist approach.

Between the seventh and fifteenth centuries, Kurdistan was occupied several times by waves of tribal conquerors who sowed destruction and undermined Kurdish social and political structures or caused them to collapse. These were the Arab tribes that propagated Islam; the Seljuk Turks; the Khwarizmian Turks, who launched a brief invasion during the thirteenth century; the Mongols; and, in the fourteenth and fifteenth centuries, the "Black Sheep" (Qaraqqoyunlu) and "White Sheep" (Aqqoyunlu) Turkmen tribal dynasties. Whereas there was no mass migration of pastoral Kurdish nomads beyond the mountains of Kurdistan and its environs, the Arab tribal pastoral nomads bore their religious ideology throughout the entire Middle East. The Turkish and Mongol nomads launched mass migrations that exceeded by far their former areas of nomadism.

In spite of vast differences between them, the Muslim conquest, the takeover by Seljuk Turks, and the brief Mongol conquest were all carried out by nomadic tribal entities based outside Kurdistan. The Kurds benefited from the organizational and political superiority of emergent states, and the Arab invasion brought the ideological message of Islam and the first stirrings of a high written language. These waves of migration by large tribal groups were accompanied by the development of distinctive political frameworks and cultural characteristics.

The majority of Kurdish tribes settled or wandered (mostly by way of pastoral seasonal migration) within the Zagros and Taurus ranges, in the Syrian Desert, to the west of the heights of Iran, and in the southern Caucasus. Their geographical and political weakness allowed successive waves of conquerors and their rulers to enjoy an advantage over them.

TRIBAL KURDISH DYNASTIES
AND THE RISE OF THE TURKS

During the central period of medieval Islamic history, in the time of the Umayyad Caliphate (661–750), when the Muslim state was centered in Damascus and the Abbasid Caliphate (750–1258) was centered in Baghdad, the Kurds were a rebellious element, difficult to control. Kurdish revolts and raids are mentioned in 702 under Governor al-Hajaj, who suppressed and punished the tribes.[7] Noteworthy during the Abbasid period was the revolt by Kurdish tribes in 839 in the area of Mosul and Tikrit, during the reign of Caliph al-Muʿtasim (833–842).[8] Kurds participated in the Revolt of Zanj (869–883), a social uprising of slaves brought in from East Africa, joined by the lower strata and by Bedouin and Kurdish tribes who sought to shake off the Abbasid yoke.

The weakening of the Abbasid state, beginning in the tenth century, and its inability to maintain effective rule allowed the Kurdish tribal dynasties to grow stronger, to compose supertribal structures (the emirates), and to impose their rule on weaker population groups—smaller or more fragmented tribes and settled nontribal peasants. In periods when the power of the Muslim state declined or when Kurdish dynasties became embroiled in struggles for succession that weakened their grip, tribal anarchy prevailed, with numerous highway robberies and raids on permanent settlements. Eventually, the signifier *kurd* acquired the connotation of "robber."

Between 959 and 1095, the Hasanwahids, a dynasty of emirs of the Barzikani tribe, acquired and retained control of Shahrizur (around the modern city of Slemani, or Sulaymaniyya) and extensive parts of the Zagros Mountains east of Shatt al-Arab and the Tigris and Euphrates Valleys and northward to southern Azerbaijan. The Hasanwahids were protégés of the Buwayhid sultan Rukn al-Dawla (935–976), who effectively ruled the Abbasid Empire.[9] This dynasty was forced out by another Kurdish dynasty, the ʿAnnazids, or Banu ʿAnnaz (990–1116), whose territory was centered on Kermanshah and extended from Shahrizur into the Mandali area in the mountains east of the lower Euphrates, on the border between modern-day Iraq and Iran.[10]

In the midtenth century, the Shadadid (Shadyanid) Dynasty (951–1075) rose to power. Based in the cities of Dvin and Ganja, this dynasty controlled the southern Caucasus, between the Araxes and Kur Rivers, and the border area between modern-day Turkey, Iran, and northern Iraq. Another branch of this dynasty continued to control the area around the city of ʿAni, on the Armenian border, apparently until the end of the twelfth century.[11] In the late tenth century, the Kurdish Marwanid (Banu Marwan) Dynasty took power (984–1083), against the background of the weakened rule of the Bu-wayhid sultans in Baghdad, after the death of ʿAdud al-Dawla in the conflict against Sultan Samsam al-Dawla and his Kurdish allies, the Hamdanids. The dynasty's founder, Bad Abu ʿAbdallah ibn Dustak al-Kharbuti, took control of the cities in central and western Kurdistan: Jazirat Ibn ʿUmar, Diyarbakir (Amed), Nasibin, and Mayyafariqin.[12]

The important Marwanid ruler Nasir al-Dawla Ahmad abu Nasir bin Marwan (1011–1061) gained recognition for his rule in Diyarbakir under the sovereignty of the Abbasid caliph and subject to the Buwayhid sultan al-Dawla (1012–1021), who was the effective ruler in Baghdad and of the Abbasid state.[13] The long years of his rule were noteworthy for their economic and cultural development. With his assistance, mosques, hospitals, and bridges were built, and ʿulema and poets lived and worked in his court.

Beginning in the ninth and tenth centuries, the Kurdish emirates and tribes had to contend with extensive incursions by Turkish tribes, which became the central force in the Abbasid Empire. The Kurdish dynasties declined as a result of this penetration by Turkish tribes from the Oguz group, especially under the leadership of the Seljuk Dynasty. In the early eleventh century, the Oguz tribes took over entire areas of Kurdistan. Between 1020 and 1041, Turkish tribes raided the Kurdish-populated areas of Azerbaijan, the Hakkari area, and the cities of Diyarbakir and Hamdhan. During that century, they conquered most of the territory of Kurdistan, Iraq, and the southern Caucasus.[14] In 1054–1055, Nasir al-Dawla bin Marwan was obliged to recognize the sovereignty of the Seljuk ruler, Tughril Beg (990–1063). In the following year, the ruler of the Shadadid Dynasty in Ganja, in the southern Caucasus, also swore fealty to the Seljuk governor.[15]

The final takeover of Kurdistan by the Seljuks took place after the Battle of Malazgird (Malazkird) in 1071 (AH 463), in which the Seljuks vanquished the Byzantine emperor Romanus IV Diogenes (1068–1071). In that battle, many Kurdish tribes fought on the side of the Seljuks, who became the principal Muslim force to fight against the Christians of the Byzantine

Empire and Armenia.[16] At the same time, against the weakness of the Abbasid caliph and the Buwayhids, who were the central power in Baghdad and served as sultans, the Seljuks—who were formally subordinate to the Abbasid caliph—became the strong force in the Abbasid state and Abbasid court. The Seljuks, led for many years by Sultan Alp Arslan (1029–1072), defeated the Kurdish Shadadid Dynasty in 1075. The Marwanid Dynasty was also conquered by the Seljuks, who appointed members of the Marwanid Dynasty as governors of cities and areas on their behalf until the late twelfth century. The last cities and fortresses controlled by the Marwanids, in the al-Jazira area, were taken over in 1083.[17]

The Seljuk rulers had difficulty imposing sovereignty on the mountainous areas of Kurdistan, where Kurdish fortresses and autonomous tribal areas continued to exist. Atabeg Imad al-Din Zanji was forced to devote many years to the attempt to reconquer the fortresses. The historian Ibn al-Athir, who was loyal to the rulers of the House of Zanji, notes the conquest of many Kurdish fortresses in the al-Jazira, Mosul, and Hakkari areas in HA 526 (AD 1122–1123).[18] The Kurds continued to rebel and to launch raids on roads and permanent settlements. The Seljuk and Zanji administrations attempted to push them back into the mountains and forests, far from the main roads, and in some cases they were forced to retake areas and fortresses that they had previously conquered.[19]

Ibn al-Athir describes Kurdish society as one based on pastoral tribalism and tribal emirates with small urban centers. The tribes and the emirates tended to throw off the yoke of central rule whenever the state showed weakness, and they made repeated efforts to maintain their autonomy. The same picture of a tribal society is drawn in books by the historians Ibn Khaldun and Bitlisi.[20]

In most chronicles, Kurds as a group are mentioned together with Arabs, in phrases such as "Arabs and Kurds." The reference should not be understood in the modern national-ethnic sense; rather, it is a sociological designation for the pastoral tribal population groups, belligerent and partially nomadic, who were recruited into conflicts by the Turkish governors and the states they controlled. One account mentions Kurdish fortresses—for example, in the Mosul and 'Amadiya areas and near Hakkari, southeast of Lake Van. In contrast to the seventh century, the quasi-feudal social pattern appears to have been more common in the twelfth century. The Seljuks had to contend not only with Kurds as a pastoral, belligerent tribal population but also with the non-nomadic Kurdish emirates that controlled small urban centers such as Diyarbakir, 'Amadiya (Amed), Hakkari, Shahrizur, and Dinavar.[21]

In spite of the collapse or subjugation of the Kurdish dynasties by the Seljuk Turks in the eleventh and twelfth centuries, some Kurdish families who had become integrated into the system acquired status and power under the Seljuks and the Zanji Dynasty. The Zanji clan was originally under Seljuk protection and became an independent dominant power in Syria and northern Iraq during the twelfth century. The best known of the Kurdish families who found their place in the Zanji government was that of Salah al-Din al-Ayyubi, known as Saladin. His grandfather, who came from the town of Dvin, northeast of the Araxes River, was appointed governor of Tikrit by Atabeg Imad al-Din Zanji. The rise of the al-Ayyubi family, who apparently had previously served the Shadadids, followed the decline of the latter and resulted from the family's ability to forge ties with the House of Atabeg Zanji.

In the Muslim world, Saladin is perceived as the Muslim leader who succeeded in repelling the invasion by Frankish Crusaders at Hittin in 1187. In the twentieth century, he became the myth of the Arab national hero; as such, his image was exploited by nationalist regimes in Egypt under Gamal 'Abdel Nasser, in Syria under Hafez al-Assad and the Ba'th Party, and in Iraq by pan-Arab nationalists during the Hashimite monarchy and later under Saddam Hussein. Many Kurds were among the officers and soldiers in Saladin's Muslim army. Bitlisi mentions the Ayyubids as a Kurdish dynasty. In fact, they were the most powerful Kurdish dynasty in the history of Islam. Although they were linguistically and culturally Arabized and their center of power was in Egypt, far from Kurdistan, they were perceived as Kurds, distinct from the Turks. Saladin's actions, in fact, were based on his own Islamic convictions and political interests. The motives of the Kurds among the fighters and commanders of his army were not nationalist in the modern sense, but Islamic; their loyalty was to Islam and to the person of Saladin. Nonetheless, the awareness of Kurdish distinctiveness vis-à-vis the Turks and Kurdish-Turkish relations was preserved. Saladin's appointment as commander of the expeditionary force dispatched by the Zanjis, the rulers of Damascus, following the death of his uncle Shirkuh was made possible by the support he received from Kurdish commanders in the army, who united in backing him against the Turkish commanders.[22]

The Ayyubids were also interested in extending their influence in the Caucasus Mountains and the heights of Armenia, from which the family originally came.[23] In Arab sources, they are described as coming from an illustrious Arab dynasty. It is even possible that the Ayyubids viewed themselves as an Islamic dynasty and preferred to claim an Arab heritage because of the negative image of the Kurds.[24] In the twentieth century, the Kurdish national movement fostered the myth of Saladin as the Kurdish national hero and defiantly pronounced to the Muslim Arabs and the Turks that the Kurds had saved Islam from the Crusader invasion and now the Arabs and Turks were repaying good with evil by preventing the Kurds from accomplishing their legitimate national ambitions.

The incursions by the Khwarizmians in the thirteenth century and by destructive Mongol invasions in the thirteenth to early fifteenth centuries decimated the population of Kurdistan, damaged its social structure, and destroyed the small cities that served as the centers of the emirates. The frontier of the Mongol-Mameluke struggle ran along the Euphrates.[25] The raids and battles emptied extensive areas in southwest Kurdistan, and the repeated destruction of permanent centers, cities, and villages eventually reinforced tribal social patterns and the pastoral and nomadic character of the Kurds. Only a few written sources and a handful of studies on this period exist.

In the fourteenth century, two Turkmen tribal military dynasties, the "Black Sheep" (Qaraqqoyunlu) and "White Sheep" (Aqqoyunlu) tribes, gradually gained strength in Kurdistan.[26] However, it was only after the death of the Ilkhani Mongol ruler Timur Leng (Tamerlane) in 1404 that the Turkmen dynasties became the ruling power in Mesopotamia, parts of Iran, and Kurdistan. Their weak control of Kurdistan helped the Kurdish emirates to recover. The relations between the Turkmen military tribal elites and the Kurdish tribal society were essentially unstable. The Turkmen rulers accepted the autonomous, and at times even independent, status of the Kurdish tribes and emirates, which accepted Turkmen rule and the trading and migration patterns practiced by the Turkmen tribes.[27] Prominent among the Kurdish forces was the Ayyubid Dynasty, which controlled Hasankeyf in the service of the Turkmen rulers.[28]

During the fifteenth century, conflict broke out between the two Turkmen dynasties. It was joined by the Kurdish emirates and tribes, many of which were allies, and indeed vassals, of the Black Sheep Dynasty.[29] As early as the first stages of its rise to power, in the years 1420–1436, the White Sheep confederation was forced to take on the Kurdish tribes and emirates that were allied with the Black Sheep,[30] but they had the help of the Kurdish tribes and emirates they now ruled.[31] In 1467 the leader of the Black Sheep was defeated by Uzun Hasan, the leader of the White Sheep. Even after his victory, he was forced to send most of his troops to fight against the Kurds in 1468–1469.

Following their victory, the White Sheep took over most of Kurdistan and Azerbaijan and established their capital in Tabriz. Because the majority of Kurdish emirates and tribes were allies of the Black Sheep, the White Sheep leaders sought to eliminate the families of Kurdish emirs and tribal leaders and appointed governors to take charge.[32] Some Kurds found places in the court of the White Sheep rulers, but relations between the Turkmen military tribal elite and the Kurdish emirates and tribes were unstable, suspicious, and fraught with violent clashes. Against the background of the loose and unstable White Sheep regime, the more or less independent Kurdish emirates, especially the Emirate of Bitlis, grew in strength. Even so, there was no uniformity in their actions. Each tribe and each emir maintained an independent relationship with the Black Sheep and subsequently with the White Sheep. In the early sixteenth century, the Shiʿite Safavid Dynasty came to power in Iran. The Shah, who united Iran under his rule, overturned the White Sheep Dynasty.

Between the Arab Muslim conquest in the seventh century and the Safavid and Ottoman conquest in the sixteenth, Kurdish emirates continued to exist, and in local discourse the signifiers *kurd* and *akrad* acquired distinctive characteristics, as did the population groups to which they referred. Nevertheless, the time was not yet ripe for the development of Kurdistan's emirates and the tribal society into a state. Throughout the two centuries of rule by the strong Umayyad and Abbasid states, which benefited from Islamic religious legitimacy, the Kurdish tribes and emirates were contained within the hegemonic Islamic culture, the Arabic and Persian languages, and the dominant states.

CHAPTER 2

THE ERA OF OTTOMAN AND IRANIAN RULE

KURDISTAN DIVIDED BETWEEN THE OTTOMAN EMPIRE AND SAFAVID IRAN

The major change in the history of Kurdistan took place in the early sixteenth century, with the growth of the Iranian state under the Shi'ite Safavid Dynasty, the eastward expansion of the Ottoman Empire, and the beginning of the long conflict between them. In 1501, Isma'il (Esmail) bin Haydar, the leader of a mystical Sufi order (the Safawiyya Sufis) who had elevated his tribal-Sufi family into a political dynasty, rose to power in Iran and imposed Safavid rule on the country, which lasted until 1722. He unified Iran, transforming it into a strong state and then an empire, and adopted the title of "Shah." Under Shah Isma'il's rule, Iran took shape as a Shi'ite state in religion and a Persian state linguistically and culturally.

In Kurdistan, the Safavid Iranian state put an end to the Turkmen White Sheep Dynasty, which had controlled most of the area since 1476, and took control of the lands as far as Diyarbakir in the west. The expanding Shi'ite Iranian state received increasing support among the Qizilbashis, a mystic sect close to the Shi'a that was influential among the Turkmen tribes in Anatolia and presented a challenge to the Ottoman Empire. In view of the Shi'ite and Qizilbashi threat, Sultan Salim I (1512–1520) opened a new front in the east, in addition to the Empire's ongoing struggle in the west against the Christian states of Europe, primarily the Habsburgs. The Sunnite Ottoman state, which up to that time had devoted most of its attention to a holy war against Christian armies in Europe, was now forced to deal with the Shi'ite Safavid challenge. Sultan Salim's move eastward led to the Ottoman conquest of most of the Arabic-speaking areas in the early sixteenth century. In the east, the Ottomans had to contend with two strong, cohesive rivals: the Mamelukes of Egypt and the Shi'ite Safavids of Persia. The Ottoman-

Iranian struggle was the central international conflict in the Muslim world until its penetration by Western powers in the nineteenth century. It lasted for more than 300 years, from 1514 until the Treaty of Erzurum in 1823, and was principally fought in the territory of Kurdistan.

The cooperation between the Kurds and the Ottomans was the achievement of the Kurdish statesman and courtier Mevlana Idris Bidlisi, who was the secretary of the last White Sheep ruler before that dynasty was eliminated by the Safavids; he subsequently served in the court of the Ottoman sultan Bayazid II (1481–1512) and in that of his heir, Sultan Salim I.[1] On the instructions of Sultan Salim I, Bidlisi persuaded the eighteen strong Kurdish emirs of the areas of Cemiskezek, Bitlis, Palu, Hasankeyf, Baradost, Baban, Soran, 'Amadiya (Bahdinan), and Chizire (Cizire, al-Jazira in Arabic) to support the Ottomans. The pro-Ottoman preference of many Kurdish emirs and tribes resulted from recognition of Ottoman power and of their common interests against the Qizilbashis. The Qizilbashis, allies of the Safavids, admired Shah Isma'il and were perceived by the Ottomans as having deviated from Sunnite Islam toward the Shi'a.

A major Turkmen Qizilbashi revolt against the Ottomans broke out in eastern Anatolia toward the end of the reign of Bayazid II and was only suppressed by his successor, Salim I. The revolt created a risk to the rearguard of the Ottoman army while it was still fighting the Safavids. The rivalry and clashes between the Kurdish emirs and tribes and the Turkmen Qizilbashis continued throughout the sixteenth century.[2] It is also possible that the decentralized nature of Ottoman rule over peripheral areas made it easier for the Kurds to accept it, in the hope that they could maintain their autonomy. As they saw it, the Ottoman policy of cooperation with the existing emirs and rulers in Kurdistan was preferable to the Safavid policy of expelling the strong Kurdish emirs and rulers and nurturing marginal families who would be dependent on the Safavid regime.

Following the Safavid victory in the Battle of Chaldiran in August 1514, the Ottomans took over large parts of Kurdistan. A few months later, in the winter of 1515, when the Ottoman army encountered difficulties from the reorganized Qizilbashis, who besieged Amed (Diyarbakir), it was the forces of the Kurdish emirs and tribes, led by Bidlisi, who helped the Ottomans to contend with their rivals.[3]

Generally speaking, during the sixteenth century the Emirates of Bitlis, Bahdinan ('Amadiya), Baban, Hakkari, and some of the Mukri tribe (in the Mahabad area southwest of Lake Urmia) accepted the official sovereignty of the Ottoman sultan. At times, however, they were also forced to pay tax to the shah of Iran. They maneuvered between the rulers of the two states and even transferred their loyalties from one side to the other according to the best strategy for preserving the status of the emirs and the autonomy of the emirates. The Ottomans and Safavids, for their part, intervened in the emirates' internal struggles. For example, Sharif Khan of Bidlis (Bitlis), who was persuaded by Idris al-Bidlisi to support the Ottoman sultan, transferred his support to the Safavid shah in 1532. That shift was part of his struggle against members of his family inside the emirate. In response, the Ottomans intervened in favor of his rivals and killed him.[4] The Safavids again took over most of Iraq in the 1530s, even conquering Baghdad in 1534 and holding it for some time.

Although the Kurdish emirates and tribes suffered from the wars, the situation enabled them to maneuver and made them an important border force to help guard the Ottoman border against the Safavids. Only the strong Ardalan emirate and most of the Mukri tribe became protégés of Iran. The emirs of Ardalan married into the Safavid royal house and during the sixteenth, seventeenth, and early eighteenth centuries fulfilled important functions in the Safavid court. In 1639 a border agreement, the Treaty of Zuhab (Qasr e-Shirin), was signed between the Ottoman Empire and Safavid Iran. It formalized the division of Kurdistan between the two powers, who viewed Kurdistan as a peripheral border area far from their centers of power. In spite of the agreement, the Ottoman-Persian wars continued until the Treaty of Erzurum in 1823.

THE KURDISH EMIRATES UNDER OTTOMAN AND SAFAVID RULE

The Kurdish emirates enjoyed varying degrees of autonomy under Ottoman rule. The unique conditions of the Ottoman Empire and the largely decentralized nature of Ottoman government created conditions in which the Kurdish tribal emirates could flourish. Their tribal sociopolitical patterns, which were centered on a strong tribe or clan and the exercise of sovereignty over other tribes and nontribal population groups around them, predated the Ottoman and Iranian conquests and may even have been present prior to the Muslim conquest. Although these Kurdish political frameworks were not "nationalist" in the modern sense, they were nevertheless perceived by the population of the time as Kurdish—that is, as having Kurdish distinctiveness. The scholar Amir Hassanpour coined the phrase "feudal nationalism" to describe the Kurds' development.[5]

The Ottoman Empire needed the strength of the Kurds against Iran. Their location on the front lines of the ongoing battle between the Sunnite

Ottoman Empire and the Shi'ite Iranian state gave them special importance. The decentralized and often weak Ottoman rule enabled the Kurdish emirates to maneuver and to exert influence in both Baghdad and Mosul as well as on the relationships between various local forces and the Ottoman *valis* (governors of administrative areas). Although the emirates were under the sovereignty of the Ottoman sultan, they were assisted in their conflicts with the Ottoman governors in Baghdad, Mosul, and elsewhere by governors on behalf of the Iranian shah in the Kermanshah and Tabriz areas.

After taking over Kurdistan, the Ottomans established the province of Kurdistan (*vilayet* Kurdistan), which included seventeen Kurdish emirates, the heads of which had the status of *sanjak bey* (district governor with some degree of autonomy). In contrast to other Ottoman *vilayets*, which were divided into districts (*liwas*), the Kurdish emirates had the special status of an *eyelet*, reflecting their autonomous nature. In the list of Ottoman provinces, dating from 1527, cited by the scholar I. Metin Kunt, the emirs of seven emirates are defined as the great emirs of Kurdistan.[6]

The Kurdish emirates in the Ottoman Empire were embroiled in struggles among themselves, and their relationship with the state was complex. Their degree of autonomy depended on the power of the central government to impose effective rule and the ability of the Ottoman *valis* to maneuver vis-à-vis local forces. During periods when strong moves were made in Istanbul to reinforce the central administration in the provinces, the emirates became less autonomous. Nevertheless, the struggles and rivalries between the emirates and tribes, their lack of any national consciousness, and their acceptance of the Islamic Ottoman discourse prevented any significant unification of the Kurds.

As early as the midsixteenth century, Sultan Sulayman the Magnificent conquered the strong Emirate of Cemiskezek (or Chamishgazak, between Mount Ararat and east Dersim, east of the northern Tigris River), which had existed since the thirteenth century. A dispute within the ruling family following the death of the strong ruler Pir Hüseyin enabled the Ottoman sultan to divide the lands among the emir's sons and thus to eliminate the emirate, which became subordinate to the Ottoman *sanjaks* (administrative districts). During the seventeenth century, the emirates' autonomy was gradually reduced and the Ottoman regime's control over at least some of them became stronger.[7]

None of the Kurdish emirates became strong enough to impose effective sovereignty upon other emirates and tribes, and none became a focus for the growth of central political power in Kurdistan, in part because of Ottoman policy, which was to exploit the struggles within the emirate ruling families and intertribal rivalries in order to prevent the emergence of a rival authority. Sharaf al-Din Bitlisi (Bidlisi), in his book *Sharafnama*, lists the central emirates in his day (the second half of the sixteenth century): Hakkari, Soran (Sohran), Baban, Ardalan, Hasankeyf, Bitlis (Bidlis), Chizire (Cizire, al-Jazira), Bahdinan (Bhadinan), Mush (Muks), and Cemiskezek (Chamishgazak) in the Dersim-Tuncheli area.[8]

The importance of the Kurdish emirates and tribes to the Ottoman Empire as a barrier against Iran, on the one hand, and the difficulties of imposing effective rule over them and the decentralized nature of the Ottoman regime, on the other, gave the emirates room to maneuver during the sixteenth, seventeenth, and eighteenth centuries, become more economically prosperous, and develop varying degrees of autonomy. During the seventeenth century, especially the first half, the Kurdish emirates reached a zenith of prosperity and power. The most prominent among them was the Emirate of Bitlis (to the south and west of Lake Van), which was controlled by strong, broad-minded, and apparently well-educated emirs from the House (or clan) of Rojiki (Rozhiki) and Bahdinan. Another emirate, Hakkari, to the east of Lake Van, played a role in the Ottoman-Safavid rivalry; however, its power was limited by the conflicts within its ruling clan.

According to the historical narrative of the emirs of Bitlis from the Rojiki (Rozhiki) tribe, they were a branch of the Marwanid Dynasty, which took control of the city of Bitlis during the tenth century. Until the late fifteenth century, they remained under the patronage of stronger forces, the Turkish and Turkmenian Dynasties. Only after the death of the Turkmen White Sheep ruler Uzun Hasan in 1473 did the Emirate of Bitlis become independent in real terms. In the early sixteenth century, the emirate joined the Ottoman forces of Sultan Salim I, and its emirs gained recognition and were awarded the title of "Noble Khan."[9] In 1530–1531, however, the emirate switched allegiance to the Safavid side, a move that led to its conquest by the Ottomans. The period of greatest prosperity in Bitlis began in 1578, when Sultan Murad III restored the emirate's autonomy and installed Sharaf al-Din Bitlisi (Bidlisi), a member of the Rojiki tribe and the author of the *Sharafnama*, as emir.[10] Under the talented and educated emirs of Bitlis, the emirate flourished.

Among the most important sources of information on the situation in seventeenth-century Kurdistan is the *Seyahatname* (*Book of Travels*) by Evliya Chelebi (Celebi) (1611–1685), an Ottoman official who made three long journeys through Kurdistan between 1640 and 1656. Chelebi describes Kurdistan from a geographical point of view; his descriptions are similar to those of al-Bitlisi's *Sharafnama* some fifty years earlier. Chelebi points out the strategic importance of the emirates to the Ottoman Empire as a barrier against Iran.[11] He visited twelve Kurdish emirates, some of which had already lost their autonomous status and become Ottoman *sanjaks*, with governors appointed by Istanbul. He describes the situation in the city of Diyarbakir, which had become the center of an *eyelet* that was controlled directly by an Ottoman governor and extended over most of the land area of Kurdistan.[12]

Chelebi describes a flourishing economic and cultural life, urban development, and military might among the Kurdish emirs. In the small urban centers, a stratum of merchants, craftsmen, and *'ulema* had developed, and religious and cultural life revolved around mosques, *medresat* (religious colleges), and the courts of the emirs. The strongest and most prominent emirates of that time were Bitlis and 'Amadiya (Bahdinan). During his third journey, in 1655–1656, Chelebi visited the Emirate of Bitlis twice. On his first visit, he was the guest of Emir 'Abd al-Khan Rozhiki; on his second, he accompanied his uncle, Malik Ahmad Pasha, the Ottoman governor of Van, on a campaign that ended 'Abd al-Khan's rule and the autonomy of Bitlis. According to Chelebi's description, Bitlis in the midseventeenth century had 1,200 shops and workshops. It was a cultural hub with mosques and *medresat*, and influential Sufi orders—the Naqshbandiyya and the Bakhtashiyya—maintained centers of religious and intellectual activity. The emirs of Bitlis owned 13 *zeamet* and 124 *timars*, feudal estates that were granted by the Ottoman sultans to the emirs and other local rulers in exchange for military services.

Chelebi describes the special, quasi-Renaissance character of Emir 'Abd al-Khan Rozhiki, the ruler of Bitlis, who was a man of considerable education and broad intellectual interests; a linguist and patron of the arts and sciences, he was talented in architecture, poetry, medicine, and drawing.[13] According to Chelebi, 'Abd al-Khan's library contained thousands of books in Persian and Arabic and hundreds of European books, mostly in French, on geography, physics, astronomy, and medicine. *'Ulema* who wrote poetry in Kurdish were active in his court.[14] Chelebi notes that the emir had the ability to call up 70,000 fighters (a figure that seems somewhat exaggerated). European travelers who visited the area in the seventeenth century also gained the impression that the emirate was independent for all intents and purposes, with a military force of 25,000 cavalrymen.

'Abd al-Khan's status was strengthened following a visit to Bitlis by Sultan Murad IV in 1635, as part of the Sultan's efforts to enlist the support of the Kurdish emirates in the Ottomans' war against Safavid Iran.[15] Bitlis more closely resembled the capital of an autonomous feudal vassal state than a district within an empire. In his travel account, a French traveler, Jean-Baptiste Tavernier, who visited Bitlis in 1655, mentions its strength and wealth and relates his (mistaken) impression that its ruler was not dependent on either the Ottoman sultan or the Iranian shah.[16] A description of the military power and prosperity of the Emirate of Bitlis several decades earlier appears in a book by the Italian traveler Pietro Della Valle, who passed through Kurdistan in the early seventeenth century and provided a detailed description of its political situation and cultural, social, and religious characteristics. According to this account, the emir of Bitlis enjoyed independence and could call up a force of 12,000 cavalrymen.[17]

The prosperity and power of Bitlis came to an abrupt end in 1655, following a clash between its emir, ʿAbd al-Khan, and Malik Ahmad Pasha, the powerful Ottoman governor of Van, who wanted to establish a dominant, effective Ottoman rule and to weaken strong autonomous forces such as Bitlis. He worked through Emir ʿAbd al-Khan's rivals in his own family and among the tribes and notables who sought to free themselves from his control. Malik Ahmad exploited a dispute between himself and the *sanjak* governor, Emir Muhammad Beg of Malazgird, who was subordinate to the Ottoman governor. A complaint by Muhammad Beg about a raid launched by ʿAbd al-Khan and other complaints by merchants from Van about taxes and confiscations of their goods in Bitlis gave Malik Ahmad cause to draw on the power of the Ottoman Empire and of ʿAbd al-Khan's Kurdish rivals to end al-Khan's rule and destroy the autonomy of his emirate.[18] ʿAbd al-Khan was also accused of heresy and of connivance with the Yazidis, who were considered heretics by Sunnite Muslims. (In fact, there were some Yazidi tribes among his Kurdish allies.[19]) Chelebi, who was in the service of the Ottomans, describes the battle to take Bitlis in his book.

Thus, in spite of all of its strength, Bitlis, as an emirate, was unable to withstand the power and political skills of the Ottoman Empire. In 1655, aided by Kurdish forces from Hakkari, the Ottomans conquered Bitlis, looted the city, and overturned the once-strong rule of ʿAbd al-Khan, who was forced to flee. Malik Ahmad Pasha appointed his young son, Ziyad al-Din, as a puppet emir dependent on the Ottoman governor. (A short time later, Ziyad al-Din was murdered by his older brother, who was apprehended and executed.) The emirate continued to exist, but with limited autonomy, under the sovereignty of Ottoman governors.[20] The Ottoman conquest of Bitlis and the end of ʿAbd al-Khan's rule demonstrated the success of the Ottoman Empire in reducing the autonomy of even the strongest Kurdish emirates and preventing their transformation into strong, self-governing political forces independent of the central regime.

Another important emirate was Bahdinan (Badinan), whose borders changed a number of times over the years. For various periods during the sixteenth through the eighteenth centuries, its authority extended over portions of the Hakkari area to the east and southeast of Lake Van, and the environs of the cities of Aqra, 'Amadiya, Zakho, and Barzan, all of which were included in the Iraqi state in the twentieth century.[21] The Emirate of Bahdinan maintained a complex relationship with the Yazidis and with the Jalili Dynasty of autonomous governors of Mosul. Internal struggles in the family of the Bahdinan emirs weakened the emirate and enabled the Ottomans to intervene in its affairs. The emirate reached the height of its power in the mid-eighteenth century. Crippled by internecine strife and by the defeat of its protégés and allies, the Yazidis, the emirate collapsed under an onslaught by Muhammad "Kor," the emir of Soran, who conquered 'Amadiya in 1833 and ended the Emirate of Bahdinan.

None of the emirates, however powerful and prosperous in their region, developed beyond the feudal stage. Although the Ottoman Empire lapsed into stagnation and weakness in the eighteenth century, the relative strength of the well-organized Ottoman and Iranian states, both of which commanded military forces, consistently overcame the Kurdish tribal emirates, which never developed common interests. They gradually lost their autonomous status and began to decline in number. In fact, Kurdish society never fully progressed from the tribal to the supratribal stage. Tribal and emirate socioeconomic relations continued to coexist, with families and clans of emirs preserving their tribal affinities.

THE EMIRATES OF BABAN AND ARDALAN AND THE OTTOMAN-IRANIAN STRUGGLE

In Iran under the Safavid and Qajar Dynasties, the autonomous Emirate of Ardalan played a role in the conflict between the Iranian state and the Ottomans. In the sixteenth century and the first half of the seventeenth, the main rivalry among the Kurdish emirates was between Ardalan, dominated by the Iranian Safavids, and Bahdinan, which was subject to the Ottomans. Bahdinan was gradually diminished, however, and lost its importance as a border force with the rise of Baban, a more southerly emirate that became, during the second half of the seventeenth century, the principal rival of Ardalan.

From the midseventeenth century until their disappearance in the nineteenth century, the Emirates of Ardalan and Baban were at the very heart of the struggle between Iran and the Ottomans. Both the emirates and the families of the ruling emirs became battlegrounds between the two regional powers and were important secondary players. The Emirate of Ardalan was a vassal of Iran, and the emirs of the House of Baban were mostly under Ottoman domination. At times they served as tools in a proxy war between the Ottomans and Iranians—initially under the Safavid Dynasty, and then from the late eighteenth century under the Qajars. At the same time the Ottoman *valis* of Baghdad and the shah of Iran intervened in and exploited the struggles for succession inside the emirates, especially in the House of Baban. Although Baban was under Ottoman dominance, members of its ruling house approached Iran for help in family struggles. The Iranian rulers took advantage of this opportunity to damage the Ottomans by supporting adversaries and competitors of the pro-Ottoman emirs in the House of Baban.[22]

Ardalan, whose capital was Sinna (Sanandaj), was the only emirate that retained its autonomy under Iranian rule. It was a strong vassal state of the Safavids, and the heads of the House of Ardalan married into the Safavid Dynasty. Ardalan's emirs (who claimed descent from the ancient Medes) exercised influence in the shah's court and on a number of occasions performed central functions there. According to Emir Sharaf Khan al-Bitlisi (Bidlisi) and Mehrdad Izady, the emirs of Ardalan were descendants of the Marwanid Dynasty, but from a different branch than the House of Bitlis.[23] The Kurdish dialect commonly spoken in the emirate and throughout southeast Kurdistan was the Gorani dialect. A considerable portion of Kurdish poetry was written in it. From the religious standpoint, the Kurdish population of the emirate included not only Sunnite Muslims but also some prominent members of the Ahl al-Haq sect, which combined Shi'ite Muslim and Zoroastrian elements.

Ardalan's northern neighbors were the Jaf and Mukri tribes. The major tribal confederations—Mukri, Jaf, and Hawrami—succeeded in retaining their tribal autonomy by virtue of their strength and importance to the Safavids and later the Qajars against the Ottoman Empire and its Kurdish allies. Although these tribal groups did not develop into emirates, they enjoyed tribal autonomy in certain periods and, in others, were dominated by the Emirate of Ardalan or by the Iranian state. Forces from the Emirate of Ardalan and the Mukri tribe that fought alongside Shah Tahmasp I (who ruled Iran from 1524 to 1576) inflicted a severe defeat on the Ottomans in 1538 and blocked the Ottoman attempt to break through the Zagros Mountains eastward. During the brief reign of Isma'il II (1576–1578), the emirs and tribes remained loyal to the Safavids; after his murder, however, with the weakening of the Safavid state and its allies the Qizilbashis, the Kurdish revolts be-

gan. In cooperation with the Ottoman governor of Van, militias of Kurdish tribes and magnates raided cities under Safavid control in southwestern
Azerbaijan.[24]

In the area to the east of Rawanduz, south and west of Lake Urmia, the
powerful Safavid shah ʿAbbas I (1588–1629) took measures to suppress the
power of the Baradost and Mukri tribes, which had maneuvered between
the Safavids and the Ottomans. Emir Khan Baradost (or Khani Lapzerin),
the powerful leader of the Baradost tribe, had an up-and-down relationship
with the Safavids that was influenced by the struggles between the Kurdish
tribes and the Qizilbashis, most of them Turkmen, who were loyal to the
Safavid shah. Emir Khan tried to preserve his near-independence as the Iranian and Ottoman Empires and the Turkmen tribes expanded. ʿAbbas I recognized the hereditary right of Emir Khan to rule the Baradost and Urmia
region. In 1608, however, when Emir Khan built the fortress of Dimdim,
which dominated the access from Urmia to Mahabad, ʿAbbas I treated this
as rebellion, and his army opened an offensive against Emir Khan and his allies, who were mainly the strong Mukri tribe.

As part of the military moves intended to impose sovereignty on the
Kurdish tribes and emirates inside Iran, the Iranians besieged Dimdim from
November 1609 until the summer of 1610. They overcame its Kurdish de-
fenders only after the last fighter was killed, and the women committed sui-
cide by jumping off the cliffs of the fortress. The Kurdish poet Faqi Tayran
(1590–1660) commemorated the event and helped to transform it into a popular myth of Kurdish heroism. In the twentieth century, the story would be
adopted as a myth of national heroism by the Kurdish national movement.[25]
A pro-Safavid chronicle devoted to Shah ʿAbbas I, written shortly after these
events by a Safavid official, describes the siege and conquest of Dimdim and
the suppression of the revolts by the Mukri and Baradost tribes; that ver-
sion, however, does not mention the heroic fall of the fortress.[26] The Mukri
and Baradost tribes revolted against the Safavids again in 1624, and their
leaders swore allegiance to the Ottomans.[27]

Parallel to measures aimed at subjugating the independent authority of
Kurdish tribes, Shah ʿAbbas I made efforts to enlist their support as a fighting force against the Ottomans in the west and against the Uzbek invasion from the northeast. The Safavids' closest ally was the Emirate of Ardalan. A powerful ruler from the House of Ardalan, Khan Ahmad Khan,
married Shah ʿAbbas's daughter and became one of his confidants. Even
the emirs of Ardalan, however, continued to maneuver between the Safavids
and the Ottomans. Ardalan's great rival, the Emirate of Baban, as a general
rule was subordinate to the Ottoman sultan. The prominence of this house

as an important ally of the Ottoman Empire against Safavid Iran and the House of Ardalan began as early as the seventeenth century. In 1694, Sulayman Babba, the powerful leader of Baban, succeeded in conquering large portions of Ardalan until he was defeated by a combined army of the Iranian shah and Ardalan. In gratitude for his services to the Ottoman Empire, Sulayman was given a splendid reception in Istanbul in 1695 and awarded the title of "Bey," and the Emirate of Baban, whose borders had been expanded, was given the status of a *sanjak*. The emirs of Baban, like those of Ardalan, frequently maneuvered between the empires; in so doing, they allied themselves at times with the Safavids. The House of Baban—or Babba, as it was called before the end of the eighteenth century—was generally loyal to the Ottomans, who considered them a force that could hold back Ardalan, the vassal of the Safavids and Qajars.[28]

In the early eighteenth century, the Safavid Dynasty weakened and eventually crumbled. The Ottoman Empire exploited its rival's weakness and invaded it in the 1720s. Forces of the emirs of Baban, in the service of the Ottomans, conquered the city of Sinna (Sanandaj), the capital of Ardalan, and took over the emirate. Their control continued until the end of the decade, when they were chased out of Ardalan by the Iranian army of Nadir Shah, who succeeded in unifying Iran for a short period in the mid-eighteenth century and assumed the title of "Shah" from 1736 until his death in 1747. Ottoman weakness in the eighteenth century helped Nadir Shah to forge alliances with the heads of the House of Baban and to intervene in the emirate's internal struggles. In 1743, Salim Baban obtained the support of Nader Shah against Sulayman Babba, who was backed by the Ottomans. In that conflict, Sulayman Babba took the upper hand.

After the death of Nadir Shah in 1747, his heirs became embroiled in a struggle for succession that led to their losing control of Iran. Only the northeastern areas of the former Safavid Empire remained subject to them. The weakness of Nadir Shah's heirs enabled Karim Khan Zand (1705–1779), a member of one of the Lur tribes—considered Kurdish by a number of scholars—to rise to power as the Kurdish ruler of Iran.[29] Zand succeeded in taking over most of Iran's land area and established a relatively strong regime, which remained in power from 1750 to 1779. His closest ally was the *vali* of Ardalan. However, Iran's weakness after Nadir Shah's death was exploited by Sulayman Nawaub Babba (1754–1765), who invaded Ardalan's capital in 1762.[30] Karim Khan Zand's heirs lost control of Iran, and the emirs of Ardalan transferred their support to the superior force of Agha Muhammad Khan.

After conquering Iran in 1794, Agha Muhammad Khan assumed the title of "Shah" in 1796 and founded the Qajar Dynasty. The emirs of the House of Ardalan helped the Qajars rise to power. Their close connections with the Qajar court, including the marriage between the daughter of Fath ʿAli Shah and the son of the Emir of Ardalan, gave the House of Ardalan a special status in the Shah's court, but also enabled the Qajars to intervene in the internal affairs of the emirate, especially in succession conflicts.

The long reign of Fath ʿAli Shah began in 1797 and continued until his death in 1834. The fact that Ardalan was an important ally gave the emirate special status in the Qajar court. The emirate's power and prosperity in the early nineteenth century are mentioned in the writings of John MacDonald Kinneir, a British colonel who at the time was the political aide of General Sir John Malcolm, the head of the British delegation to the court of the Shah in Tehran.[31]

Unlike the House of Ardalan, the emirs of Baban were not close to the court to which they owed their loyalty—the Ottoman court in Istanbul. Their struggles for survival were against the Ottoman *valis* and other local forces: the Mamelukes in Baghdad, the House of Ardalan, and the Iranian governors of nearby districts in Shahrizur. Until 1784, the capital of Baban was the village and fortress of Qalʿa Chilawan. In that year, however, the city of Sulaymaniyya was established and became the capital of Baban. By 1820, the city had a population of 10,000.

During the later eighteenth and early nineteenth centuries, the emirs of Baban played an influential role in political events in Baghdad. At the same time, they were subject to the influence and intervention of Ottoman governors in their family conflicts. The struggles and factions within the Baban family were exploited and intensified by the involvement of the Ottoman governors in Baghdad, as well as by the Qajar shah and his vassal, the House of Ardalan. In one example, the powerful governor of the emirate, ʿAbd al-Rahman Baban, was ousted and fled from Sulaymaniyya, but subsequently regained control of the city. This sequence of events repeated itself five times during his rule, which was constantly beset by struggles with his rivals within the family (1789–1813).[32]

THREE CENTURIES OF KURDISH POETRY AND LANGUAGE

A Kurdish written language and poetry began to develop in the emirates in the fifteenth century. Poets who are viewed as Kurds, such as Baba Tahir Hamadani, who wrote in a Lur dialect that is also considered a Persian dialect, were active as early as the tenth century, if not before.[33] During the fifteenth through eighteenth centuries, however, Kurdish poetry flourished, especially in the courts of the emirs and in emirates that enjoyed periods of stability and economic prosperity. Many of the poets were ʿulema, but some belonged to aristocratic families. The most prominent fifteenth-century Kurdish poet was ʿAli Hariri (Eli Heriri) (1425–1495), from the Hakkari area.[34] Well-known later poets included Malaye Jaziri (1570–1640) and Feqiye Teyran (Faqi Tayran) (1590–1660).[35]

An author who in addition to poetry composed a Kurdish-Persian-Arabic dictionary was Ismaʿil Bayazidi (1654–1709). Other poets were Sharif Khan of the family of the emirs of Hakkari (1689–1690 to 1748–1749), who wrote in Arabic and Persian, and Murad Khan (1737–1738 to 1784–1785), who wrote romantic and erotic poems.[36] Much Kurdish literary writing has come down to us from the Emirate of Ardalan, where Kurdish writing was in the Gorani dialect. Literary works were also written in Persian, but with Kurdish heroes.

Two great works of Kurdish literature from the sixteenth and seventeenth centuries are the *Sharafnama*, a history of Kurdish states and emirates written in Persian, and *Mam u Zin*, a poetic epos written in Kurdish. These two works became foundational in the shaping of Kurdish identity and provided a historical and cultural foundation for the rise of modern Kurdish nationalism. Both spoke to Kurdish distinctiveness and identity vis-à-vis the "others."

In 1595, Sharaf Khan al-Bitlisi, the ruler of the Emirate of Bitlis, published a detailed chronicle of the dynasties of Kurdish emirs and rulers. Bitlisi was initially a vassal of the Safavids. Shah Tahmasp I subsequently appointed him governor of Gilan, to the south of the Caspian Sea.[37] Shah Ismaʿil II gave him the title of "Emir of the Emirs of the Kurds" (*amir al-umara al-akrad*). In this role, he was involved in the struggle between rival factions in the Shah's palace and was forced to contend with the heads of the Qizilbashis. His status weakened, Bitlisi was banished from the palace and appointed governor of Nakchivan in the Caucasus. After the death of Ismaʿil II, Bitlisi switched to the Ottoman side in 1578 and was appointed governor of Bitlis by the Ottoman sultan Murad III. In that capacity, he led the Kurdish tribes against the Safavids. At the end of the 1580s, he apparently abdicated his emirate rule in favor of his son and devoted himself to his book, which he wrote in Persian, the cultural language of the time.[38]

The book's orientation is pro-Ottoman; it was written in the context of the Ottoman-Iranian struggle, during the reign of the powerful Safavid shah ʿAbbas I. Bitlisi considered history to be the history of rulers and ruling dynasties. Although the book is not nationalist in the modern sense, it nevertheless conveys a sense of Kurdish ethno-political distinctiveness, however fragmented: a large number of emirates and dynasties of emirs had to be taken into account by the states warring for control of Kurdistan.[39] The four parts of the book review the rulers and dynasties according to their degree of independence, beginning in the first part with those that were independent and powerful, such as the Ayyubids.[40] The second part is devoted to rulers who were not independent but whose status was sufficiently high that their names were mentioned in the *khutbeh* (sermons) on Fridays in the mosques and they minted their own coins. The third part is devoted to all the remaining Kurdish rulers, and the fourth part deals with the rulers of the Emirate of Bitlis. The book played an important role in the late history of the Kurds in that it provided a source of memory and imagery for the dynasties of Kurdish emirs, as well as proof that the Kurds had played a role in history. The book was apparently known by at least some of the emirs, and probably by Kurdish *ulema* as well. According to a British traveler in the early nineteenth century, the Emir of Ardalan was familiar with it.[41]

As a work that deals with *ta'ife Kurdiye*—the Kurdish nation or community—the book reinforced a sense of Kurdish distinctiveness, at least among the literate members of the tribal elites and emir dynasties.[42] Bitlisi defined ethnographically and socially the Kurdish lands and the Kurdish imagined community. Yet, as we have seen, the political and social conditions under which any of the Kurdish dialects could have evolved into a dominant position never developed.

During the fifteenth through the eighteenth centuries, poets and *ulema* who wrote in Kurdish were active in some of the Kurdish emirates, and some *ulema* apparently used Kurdish for religious studies in *medresat*. Kurdish poetry in the Gorani dialect flourished during the sixteenth, seventeenth, and eighteenth centuries in the Sinna (Sanandaj) area, east of Sulaymaniyya and north of Kermanshah, which is now in Iran.[43]

A zenith of intellectual and literary activity was the poem *Mam u Zin*, written in the Kurmanji dialect by Ahmad-i Khani (1660?–1707)—one of the most important Kurdish poets and an *alim* (clergyman) with a leaning toward Sufism—and published in 1695.[44] The poem revolves around a love story that has appeared in several versions throughout the Arabic- and Persian-speaking Muslim world. This particular work, however, is written in a Kurdish dialect and exhibits definitive expressions of early Kurdish nationalism. In one of the poem's sections, Ahmad-i Khani explains that he wrote it in Kurdish because Kurds, like other peoples, need a book of their own. In other words, he refers to the Kurds as a group with a defined identity. At the same time, he apparently considered only the Kurmanji-speaking Kurds to be Kurds: as he saw it, the signifiers *Kurd* and *Kurmanji* were congruent.[45]

The last sections of the work include poetic descriptions of the tragic geopolitical situation of the Kurds relative to the Turks, Persians, Arabs, and Georgians:

> *Look, from the Arabs to the Georgians*
> *The Kurds have become like towers.*
> *The Turks and Persians are surrounded by them.*
> *The Kurds are on all four corners.*
> *Both sides have made the Kurdish people,*
> *Targets for arrows of fate.*
> *They are said to be keys to the borders,*
> *Each clan forming a formidable bulwark.*
> *Whenever the Ottoman Sea [the Ottomans] and the Tajik Sea [the Persians]*
> *Flow out and agitate,*
> *The Kurds get soaked in blood*
> *Separating them like an isthmus.*[46]

The explicit reference to the Kurds as a collective is a clear expression of the concept of a Kurdish identity different from that of "others." Popular characters in the poem also express a Kurdish personal identity:

> *I am a peddler, not of noble origins,*
> *Self-grown, not educated.*
> *I am a Kurd from the mountains and distant lands.*
> *These are a few stories from the Kurdavari* [Kurdish way of life] . . . [47]

The poet subsequently bewails the division of Kurdistan and expresses longing for a Kurdish ruler who will unite the Kurds against their Turkish and Tajik enemies—in other words, for Kurdish political and military might. This passage may have been a response to the destruction of the Emirate of Bitlis by the Ottomans:[48]

> *If the Kurds had a king . . .*
> *These Rumis [Ottomans/Turks] would not defeat us,*
> *We would not become ruins in the hands of Owls,*
> *We would not become doomed, homeless,*
> *Defeated by the Turks and Tajiks [Iranians] and subjugated by them . . .*
>
> *If we had a king*
> *And God befitted him a crown,*
> *And success had been appointed for him,*
> *A fortune would appear for us . . .*[49]

Khani laments the lack of unity among the Kurds and says:

> *If we were united*
> *Then we would subjugate them all*
> *The Rumis [Turks], Arabs and Persians*
> *Would all serve us . . .*[50]

Again, this is an early expression of one of the characteristics of modern nationalism: the ambition for statehood on the basis of a collective identity. Long before the rise of modern nationalism, Khani used the terms "Kurds," "Arabs," "Persians," and "Turks," not to refer to religious communities, but in the ethno-national sense. He referred to "the Kurds" in the sense of an "imagined community," the term coined in the twentieth century by Benedict Anderson.[51] The poem is the most important expression of the Kurdish political consciousness. Khani justified the writing of the poem in Kurdish as a need to show "others" that the Kurds had a history, a culture, and a literature:

> *So that people won't say that the Kurds*
> *Have no knowledge and have no history;*
> *That all sorts of peoples have their books*
> *And only the Kurds are negligible.*[52]

Khani believed that a cultural revival would arise under a Kurdish political ruler that would metaphorically resurrect the long-dead Kurdish poets Malaye Jaziri (Chizri), ʿAli Hariri (Eli Heriri), and Faqie Teyran, who were probably almost forgotten in his era:

> *If we had for us an owner*
> *Highly generous, versed in good speech,*
> *Science, arts, perfection, and prudence,*
> *Poetry, lyrics, books, and verse collection,*
> *These genres would become acceptable to him.*
> *I would see the banner of rhythmic [??] speech*
> *Raised high on the top of universe.*
> *I would have brought back to life Mele Cizri,*
> *Resurrected Eli Hariri,*
> *Would have given such pleasure to Feqiye Teyran*
> *That he would have stayed forever overwhelmed with joy.*[53]

Beginning with the first proponents of the modern Kurdish national movement in the early nineteenth century, this poem—which was edited and republished by one of the forerunners of modern Kurdish nationalism, the poet Haji Qadir Koyi (1815–1897)—has been adopted as a national epos.[54]

In addition to *Mam u Zin*, Ahmad-i Khani compiled the first Kurdish-Arabic dictionary and wrote a book in Kurdish on the principles of the Islamic faith. These works conferred on the Kurdish language—and more precisely, on the Kurmanji dialect—the status of a language in which it was possible to express the tenets of Islam and to write high poetry. His book on the Muslim religion was not the first of its kind: another on the same subject had been written in Kurdish as early as the fifteenth century.

Both *Mam u Zin* and the *Sharafnama* were well known among educated Kurds, principally 'ulema, and in the courts of the emirs. Both were expressions of Kurdish proto-nationalism or early nationalism and Kurdish distinctiveness. In addition to tribal, dynastic, and sometimes religious identities, an identity (albeit sometimes vague) of Kurdishness was also associated with the tribes and clannish dynasties of emirs. These works of literature helped strengthen and perpetuate that sense of identity, even as the tribal experience remained paramount. Both works—written in circumstances that included the tribal fragmentation of Kurdistan, its division between the Ottoman Empire and Iran, and the evolving sense of Kurdish cultural-ethnic and political distinctiveness and identity in contrast to the surrounding Ottoman-Turkish, Arab, Iranian, Armenian, and Georgian cultures and identities—included criticism of the divisions among the Kurds and of their lack of unity and central leadership.

These literary trends could not, however, be sustained. None of the emirates was capable of imposing upon the others a sovereignty that would have fostered the collective identity and common interests critical to creating a state-building dynamic and constructing a nation. No Kurdish ruler, and no other political or social entity, had any interest in nurturing Kurdish as a language of administration and written culture. Although several emirates acquired considerable political and military power for various intervals—for years or even, at times, for decades—the Ottoman authorities, fearing that peripheral forces would grow too strong to be manageable, took measures to weaken them from time to time and even destroyed emirates and dynasties that became powerful enough to pose a threat. In the absence of conditions in which an urban bourgeoisie or supratribal leadership could develop, the Kurdish emirates and tribes could not unite around a common interest and oppose the Ottoman state.

The Kurdish language also suffered from the historical vigor and reach of Arabic, Turkish, and Persian. The centrality of the Arabic language to the growth of Islam, as reflected in the Koran and Hadith literature, the development of the Islamic religion and culture, and the establishment of an Arab Muslim state—primarily during the reign of the first caliphs and the period of the Umayyads, who were culturally Arab—conferred a hegemonic status on the Arabic language. Persian adopted the Arabic alphabet instead of the original Persian script, but nevertheless remained independent enough to find a place in the Muslim world as the language of high and refined culture and, to a great degree, of Shi'ite religious discourse. The power of the Turkish tribes in the Muslim world beginning in the eleventh century and the hegemony of the Ottoman state after the fifteenth century transformed the Ottoman Turkish language—which also adopted the Arabic alphabet— into the discourse of government and administration.

The absence of a written high Kurdish language during the seventeenth century, as well as the dominance of the Arabic-speaking state, relegated local Kurdish dialects to a position of inferiority. Arabic was the language of religion and law, Turkish was the language of administration and the state, and it was Persian, the language of high culture, in which the Kurdish *ulema* expressed themselves and created works of literature. In the absence of any Kurdish social stratum or ruler willing or able to nurture any of the Kurdish dialects, none of these became standardized as the "correct" Kurdish language or as a means of disseminating a Kurdish cultural heritage. The dialects were used exclusively for day-to-day speech, folk tales, and poems.

The first stirrings of a written high Kurdish language, primarily as poetry in the Kurdish emirates, remained embryonic. Kurdish poets continued to write poetry in Kurdish, but none of the dialects developed beyond everyday communication. The literation of Kurdish society—the most important driver of modernization—started in the late nineteenth century in Turkish, Arabic, and Persian. Kurdish students in Ottoman, Iranian, and (after World War I) Turkish schools learned to read and write in those languages. Even in Iraq, where Kurdish was taught in some schools, a considerable proportion of Kurdish students attended Arabic schools. In the early twentieth century, this linguistic weakness placed the Kurdish national movement at a disadvantage compared to the Arab, Turkish, and Iranian national movements.

CHAPTER 3

THE DEMISE OF THE KURDISH EMIRATES IN THE NINETEENTH CENTURY

INTERNATIONAL CHANGES AND OTTOMAN REFORMS

Between the sixteenth and early nineteenth centuries, political life in Kurdistan was conducted in the context of internal developments in the Ottoman Empire and Iran, as well as in the region dominated by those two powers. In the early nineteenth century, regional conditions changed and both of these major states began a series of internal reforms and transformations. Two changes had an impact on the Kurdish emirates: first, the reforms in the Ottoman Empire during the reign of Sultan Mahmud II, especially the policy to increase central bureaucratic control over the autonomous forces in the provinces; and second, the transformation in international relations, particularly the end of the Ottoman-Iranian wars with the 1823 signing of the Treaty of Erzurum. The end of hostilities between the two states made the emirates (especially Baban and Hakkari on the Iranian border) less militarily important against Iran and dampened their ability to maneuver occasionally between the two powers.[1]

Additionally, since the beginning of the nineteenth century, Russia and Britain had become influential in regional relations and in the domestic affairs of the Ottoman Empire and Iran. These regional and international changes, as well as those within the Ottoman Empire and Iraq, were a direct and indirect consequence of the influence exerted by the colonial Western states; of the spread of capitalism and modernization in western Europe and its impact on the non-European world; and of the responses of local forces and societies.

In the last years of the reign of Catherine the Great, Czarina of Russia, and during the reign of her heir, Czar Pavel (Paul) I (1754–1801, ruled 1796–1801), Russia took control of much of the Caucasus. The relative proximity of Russia and its initial probes of Iran and Kurdistan caused concern in Britain and affected British relations with Iran and the Ottoman Empire. At the same time, the growth of the British-owned East India Company's economic interests in the Persian Gulf compelled Britain to intensify its activities in Mesopotamia and Kurdistan in order to block any Russian penetration. Preserving the existence, unity, and strength of the Ottoman Empire so that it could act as a barrier to Russian expansion southward toward the routes to India, or even close to India itself, became a coherent diplomatic strategy in the 1830s. For Kurdistan, the relevant regional arena changed from a bipolar to a quadrilateral one in which Russia and Britain played a role as well as the Ottoman Empire and Iran.

This development also affected the conditions within the Ottoman Empire that had enabled the autonomous Kurdish emirates to exist. As part of its policy to preserve the Ottoman Empire's stability, Britain supported the Ottoman reforms, which among other things were intended to reinforce centralized control and to subdue autonomous local forces—such as the Kurdish emirates. The strengthening of the centralist Ottoman regime during the reign of Sultan Mahmud II (1808–1839) and the period of the Tanzimat reforms (1839–1876) led to the ouster of Dawud Pasha (who ruled from 1816 to 1831), the powerful Mameluke ruler in Baghdad, and to the defeat in 1831 of the Mamelukes as a local force. In 1834 the Ottomans wiped out the House of Jalili, which had controlled Mosul.[2] At the same time, the power of the Bedouin tribal federations declined.

The elimination of the Mamelukes and the weakening of the Bedouin federations demolished the local political arena in which the Kurdish emirates had enjoyed the freedom to maneuver between local forces and the Ottoman governors. The administrative reforms and the moves against various autonomous local forces led to a confrontation between the emirates and the superior power of the Empire.

Another change resulted from a shift in the relations between Muslims and Christians. The tensions between the two religious groups in the Ottoman Empire increased as a result of the Empire's penetration by Western powers, the natural ties between the Western powers and the Christian communities there, and the socioeconomic implications of the influence of Western capitalism on the Christians' economic situation. These religious tensions exacerbated the tensions and conflicts in Kurdistan between the agricultural-pastoral, mostly tribal Kurdish population and the permanently settled, nontribal peasants, merchants, and craftsmen, many of whom were Assyrian and Armenian Christians who were also the vassals and protégés of Kurdish emirs. Muslim-Christian relations at times reflected socioeconomic and ecological divisions, and in Kurdistan these tensions took the form of Kurdish-Armenian and Kurdish-Assyrian rivalry.

THE KURDS AND RUSSIAN INFLUENCE

The first contacts between Russia and the Kurdish tribes were forged as a result of the Russian expansion into the southern Caucasus during the reign of Czar Pavel I and the wars fought by Russia against Iran and the Ottoman Empire in the late eighteenth and early nineteenth centuries. At the end of the eighteenth century, Russia began to get more involved in the Caucasus. In 1801 it extended its patronage to the Kingdom of Georgia, which had sought its protection against the Ottomans.

The founder of the Qajar Dynasty, Agha Muhammad Khan (1742–1797), who proclaimed himself "Shah" in 1796, wished to restore to Iranian control the territories the Qajars had controlled under the Safavid Dynasty. Agha Muhammad's aspirations, as well as his attempts to resume tax collection, led Kurdish tribes and magnates in the Caucasus to cooperate with Russia. The links between Russia and the Christians in the area and the nature of the Russian army as a Christian force put a halt to this cooperation; nevertheless, this phenomenon was to repeat itself in the wars between Russia and Iran between 1804 and 1813 and again between 1826 and 1828.[3]

During the Russian-Ottoman War of 1828–1829, the Kurds and the Russians began to cooperate. The Kurds fighting on the Russian side were more prominent during that war than in any other Russian-Ottoman war. The talented but cruel Russian commander General Ivan Fyodorovich Paskevich (1782–1856) pursued a policy of active cooperation with the mountain tribes that were resisting Ottoman attempts to impose sovereignty over the southern Caucasus. As the Kurds saw it, this was an outcome of their opposition to both the centralization being imposed by the Ottoman government and Sultan Mahmud II's administrative reforms, which would limit the autonomy of the emirates. In the course of that war, some 3,000 Kurdish cavalrymen from the Yerevan area, under the command of Husayn Agha, allied with the Russians and played a significant role in the fighting against the Ottomans. The emirates further to the south, Soran (Rawanduz), Hakkari, and Botan, remained neutral and did not come to the aid of their sovereign, the Ottoman sultan.[4]

Both the Ottoman Empire's weakness and defeats and the rise of Russia and Britain were closely watched by the Kurdish emirs, who may have been committed to the Ottoman sultan but in practical terms were loyal to the interests of their own tribes and emirates. Various Kurdish forces also cooperated with Russia during the Crimean War (1853–1856) and in a Kurdish revolt led by Yezdansher. Other Kurdish forces, however, maintained their loyalty to the sultan. Local Kurdish tribes and leaders cooperated with Russia or with the Ottomans depending on their own interests. The Kurdish tribes that remained loyal to the sultan burned and looted Armenian churches and villages with Ottoman encouragement. At times, local tensions between Kurdish Muslims and Armenian Christians—which also had a socioeconomic element—gave the Kurds a motive to demonstrate their support of the Ottoman Empire, either because they identified with it as Islamic or because of a desire to settle old scores with the Armenians. Russian military commanders had pragmatic, tactical reasons to cooperate with the Kurdish tribes; at the same time, cooperation with the Armenian Christians was a basic component of Russian activity in the area, and the Armenians were generally perceived as allied with Russia.

THE WEAKENING OF THE EMIRATE OF BABAN

In the early nineteenth century, the principal Kurdish emirates were Baban, Soran (sometimes called after its capital, Rawanduz), Botan (Bohtan) in the areas of Diyarbakir (Amed), Chizire (Jazira), and Nuseibin. Other emirates included Hakkari, to the east and south of Lake Van on the Iranian border, and Bahdinan (sometimes called after its capital, ʿAmadiya), which extended between Zakho in the west and the Great Zab River in the east. Hakkari and Bahdinan became progressively weaker, and their autonomy was limited as a result of internal struggles and pressure from the Ottoman authorities and the rulers of stronger emirates.

After the Ottoman-Persian wars, the Emirates of Baban and Hakkari lost their importance, and their ability to maneuver vis-à-vis the Ottoman government was curtailed. Baban had relatively more influence on decisions in Baghdad, but both Baban and Hakkari lost their status and strength (*inter alia*, as a result of internal struggles), and both emirates were finally overthrown in the 1830s.

The writings of Claudius Rich, an agent of the East India Company in Basra and Baghdad, are an important source of information about the political situation of the House of Baban and the relations between various local forces in Basra, Baghdad, and southern Kurdistan in the last two decades of the nineteenth century.[5] The Emirate of Baban arose in the midseventeenth century; Sulaymaniyya, its urban center, was established in 1784. The emirs of the House of Baban played an important role in the complex politics of Baghdad. The forces active in the local political arena included the local Mameluke rulers; the *valis*, who were appointed by the Istanbul government in an attempt to extend central control over the *vilayets* of Iraq; and the powerful Bedouin tribal federations, which at times controlled most of the roads. The relative proximity of Baban to Baghdad, the emirate's military power, and its status as an essential barrier to the influence of Iran— as well as the internal struggles within the House of Baban, which were exploited by both Iranians and Ottomans—created a complex network of connections and influences between Baghdad and Sulaymaniyya. Generally speaking, the emirs of Baban preferred the *valis* in Baghdad to be sent from Istanbul rather than appointed from among the Mamelukes. As the House of Baban saw it, a *vali* who was appointed in Istanbul and had to contend with the Mamelukes and the tribal federations in order to maintain his status was better than one selected from among the strong rival forces. At times, it was preferable for the emir in power to be directly subordinate to the Sublime Porte in faraway Istanbul, which only loosely controlled the area, rather than to the heads of the Mamelukes or to the Ottoman governors in Baghdad, which was much closer to Sulaymaniyya. The attempts by Dawud Pasha, the Mameluke ruler in Baghdad, to take over Mosul gave rise to intermittent collaboration between the House of Jalili (the dominant force in Mosul) and the House of Baban against the Mamelukes in Baghdad.[6]

In the early nineteenth century, the strong man of the House of Baban, ʿAbd al-Rahman (1789–1813), continued to maneuver between the Mamelukes in Baghdad, the Ottoman government in Istanbul, the emirs of Ardalan, and the Iranian state. At times, he achieved a degree of influence in Baghdad and could engineer the rise or fall of the Ottoman *valis*. However, against the background of the convoluted struggles within the House of Baban, he was forced to flee from Sulaymaniyya to Iran no less than five times.[7]

In 1805, when ʿAbd al-Rahman fled to Iran to escape the coalition between the Mameluke and Ottoman forces in Baghdad and the rivals within his own family, headed by Khaled Baban, the Iranians were glad of the opportunity to boost their status in Sulaymaniyya and the Shahrizur area. With the help of the Shah, ʿAbd al-Rahman returned to Sulaymaniyya and reassumed his rule of the emirate in 1806. The appointment of the powerful Mameluke Küçük Sulayman ("Sulayman the Little") to the post of *vali* in Baghdad (from 1808 to 1818) led to the renewal of the struggle between ʿAbd al-Rahman and the Mameluke Ottoman government in Baghdad. ʿAbd al-Rahman fortified mountain passes in the direction of Sulaymaniyya in order to strengthen his autonomous status vis-à-vis the Mamelukes and the Ottoman governors in Baghdad.[8] This conflict centered on efforts by the Mameluke-Ottoman government to impose sovereignty over the emirate, whose relative proximity to Baghdad, location on the Iranian border, and ability to call up a significant military force gave its leaders a stronger position in the power struggles in Baghdad. When Küçük Sulayman rebelled against the central Ottoman government in 1810, the emissary who arrived from Istanbul to organize the forces to defeat Sulayman suggested appointing ʿAbd al-Rahman as the Ottoman *vali* in Baghdad. ʿAbd al-Rahman refused, probably fearing that if he absented himself from Sulaymaniyya, his status would be weakened, as would that of his family group, relative to his internal rivals.[9]

Mahmud, the son of ʿAbd al-Rahman, became emir after his father's death in 1813 and played a part in the conflicts that led to the rise of Dawud Pasha, the last of the strong Mameluke governors of Baghdad (1818–1831). Dawud Pasha developed and promoted the area under his control. He rebuilt the city walls and began to improve the condition of Baghdad's streets; at the same time, he established a textile plant and a weapons factory.[10]

The House of Baban, as a general rule, was subject to Ottoman sovereignty. But its constant internal struggles were exploited by the Qajars of Iran and the emirs of Ardalan. At times, members of the House of Baban would seek assistance and protection from Iran or an alliance with the emirs of Ardalan. This incessant strife and the frequent interventions weakened the House of Baban and from the early 1820s led to its subordination to either Ottoman or Iranian rule and the restriction of its autonomy. Although the Baban emirs were nominally under the sovereignty of the Ottoman sultan, until the 1830s they also paid tax to the Qajar shah of Iran.

Woven into the struggles within the House of Baban was an episode in the rise of the Sufi order known as Naqshbandiyya-Mujaddidiyya, which during the nineteenth century developed into one of the most influential streams of religious ideology in Sunnite Islam. Shaykh Mawlana Khalid (1779–1827), the founder of the Naqshbandiyya-Mujaddidiyya order, was born in Shahrizur (near Sulaymaniyya). After studying in India, he returned to Kurdistan in 1811 and moved back and forth between Kurdistan and Baghdad until 1822. Between 1811 and 1813, he was a protégé of Emir ʿAbd al-Rahman, who, along with his son Mahmud, apparently gave the Shaykh their protection at the time of the ongoing strife with their domestic rivals and with the Mameluke-Ottoman governors in Baghdad. Mawlana Khalid's activity and increasing influence over the heads of the House of Baban led to tension with the head of the dominant Qadiri order, Shaykh Maʿaruf Nudahi al-Barzinji (1761–1838), who was also influential in the court of Baban.[11] As a result of the ensuing struggle, Mawlana Khalid was forced to leave Sulaymaniyya in 1813. In 1817 he returned to Sulaymaniyya, but in October 1820 he had to leave again under cover of darkness, traveling first to Baghdad and then to Damascus.[12]

During the 1820s and early 1830s, the emirate continued to be torn between the Ottomans and the Iranians. The Iranian involvement in the emirate, however, ceased with the death of the powerful Qajar shah of Iran, Fath ʿAli Shah, in 1834. The end of the Ottoman-Iranian wars deprived the Emirate of Baban of its importance as a barrier between the Ottoman Empire and Qajar Iran, and the defeat of the Mamelukes in Baghdad in 1831 by forces loyal to Sultan Mahmud II further diminished the emirate's ability to maneuver. While Emir Sulayman Pasha (1828–1838) still maintained a small regular army of his own, the position of the emirate as a whole, relative to the Ottoman Empire, grew weaker and weaker. An attempt to reduce the emirate's size and the power of the House of Baban was opposed by Emir Ahmad Pasha (1838–1847) and led to a clash—apparently very limited—with the forces of the Ottoman *vali* in Baghdad, Najib Pasha, in 1847. Ahmad Pasha was ousted, and the Ottomans appointed his brother to replace him. The House of Baban continued to head the emirate, but the emirs were appointed by the Ottoman authorities, and their autonomy was gradually cut back until it disappeared completely in 1851 with the appointment of Ismaʿil Pasha, a Turkish officer, as *kaymakam* (district governor) of the area.[13]

THE RISE AND FALL OF MUHAMMAD KOR OF SORAN

With the weakening of the Emirate of Baban, the most prominent remaining emirates were Soran, headed by a strong ruler, Emir Ibrahim, and Botan, whose capital was Jazira and which was headed by Emir Bedir Khan. The Emirates of Hakkari and Bahdinan were embroiled in internal struggles within the clans of the ruling emirs. The rest of Kurdistan consisted of a network of smaller tribes and local khans.

Muhammad "Kor" ("the Blind"—so-called because he was blind in his left eye) inherited the Emirate of Soran from his father Ibrahim in 1813. It is unclear whether Ibrahim, who was then old and sick, abdicated in his son's favor or was ousted by him. Initially, Mohammed Kor overcame his rivals in Soran, killed those relatives whose disloyalty he suspected, and increased his control over the emirate until 1826. He developed and fortified Rawanduz and established a *diwan* (advisory council) there. Known for his religious devotion, he obtained the support of the ʿulema. During the 1820s and early 1830s, the Emirate of Soran under Muhammad Kor became the central power in southern and central Kurdistan. Initially, he succeeded in im-

posing his sovereignty upon the tribes in the Rawanduz area and on the sur-
viving remnants of the Emirate of Hakkari. In the early 1820s, he expanded
his control southward to the Little Zab River and also northward; he threw
out the governors of the declining Emirates of Baban and Hakkari and conquered the cities of Erbil and Koy Sanjaq. By the mid-1820s, he had forced
his sovereignty upon the Emirate of Hakkari and on the Baradost, Sorchi,
and Mamish tribes.[14] In 1831, when a confrontation broke out between the
central Ottoman government and Dawud Pasha, the Mameluke governor of
Baghdad, Muhammad Kor assisted the Ottoman commander, ʿAli Riza Pasha, who defeated the Mameluke rulers in Baghdad.[15]

In 1831, Muhammad Kor exploited the weakness of the Emirate of Bahdinan and attacked the Yazidis, who were the protégés and allies of Bahdinan
at the time. In 1833 he took over its capital, ʿAmadiya, and most of its territory and ousted its ruler, Emir Ismaʿil Pasha.[16] Muhummad Kor thus put
an end to the old emirate, which had been declining since the 1780s because
of internal struggles and against the background of the tensions and complex relationship with the Yazidis and the Jalili Dynasty, the rulers of Mosul.[17] The conquest was violent and included many acts of murder and looting. The victims came from all segments of the population: Kurds, Yazidis,
Christians, and Jews. By 1833 Muhammad Kor had succeeded in imposing
control over an extensive area, which included ʿAmadiya, Zakho, Dohuk,
Mardin, and Nuseibin in the west. In practical terms, the Emirate of Bahdinan ceased to exist at that time; later, during the 1840s, it was entirely sub-
ordinated to the Ottoman governor of Mosul and disappeared altogether.

Muhammad Kor established an army that included cavalry, infantry, and
an artillery unit. Most of its soldiers came from the tribes over whom he had
sovereignty or with whom he contracted alliances; however, there was also
a regular army unit. According to several sources, he was capable of calling
up 10,000 cavalrymen and 20,000 infantrymen; another source claims that
he could call up 50,000 fighters.[18] Although these figures appear to be exaggerated and have never been verified, there can be no doubt that Muhammad Kor became the strongest force in Kurdistan. At the same time, he began to develop workshops for the manufacture of swords, rifles, and even
cannons. The extent to which these plans came to fruition requires further
study. Additional signs of his ambition included the minting of coins carry-
ing his name and the mention of his name in Friday sermons in the emirate's mosques.[19]

Muhammed Kor's status and achievements in no way equaled those of
the governor of Egypt, Muhammad ʿAli (1805–1848), or even those of ʿAli
Bey al-Kbir (1728–1773), the Mameluke ruler of Egypt in the second half of

the eighteenth century. Nevertheless, his rule reflected a trend similar to trends that developed among autonomous rulers throughout the Ottoman Empire, starting in the mid-eighteenth century, and to which the Empire responded in the nineteenth century with reforms, especially the modernization and centralization of its government and administration.

By now, Muhammad Kor controlled a larger part of Kurdistan than any Kurdish emir before him. Only the Emirate of Botan, under Emir Muhammad Bedir Khan, retained its independence. Following his successful suppression of the Yazidis and conquest of Bahdinan, Muhammad Kor directed his next onslaught against Botan in 1833 and easily conquered its capital, Jazirat Ibn 'Umar. Bedir Khan's forces holed up, however, in a series of mountain fortresses, which Muhammad Kor did not succeed in taking. The resistance by Bedir Khan and his supporters, and the revolts that broke out in 'Amadiya and other places, forced Muhammad Kor to halt his offensive and to retreat.[20] The attack on the Emirate of Botan took place when the Ottoman regime was weakened by military defeats in the war against Russia in 1828 and 1829 and by the conquest of Syria by Muhammad 'Ali in 1831–1832.

In 1831, Muhammad 'Ali's army invaded Syria. The Egyptian forces, under the command of Muhammad 'Ali's son, Ibrahim Pasha, defeated the Ottoman army and advanced as far as Kutahya, about 200 kilometers from Istanbul, in northwestern Anatolia. Muhammad 'Ali viewed Sultan Mahmud II's policy of centralization and elimination of autonomous local and regional powers as a threat, and he responded by invading Syria and taking measures to bring about the replacement of Mahmud II by another Ottoman sultan who would accept his right to pass on his rule of Egypt to his descendants and who would recognize Egypt's special status within the Ottoman Empire.

At that time, the Ottoman army was in the initial stages of reorganization and modernization, following Mahmud II's violent dismantling of the Janissary Corps in 1826, both as a military force and as a sociopolitical system. The Janissaries had constituted the principal force of the Ottoman army and were also the conservative element that opposed the reforms and the modernization of the army that Mahmud II sought to promote. Accordingly, their violent elimination was intended to remove a center of power that threatened the reform-minded sultan.

Disturbed by the advance of the Egyptian army toward Istanbul, Sultan Mahmud II turned to Russia, the Ottomans' great enemy, and asked it for aid. Russia sought to exploit the crisis in order to strengthen its influence in the Ottoman Empire and to extend its rights in the Bosporus and Dardanelles. Russian troops intervened and drove the Egyptians back to Syria. This attempt to exploit the conflict and the Treaty of Hunkar Iskelesi signed by Russia and the Ottoman Empire in 1833 led Britain to step up its activity in Istanbul and to work to preserve the Ottoman Empire as a barrier to Russian infiltration of the Mediterranean Sea and the Persian Gulf. Accordingly, Britain became more interested in supporting the Ottoman reforms, which were meant to strengthen the Empire. Britain also supported the similarly intended Ottoman policy of eliminating the Kurdish emirates and other autonomous forces, which undermined the Ottoman regime and ran counter to the British interest of preserving the Ottoman Empire and reinforcing the central authority in Istanbul. In addition, during the period of Egyptian rule in Syria and in light of the Egyptian threat to the Empire, the Ottomans and the British feared that the Kurdish forces, and especially Muhammad Kor, would cooperate with Ibrahim Pasha, now the Egyptian governor of Syria.

In the summer of 1834, the Ottomans launched an offensive against Muhammad Kor.[21] His successful resistance gave him confidence, which may have inspired his attempt to take action among the Kurdish tribes in Iran. On the other hand, he may merely have wished to maneuver again between Iran and the Ottoman Empire. In fact, his move aroused suspicion among the Iranians, and the Russian consulates in Tehran and Tabriz feared that the weakening of Iran would be exploited by Britain. The rival powers Britain and Russia supported, for opposite reasons, the continued existence of the Ottoman Empire and Iran, but only as states at their mercy: remaining weak enough to enable each of the rivals to promote its own interests, but strong enough to prevent a vacuum that could be exploited by the rival state for its own purposes, primarily strategic, but also economic. Notwithstanding this internal contradiction in the diplomatic policy of the two European powers, it recurred throughout the nineteenth and twentieth centuries and the first years of the twenty-first century: the great powers in the international arena, both as a general rule and especially at decision points, have preferred to preserve Iran and the Ottoman Empire (Turkey after World War I) rather than support the Kurdish emirates or the Kurdish national movement.

The rumors of ties between Muhammad Kor and Ibrahim Pasha increased Ottoman fears of cooperation between them and moved Sultan Mahmud II to prepare a military strike against Muhammad Kor. In accordance with the Sultan's policy of destroying autonomous powers, Mehmet Reshid Pasha, commander of the Ottoman army, concentrated a large Ottoman force that reduced the areas under Muhammad Kor's control. An Ottoman offensive in the summer of 1836—whose participants, acting on

Mahmud II's orders, included not only troops brought in from Anatolia but also those led by the *valis* of Baghdad and Mosul—forced Muhammad Kor to retreat and to fortify his position in Rawanduz. His efforts to enlist Iranian support failed. The emir may have considered giving himself room to maneuver between the Ottomans and Iran. But the suspicion that he was planning to obtain the assistance of Muhammad 'Ali—and possibly of the Iranians as well—only increased the Ottoman determination to oust him.

In view of his isolation, Muhammad Kor decided to negotiate with the Ottomans. The British were also involved, and a British diplomat, Richard Wood, came to Rawanduz with a view to persuading Muhammad Kor to surrender to the Ottomans in exchange for their consent to leave him in place as governor of the Emirate of Soran.[22] When he arrived in Soran, Wood heard about the negotiations between Muhammad Kor and Iranian representatives and was informed of a rumor (apparently spurious) that an irregular battalion of Cossacks, organized in Iran with Russian assistance, would assist the Shah in providing support to Soran.[23] Wood may have attributed more importance to himself than he actually had in convincing Muhammad Kor to surrender. It appears, however, that the British sought to prevent a resumption of the war between Iran and the Ottoman Empire, in light of the latter's weakness, and to avoid a situation that Russia might exploit.

Muhammad Kor's status was undermined by the looseness of his tribal alliance. The loyalty of the Kurdish tribes depended on either the degree of his success or his ability to instill fear in them. When the Ottomans appeared to have the upper hand, his allies preferred their particular tribal interests and refrained from assisting him. Faced with Ottoman might, Mohammed Kor's tribal allies preferred to lay down their arms. In Soran itself, a dispute broke out with the *'ulema* on the subject of mentioning Mohammad Kor's name in the Friday sermons instead of that of the Ottoman Sultan. He was dealt a further blow when the *'ulema* in Rawanduz—possibly under Ottoman influence—spoke out against the confrontation with the Sultan, and the Mufti of the city issued a *fatwa* (legal verdict) that prohibited war against the Sultan.[24]

The firepower of their modernized and reorganized artillery corps gave the Ottomans a great advantage. Their ability to pull Kurdish tribes over to their side and to neutralize others that had tended to support Muhammad Kor, as well as their improved tactics (thanks to training by Prussian officers), tipped the scales. In light of Iran's unwillingness to offer him either assistance or asylum, and given his isolation in the face of Ottoman strength backed by the British, Muhammad Kor agreed to surrender and to go to Istanbul, apparently on the basis of a promise by the Ottoman commander Mehmet Reshid Pasha that if he surrendered and accepted Ottoman sovereignty, they would allow him to remain in control of Soran,[25] but with limitations on his power and on Soran's autonomy. Muhammad Kor departed for Istanbul, where he remained for some six months as the Sultan's guest. The Ottomans apparently followed through on their promise, but on his way home to Soran via the Black Sea, Muhammad Kor disappeared under mysterious circumstances. It may reasonably be assumed that he was murdered by the Ottomans.

After the death of Muhammad Kor, the Emirate of Soran was considerably weakened. Initially, the Ottomans refrained from administering it directly; they appointed Muhammad Kor's brother, Rasule, to replace him and gave him the title of "Bey." When Rasule Bey attempted to enhance his status, he was dismissed by the Ottoman governor of Baghdad in 1847 and forced to flee to Iran. The Ottomans subsequently integrated Rawanduz and the emirate's territory into the Ottoman administration and appointed its governors as they saw fit, not from a local family.[26] The Emirate of Soran and its ambitious ruler fell victim to the changes in the international arena, following the interventions by Britain and Russia and the end of the wars between Iran and the Ottoman Empire. They could not withstand the Ottoman government, its reforms, or its centralization.

EMIR BEDIR KHAN OF BOTAN AND OTTOMAN-BRITISH RELATIONS

After the fall of Soran, only Botan remained as the last of the Kurdish emirates and the strong power in Kurdistan. Its ruler, Muhammad Bedir Khan, took the Ottoman side in the Ottoman-Egyptian conflict and was given an Ottoman military rank of "Captain." Bedir Khan sought to exploit his status and ties with the Ottomans in order to increase his autonomous position within the Empire. He enjoyed the broad-based support of both Kurds—tribes and nontribal peasants alike—and Armenians, from Van in the northwest to Sulaymaniyya in the southeast. In light of the virtual disintegration of the Emirate of Hakkari, Bedir Khan extended his patronage to it.

With the end of the Ottoman-Egyptian war and the retreat of Muhammad 'Ali's forces from Syria in 1840, the tensions that Bedir Khan and the Kurdish tribes experienced in their relations with the Ottoman authorities increased. After the death of Sultan Mahmud II in 1839, the Ottoman Empire entered a new phase of reforms, the Tanzimat (Reorganization), which continued periodically over nearly forty years until Sultan 'Abd al-Hamid came to power in 1876. The Tanzimat reforms became the framework of the contentious relations between the Ottoman state and the Kurds.

With the removal of the threat presented by Muhammad ʿAli and the renewed momentum of the reforms, the Ottoman authorities sought to impose state sovereignty upon the last autonomous emirate, the very existence of which ran counter to their centralizing policy. Kurdish tribes in the Botan area refused to pay the taxes demanded by the Ottoman state. Elsewhere in the Ottoman Empire, the strength of local powers often dictated the amount of taxation. In this case, however, Bedir Khan—despite his relative strength—was contending with the Ottoman state. Another reason for the tension with the Ottomans was the mandatory service for young Kurdish men in the Ottoman army. Many Kurdish draftees, even though they were accustomed to the severe physical conditions in the mountains of Kurdistan, had difficulty adjusting to the demands of the regular Ottoman army, which had adopted Prussian patterns of discipline and training.[27] Many became ill and died; others deserted. The demands for taxation, the corruption of Ottoman officialdom, the brutality exhibited by the Ottoman army in places where local commanders had no fear of the Kurdish tribes, and the implications of the draft into the Ottoman army created an anti-Ottoman atmosphere, which increased tribal opposition to the authority of a state from which they felt alienated.

Emir Bedir Khan was essentially an independent ruler who paid taxes and lip service to the Sultan and the Ottoman state. Until 1842–1843, he seems to have been completely loyal to the Ottoman Empire. Nonetheless, the contradiction between his existential interest in keeping the emirate independent and the Ottoman policy of suppressing local autonomy led to clashes. In 1842–1843, in order to weaken Bedir Khan and emphasize his subordination to the *valis*, the Ottoman authorities established a new administrative border between the *vilayets* of Diyarbakir and Mosul. It was shaped in such a way that the majority of the lands of the Emirate of Botan were now included in the Ottoman *vilayet* of Diyarbakir, but in the south the area of Jazira was part of the *vilayet* of Mosul, under the sovereignty of a *vali* who was hostile to Bedir Khan.[28] This division of lands between new Ottoman administrative areas reflected the fundamental contradiction between the old Kurdish autonomous frameworks—the tribes and emirates—and the new centralized administrative order. The Ottoman reforms included canceling the *iltizam*, the traditional tax leasing system that had given Bedir Khan important economic advantages and power vis-à-vis both the tribal and nontribal populations.[29]

In 1844 a dispute broke out between the Ottoman *vali* of Diyarbakir and

Bedir Khan, who refused to come to a gathering initiated by the *vali* on the subject of tax collection and the draft. As Bedir Khan saw it, this was an Ottoman attempt to reduce his power and autonomy in these two important areas, which helped him to control his people and extend his authority over tribes and areas outside Botan. He set out on a campaign in the lands under his control, where he was welcomed as the Emir of Kurdistan by the Kurdish and Christian populations. His patronage of the Emirate of Hakkari, which was weak and fraught with internal disputes, led to a head-on collision with the Ottoman Empire, supported by Britain. The population of the Emirate of Hakkari was heterogeneous. In addition to the pastoral Kurdish tribes that were the mainstay of the emirate, Hakkari was home to Nestorian Assyrian Christians as well as Armenians, many of whom were settled farmers, though some belonged to pastoral Armenian tribes. The Nestorian Christians were mostly vassals of the pastoral Kurdish tribes.

In the 1830s, American and British Protestant missionaries who hoped to propagate the "true" Christian faith among the Nestorian Assyrians had begun to be active in the area. The schisms and struggles in the Assyrian Church, one of the oldest Christian denominations, were exploited by Western Christian missionaries. The Nestorian priests had maintained ties with the Vatican and the Catholic Church for centuries. In the seventeenth century, a schism occurred in the Nestorian Church. The dynamic, intensive activity of the American missionaries led to competition from the British missionaries, and this rivalry intensified the internal factionalism among the Assyrians. The American missionaries exploited the concession they had been granted for the building of churches as part of the Tanzimat reforms by erecting an impressive, fortresslike church in a prominent place in the Hakkari area. The church's formidable structure, in a remote area of small Kurdish villages with no other prominent buildings, aroused the suspicions of the Kurdish Muslim population, who feared a foreign Christian invasion and the strengthening of local Christians, whose social status was generally lower than that of Kurdish Muslims.[30]

In light of the weakness of the emirs of Hakkari and their intrafamily struggles, and possibly fortified by a sense of power resulting from the involvement of Western missionaries, a Nestorian Assyrian leader by the name of Mar Sham'un sought to free the members of his community from the control of the Kurdish emirs and tribes. He may also have been prompted by an internal struggle for the leadership of the community in which the rivals were backed by different denominations of Western missionaries. According to one source, Ottoman government officials encouraged Nur Allah Beg, the Emir of Hakkari, to impose his sovereignty on the Assyrians, who were considered to be collaborators with the Western powers.[31] Nur Allah Beg, whose weakness made him unable to contend with the Assyrians, approached Emir Bedir Khan for help. Bedir Khan was glad to be of assistance—and, in effect, to extend his patronage over Hakkari.[32] The influence on Bedir Khan of Shaykh Taha of Nehri, a Sufi shaykh and ʿalim, also appears to have played a role and to have given his actions Islamic legitimation and motivation, derived from the political balance of forces in Kurdistan.

The American missionaries and British travelers who reported these events emphasized the aspect of Islamic religious fanaticism shared by Bedir Khan and Shaykh Taha. In 1843 Bedir Khan's forces massacred the local Assyrian Christians. This tragic episode in a remote corner of the world was one of the manifestations of the growing Muslim-Christian tensions throughout the Ottoman Empire, following its penetration by Western powers, and against the background of the Empire's reforms, which in the end led to the granting of equality to Christians.

In Kurdistan, Muslim-Christian tensions and clashes manifested in Kurdish-Assyrian and Kurdish-Armenian conflicts, which at times reflected the socioeconomic gaps between the pastoral-tribal Kurdish and Turkmen population and the Christian population, who were mainly settled farmers, with some merchants and craftsmen. The granting of rights to the Christian sects, beyond those that had been customary in the Ottoman Empire, along with the increasing activity by the Western powers with whom the local Christians had become identified, changed the stable pattern of Muslim-Christian relations throughout the Empire and their complex relationships in Kurdistan. At the same time, with the exception of the missionary activity, which directly contributed to destroying the local equilibrium, Western influence in Kurdistan was indirect and resulted principally from overall developments in the Ottoman Empire and the impression that it was becoming weaker relative to Britain and Russia.

British travelers who visited Kurdistan in the 1830s and 1840s described an atmosphere of rumor and anxiety among the Kurdish population.[33] Some of the Kurdish notables expressed hope that the growing strength of Britain and Russia would liberate them from Ottoman rule. Admittedly, their suspicion of and resentment toward the Ottoman authorities had increased as centralization and other reforms seemed to threaten Kurdish tribal autonomy. At the same time, the growing feeling that the Ottoman Empire was declining, along with the increased missionary activity and the confidence it inspired in local Christian communities, strengthened the fears of the Muslim population. In slaughtering many Christians, Bedir Khan may have obtained the tacit support of the Ottoman authorities, who sought to block Western Christian activity in the Empire.[34] Nevertheless, the slaughter was reported by Western missionaries and travelers in Kurdistan and aroused strong British protests and pressure to oust Bedir Khan.[35]

The Ottomans, who had exploited Bedir Khan's power in order to harm the Christian communities, were pleased to take the opportunity to eliminate the last autonomous Kurdish emirate. Faced with growing Ottoman pressure, Bedir Khan established a coalition with Emir Nur Allah Beg of Hakkari and the magnate Khan Mahmud of Mush (Muks).[36] The conclusive military clash between the Ottomans and Bedir Khan's forces took place in 1847.[37] In spite of the emirate's considerable power and the coalition that Bedir Khan had put together, the Kurdish forces could not withstand the might of the modernized Ottoman army. The Ottoman troops enjoyed superior organization and artillery firepower and wrought destruction throughout the area. Entire settlements were wiped out and their inhabitants killed. Fear of the Ottoman army led to attempts at mediation between the combatants. A dispute broke out in Bedir Khan's camp, and his relative Yezdansher ('Izz al-Din Shir) Khan, a prominent army commander, went over to the Ottoman side, apparently motivated by a promise of a senior appointment on behalf of the Ottoman administration. Bedir Khan surrendered in 1847 and was exiled. The last of the autonomous emirates in Ottoman Kurdistan, and the last of the strong Kurdish emirs, left the stage of history.

The conflict between the Emirate of Botan under Bedir Khan and the Ottoman Empire reflected not only Western (in this case, British) influence but also the opposition to the Ottoman centralist trends and reforms in the context of the changes in Muslim-Christian relations throughout the Empire. Bedir Khan himself, after a few years of imprisonment and humiliation, was reintegrated into the Ottoman establishment and appointed governor of Crete. In 1858 he was awarded the title of "Pasha," and later he moved to Istanbul and retired in Damascus. He died in 1870. Members of his family were given Ottoman bureaucratic posts, and his descendants, who would grow up far from Kurdistan in the distant reaches of the Ottoman Empire, were among the writers of a new, more modern page of Kurdish history and made the transition from outmoded tribal solidarities to Kurdish nationalism. Some of them, starting in the late nineteenth century and continuing until the end of the 1970s, would be among the exiled activists who took up the banner of Kurdish nationalism and contributed to developing and unifying the modern Kurdish national movement. They influenced the shaping of the Kurdish historical narrative and the special importance attributed to the revolt of Bedir Khan as the harbinger of modern Kurdish nationalism.

From the perspective of Ottoman history, and especially the history of the Ottoman reforms, the revolt of Bedir Khan was one of the greatest out-bursts of resistance to the centralization and reinforcement of Ottoman rule. It was an unsuccessful attempt to preserve Kurdish autonomy under the po-litical and social conditions that represented the beginnings of moderniza-tion in the Ottoman Empire.

Between 1845 and 1849, the Ottomans suppressed all of the remain-ing tribal or strong local Kurdish leaders, such as the khan of Mush, who had maintained some degree of autonomy up to that point. In the mid-nineteenth century, the Ottoman Empire declined as the might of the West-ern powers increased. Internal political forces such as the Kurdish emirates, which had barely begun to modernize and did not benefit from any Western support, were relatively inferior to the strength and abilities of the reformed and modernized Ottoman state, government, and armed forces. In 1846 the Ottoman Empire established a province known as the *eyelet* of Kurdistan, which encompassed the areas of Diyarbakir, Van, Mush, Chizire (Jazira), Botan, and Hakkari. Although the province enjoyed a special status and was fairly autonomous, the autonomy was not conferred upon the Kurds them-selves. Rather, it consisted of broader powers for Ottoman officials—to en-able them to deal with difficult local conditions and to impose Ottoman state sovereignty more efficiently.[38]

THE REVOLT OF YEZDANSHER KHAN
AND THE CRIMEAN WAR

Russia's policy in the Balkans and the Black Sea basin was intended to achieve supremacy there. When its ambition to become the controlling power in Istanbul and to close the Bosphorus to foreign warships was met with the Ottoman Empire's efforts to withstand this pressure, the result was an outbreak of war between the Empire and Russia in 1853. Britain and France rapidly came to the aid of the Ottomans in order to prevent Russia from getting a grip on Istanbul and thus access to the Mediterranean Sea—for Britain, a strategic route to India. The war, which became a conflict between the European powers, was mainly fought in the Balkans and the Crimean Peninsula. A secondary front included the Caucasus and areas to the south, some of which were populated by Kurds.

From the beginning of the war, the Russians recruited Kurdish tribes in the southern Caucasus as irregular auxiliary forces. The weakness and de-feats of the Ottoman army by the Russians on the Caucasian front, especially in the area of Kars, inspired a broad-based but short-lived Kurdish uprising in the fall and winter of 1854–1855.[39] Among the combatants in the battles around Kars in December 1853 was an irregular force of some 15,000 Kurdish cavalrymen. Both the Russians and the Ottomans recruited Kurdish tribes in the border area. Following the defeat of the Ottoman forces that month, fourteen Kurdish notables approached the Russians with a view to reaching an agreement with them. Some of the Kurdish forces recruited by the Ottomans switched loyalties and began to fight on the Russian side. A Russian colonel, Count Mikhail Loris-Melikov, was put in charge of relations with the Kurdish tribes.[40] Another Ottoman defeat at the hands of the Russians in August 1854 severely deterred the Kurds from continuing to assist the Ottomans.[41] The Russians established two regiments of Kurdish cavalry from the Caucasus as a semiregular auxiliary force.

The most prominent Kurdish leader whom the Ottomans sought to exploit in order to enlist the support of Kurdish tribes was Yezdansher Khan. He had been a prominent Kurdish commander—perhaps the most prominent of all—in the army of his relative Emir Bedir Khan during the latter's revolt against the Ottomans in 1847. Yezdansher was persuaded or bribed by the Ottomans to change sides, along with a significant portion of Bedir Khan's army. His betrayal was a grievous blow to Bedir Khan and helped the Ottomans to eliminate the last Kurdish emirate. Although Yezdansher was given a high rank in the Ottoman army, he was disappointed by the Ottomans' refusal to grant him sovereignty over the Emirate of Botan or other areas of Kurdistan. Having no other choice, he continued to serve the Ottomans. His disappointment, however, seems to have been an important motive for his attempted revolt.

In light of their distress on the front against Russia and the Kurds' diminished willingness to fight on their side, the Ottomans put Yezdansher in charge of recruiting Kurdish forces from Chizire and Mosul as irregular units in the Ottoman army. Following their victories in the summer of 1854, the Russians dispatched a missive to Yezdansher, asking him to stop assisting the Ottomans. In the autumn of that year, the relationship between Yezdansher and the Ottomans became strained. His salary was cut back, and disputes broke out between him and various Ottoman governors.

While Yezdansher's relations with the Ottomans were undoubtedly the principal reason for the revolt, its scale reflected the economic distress in wartime Kurdistan; perceptions of Ottoman weakness following repeated defeats by the Russians, who were perceived as a rising power, contributed as well. The revolt was launched toward the end of 1854, and by February 1855 Yezdansher had taken the cities of Midyat and Bitlis. The uprising was also joined by Arabs from the Mardin area. According to Averianov, Yezdansher's forces numbered between 60,000 and 100,000 fighters. Even if these figures appear somewhat exaggerated, it was certainly a large-scale revolt. However, his tribal forces were not a regular army; they were motivated by a desire for spoils, and their loyalty was primarily tribal in nature. Moreover, his hold on the cities he conquered appears to have been weak and brief.[42]

Yezdansher sought military coordination and support from the Russians, but did not receive a response. At the same time, he corresponded with influential Kurdish notables in the areas of Van, Bitlis, and Mush. The revolt's broad scope caused anxiety among the Ottomans and the British alike, and its location—to the south of the Ottoman forces that were holding back the Russian army in the north—represented a strategic threat. In January 1855, General Williams, the British officer in charge of the Ottoman forces and the British officers in the Kars area, sent a message to Yezdansher warning him that the conflict with the Ottomans was also a conflict with Britain. Having no chance of cooperation with Russia and facing the combined pressure of the massed Ottoman troops in Kurdistan and the British threat, Yezdansher surrendered and was arrested. The precise circumstances of his surrender are not clear; he apparently preferred to avoid a violent battle with the Ottoman army.[43] Yezdansher's disorganized tribal forces crumbled upon his surrender. It is quite possible that his unstable personality, indicated in his betrayal of Emir Bedir Khan during the latter's revolt against the Ottomans in 1847, also contributed to the decline of his own revolt before any real conflict with the Ottoman forces could take place.

The abortive revolt and the developments that surrounded it reflected both the British involvement in the Ottoman Empire and the atomization of Kurdish society in the absence of any significant social or political force that could have given ethnic or national significance to the uprising. At the same time, and even though the Ottomans and the Russians considered the Kurds (and the Kurds considered themselves) primarily an assemblage of local tribes, the concept of "Kurds" had already begun to imply a tribal population with certain ethnic, linguistic, social, and cultural characteristics. The revolt gave rise to expectations of Kurdish unity on the part of one of the early harbingers of the modern Kurdish national movement, the poet Haji Qadir Koyi, whose work mentions Yezdansher.[44]

It is little wonder that the revolt led by Yezdansher has been mentioned relatively little by the spokespersons of Kurdish nationalism. After all, Yezdansher betrayed Emir Bedir Khan, switched to the Ottoman side, and contributed to the defeat of the man who has long been perceived by Kurdish nationalists as the first nationalist Kurdish leader. Bedir Khan's descendants, who influenced the shaping of the Kurdish historical narrative in the first half of the twentieth century, viewed Yezdansher as a traitor and opportunist. After a period of exile, the leaders of both revolts, however, were integrated into the Ottoman establishment and appointed to senior administrative positions in Ottoman provinces far from Kurdistan. Both Bedir Khan and Yezdansher ended up as governors under the Ottoman regime, with no commitment to Kurdish nationalism in the modern sense.

In both the Crimean War of 1853–1856 and the Ottoman-Russian War of 1877–1878, areas populated by Kurds and Armenians became one of the fronts. Admittedly, the battles and most of the military activity took place not in the heart of Kurdistan but at its edges. Nonetheless, these wars had a considerable effect on economic and political conditions, as well as on Kurdish-Armenian and Ottoman-Kurdish relations. The recruitment of Kurdish tribes by the Ottomans, the Russian efforts to gain the support of Kurdish tribes, and the increasing economic distress of the people of Kurdistan all affected the Kurdish and Armenian populations. The Armenians' identification with Russia during the Russian-Ottoman War of 1877–1878, and the growing nationalist trends among them, aroused suspicion among Ottomans and Kurds alike that the Armenians would attempt to establish a state under the protection of Russia or Britain, similar to what was happening with the Christian peoples of the Balkans.

Thus, the two significant Kurdish revolts of the midnineteenth century—one led by Yezdansher Khan and the other by Shaykh 'Ubaydallah (see chapter 4)—broke out in the context of the wars between the Ottoman Empire and Russia. The Russian-Armenian-Christian threat was skillfully exploited by the Ottomans in order to enlist the support of the Muslim Kurds for the Sultan.

CHAPTER 4

SEEDS OF KURDISH NATIONALISM
IN THE DECLINING OTTOMAN EMPIRE

THE EFFECTS OF THE DEMISE OF THE EMIRATES

The Tanzimat reforms in the Ottoman Empire between 1839 and 1876 and the Empire's integration into the nineteenth-century global market economy, which was dominated by the colonialist, capitalist Western powers, had contradictory effects on the social conditions in Kurdistan. On the one hand, the elimination of the tribal Kurdish emirates and the weakness of the Ottoman administration allowed the tribes and tribal leadership to gain strength over the course of the nineteenth century. On the other hand, the Ottoman reforms (especially the Land Registration Law of 1858) and the global capitalist market economy combined to give the tribal leaders and notables an interest in taking control of land areas in order to exploit them for market production and export.

In certain parts of Kurdistan where conditions were suitable for growing crops for export outside Kurdistan, more power accrued to the *aghawat* sector—medium-sized and large landowners, many of whom were tribal notables. This was part of a broad-based trend throughout the Ottoman Empire during the reforms in the nineteenth century: the growth of a stratum of large landowners as a result of the land registration policy and the development of the capitalist market economy. Under these conditions, the value of land increased—not as an asset and a means of personal and tribal survival, but as a means of production for market purposes and a source of big profits for landowners. Social relations also changed: tribal relations became relations between the landowner and landless—or nearly landless—peasants, some of whom belonged to the landowner's tribe.

Even as landowners became more powerful, the elimination of the autonomous emirates that had ruled over the tribes strengthened tribal frameworks and loyalties. Insecurity, anarchy, robbery, and violence increased, against the background of impotent Ottoman rule and poverty and the constant struggle for survival in the harsh terrain and climate of Kurdistan.[1]

Although the Ottomans were able to dispose of the Kurdish emirates, they were unable to establish an efficient administration in their stead. Control of the lofty mountains and deep valleys of Kurdistan was effectively achieved only by the presence of an Ottoman military force. If the force in question was small, its members feared for their lives and sought to shorten their tour of duty; if it was large, its soldiers robbed the shepherds and looted the isolated villages through which they passed. In the absence of individual security, tribalism was the social response to the harsh living conditions in the mountains of Kurdistan; individuals and small families found it very difficult to survive without belonging to strong tribal frameworks.[2]

In the vacuum that followed the elimination of the emirates, the Sufi shaykhs became more influential. At times their power extended beyond their tribal frameworks, and their patronage was sometimes sought by nontribal peasants. New tribes and clans arose around the shaykhs, who enjoyed religious prestige and sometimes acquired lands and economic assets. Though modified to some extent, the tribal patterns were basically preserved, with some tribes still headed by traditional tribal notables, while others congregated around the shaykhs. The lack of significant change in the conditions of production and survival contributed to the preservation of tribal social patterns, notwithstanding the disappearance of the emirates.

Starting in the late nineteenth century, some members of the clans and tribes that developed around charismatic Sufi shaykhs began to promote their tribal and clannish interests, while expressing a sense of Kurdish distinctiveness as an ethnic group or *ta'ife* (which can also be interpreted as "nation") and adopting nationalist concepts. The most prominent of these tribesmen—members of the Shemdinan, Barzinji, Barzani, and Talabani clans or tribes—were to play a major role in the twentieth-century Kurdish national movement. At the same time, Kurdistan's towns developed a thin stratum of merchants and civil servants in the new Ottoman regime, and a few Kurds became schoolteachers. Nevertheless, in the absence of any major change in economic conditions, tribal social patterns were perpetuated and tribal notables who had become landowners continued to dominate. The time still was not right for the rapid development of a bourgeoisie that could become a modernizing force.

Modern education developed more slowly in Kurdistan than in other parts of the Ottoman Empire. Kurdistan had no outlet to the sea, no quarries, and no products that were especially attractive to European traders (oil did not acquire importance until the last years of the nineteenth century), and so Western influences continued to be more limited than in Egypt, the Levant (Damascus, Aleppo, and Beirut), and western Anatolia.

THE REVOLT OF SHAYKH ʿUBAYDALLAH SHEMDINANI— EARLY NATIONALISM?

Unrest increased in Kurdistan during the Ottoman-Russian War of 1877–1878 and continued to grow thereafter. The war was fought on the northern edges of Kurdistan and in the southern Caucasus. The Russian army advanced toward Erzurum, Van, Ardalan, and Kars.[3] Although the Ottomans made efforts to preserve the Kurds' loyalty, in 1876, even before the war broke out, Russian consuls in the Ottoman Empire and Russian army officers in the Caucasus reported inquiries by tribal notables who wanted to help Russia against the Ottomans.[4]

The deterioration and destruction of Kurdish agriculture and pasturage as a result of the fighting and pillaging, in addition to years of drought, had given rise to severe economic distress and famine throughout Kurdistan. The weakness and inefficiency shown by the Ottoman army throughout the war, on the one hand, and the cruelty with which its units had treated the civilian population of Kurdistan, on the other, had undermined Ottoman prestige and lessened the Kurds' fear of the Empire's might. In this state of affairs, although tens of thousands of Kurdish tribesmen were serving in the regular and irregular forces of the Ottoman army, the Kurds began to long for, and even to strive for, the achievement of autonomy or even independence.[5]

In the autumn of 1878, Osman Bey and Husayn Kenan Bey, the sons of Emir Bedir Khan, who had participated in the Ottoman-Russian War of 1877–1878, began to organize the tribes in the Botan area and to renew the control of their tribal-feudal dynasty over adjacent areas. Initially, they succeeded in inciting rebellion and even repulsed an Ottoman unit that was sent to suppress the revolt.[6] Only a few tribes joined them, however, and the Ottomans had no difficulty in suppressing this local insurrection. These efforts by Emir Bedir Khan's sons failed because of tribal splits, the opposition of certain tribes to being controlled by the Bedir Khan family, and the fear of a violent response from the Ottoman regime. The revolt remained a local event, and the Bedir Khan brothers surrendered and were imprisoned. Although it was true that Emir Bedir Khan's descendants acted in accordance with their aristocratic origins, they also considered themselves Kurdish leaders and made a genuine attempt to unify and organize Kurdish resistance.[7]

Between 1878 and 1881, a series of events took place in the area of Nehri, near the border between the Ottoman Empire and Iran, including a revolt against the Ottomans and a Kurdish invasion of Iran. The background to these events was the Ottoman-Russian War of 1877–1878, the weakness of the Ottoman regime, and the overt support of Russia by significant portions of the Armenian population. The Ottomans, who were disturbed by the nationalist and separatist trends among the Armenians, attempted to convince the Kurds and other Muslims in eastern Anatolia that the Armenians intended to establish a Christian state under the protection of both Russia and Britain.

The leader of the Kurds in this complex series of events was Shaykh 'Ubaydallah of Nehri, of the House of Shemdinan.[8] A Sufi shaykh with high religious status and considerable economic power, 'Ubaydallah enjoyed the admiration and support of both the tribes and the nontribal peasants in the Shemdinan area. The prestige he enjoyed extended to the Hakkari area as well, and his influence extended even beyond the boundaries of the Ottoman Empire: he achieved a certain degree of support and renown among the Kurdish tribes and nontribal peasants in Iran.[9] His family had accumulated considerable wealth from the spice trade.[10] Shaykh 'Ubaydallah owned orchards and grazing lands that lay both in the Ottoman Empire and across the Iranian border.

The Ottoman army, which was considerably inferior to the Russian army and extremely inefficient, had a great need for irregular auxiliary forces, and the majority of them were Kurdish. Shaykhs who were leaders of Kurdish tribes and commanded Kurdish irregular forces were awarded officers' commissions. Shaykh 'Ubaydallah and Shaykh Nasir of Tello were the senior commanders of the largest Kurdish tribal forces that fought on the Ottoman side. Shaykh 'Ubaydallah commanded some 50,000 irregular Kurdish cavalrymen who were motivated by the desire for spoils and by the appeal from Shaykh 'Ubaydallah to defend Islam.

The Kurdish fighters who saw combat during the war witnessed the debility of the Ottoman army.[11] When they returned to their homes, they did not give back the rifles they had received from the army or collected on the battlefield after they were thrown down by Ottoman soldiers. Thus, at the end of the war many Kurds, especially tribesmen who had been recruited into the war, were in possession of modern rifles.[12] Both the Kurdish fears of the Armenians and the feeble image of the Ottoman regime, following its defeat by Russia, continued to grow after the war. The Kurds' fear of the Armenians increased even further after the Berlin Conference of 1878 at the end of the war, when the Western powers adopted resolutions to intervene in the Armenians' favor.

The Berlin Conference was called in an effort to prevent the undermining of the European order and to block Russia. The Western powers supporting the Ottoman Empire emphasized its commitment to protecting the Armenians and other Christians within its territory and to continuing reforms. The Ottomans and Shaykh 'Ubaydallah objected, however, to the reforms that had been forced on the Empire by the Western powers within the framework of the conference resolutions. The Kurds feared the Armenians not only because of the backing given to them by the Western powers but also because of the increased activity by Armenian nationalist-revolutionary activists and movements. The Ottomans considered the West's intervention and its arrangements for the Empire to protect Christians a grave threat that was likely to lead to the loss of Ottoman control in Kurdistan and eastern Anatolia, similar to their loss of territories in the Balkans.

Following his return from the war, Shaykh 'Ubaydallah took steps to bolster his status through complex tribal political maneuvers. As part of that effort, he attempted to form an alliance of Kurdish tribes in the eastern part of the Ottoman Empire and also, apparently, among the Kurdish tribes in Iran. From 1878, Shaykh 'Ubaydallah maintained a correspondence with the Russian and British consuls in western Iran and the eastern Ottoman Empire, as well as with American missionaries in the area. At the same time, he sent missives to the sharifs of Mecca and the khedives of Egypt, with a view to establishing ties with forces that enjoyed a broad-based autonomy within the Empire or were even essentially independent.[13]

The revolt broke out in 1879, following the prison sentences and other penalties imposed by an Ottoman *kaymakam* (regional governor) upon a group of Kurds loyal to Shaykh 'Ubaydallah who had looted a village. In response, the Shaykh called for a revolt against the tyranny of the *kaymakam*. The rumor that Shaykh 'Ubaydallah was about to launch a revolt, with the intention of taking first 'Amadiya and then Mosul, reached the *vali* of Mosul, who sent out an Ottoman military force. Eight hundred Kurdish fighters under the command of Shaykh 'Ubaydallah's son, 'Abd al-Qadir, attacked the Ottoman force but were repulsed. It seems that in the absence of a decisive military victory for either side, Shaykh 'Ubaydallah understood that his chances of overcoming the Ottomans were slim, and the Ottomans understood that it would be difficult for their army to defeat him in a frontal attack. Accordingly, the two sides attempted to reach an understanding, as part of which the *kaymakam* was dismissed from his position. In reality, 'Ubaydallah had an autonomous status, and his relations with the Ottomans were not clearly defined.

In July and August 1880, Shaykh 'Ubaydallah organized two gather-

ings of tribal leaders, prominent 'ulema, and Kurdish tribal notables. The
first conference took place in Shemdinan and was attended by more than
100 tribal leaders and notables from all over Kurdistan, including the Sivas
area in western Kurdistan. At the gathering, he announced the impending
establishment of a national alliance based on the tribes.[14] The second gathering, in August, was attended by some 220 tribal notables, landowners, and
'ulema.[15] Following these gatherings, the Kurdish League, an association
of tribal chiefs and notables, was established. One of the organizers of the
gatherings was Bahry Bedir Khan, a son of Emir Muhummad Bedir Khan.[16]

The fear of an Armenian Christian state being established under the protection of the Western powers was an important motivation for participants in the gathering. The resolutions adopted at the Berlin Conference
of 1878 were intended to block Russia and preserve the European balance of
power. At the same time, however, those resolutions reflected the Western
powers' support of the Armenians and aroused concern among the Kurds.
'Ubaydallah, as a devout Sufi shaykh of considerable religious status among
the Kurds, took steps toward a rapprochement with the Christians in Kurdistan. He appears to have been aware that in order to obtain Western support and not be considered a fanatical anti-Christian, he would have to show
a tolerant attitude toward Christians. Against the tension that prevailed in
Muslim-Christian relations throughout the Ottoman Empire, reflected locally in Kurdistan by the unease between Kurds and Armenians, the Armenian question remained one of the unresolved topics in the dialogue between Shaykh 'Ubaydallah and some of the tribes and tribal leaders.[17]

In his speech at the gathering, the Shaykh spoke against both Ottoman
Turkish and Qajar Iranian rule. He pointed out the difficulties that the Iranian army was experiencing in fighting the Turkmenian tribes and called
for assistance to the "brothers" in Iranian Kurdistan.[18] In October 1880,
'Ubaydallah's forces invaded Iran.[19] In a letter to an American physician and
missionary, Dr. Cochran, Shaykh 'Ubaydallah justified his invasion by cit-
ing, among other reasons, the suppression of the Kurds by the Shi'ite Iranian authorities, the harm done to the tribal notables, the monetary penalties imposed on the Kurdish population, and the assault on the honor of
Kurdish women by Iranian officials.[20] Shaykh 'Ubaydallah obviously had
personal reasons as well. He had loyal supporters in many tribes and villages in the area of Urmia and Sauj Bulak (Mahabad), where he and his associates owned agricultural lands and especially a large number of orchards.
In 1873 the Qajar governor had begun to collect taxes from the villages that
belonged to Shaykh 'Ubaydallah, and in 1879 the governor had arrested and
humiliated a number of notables who were loyal to 'Ubaydallah.[21]

It is quite probable, however, that in addition to local motives, 'Ubaydallah was guided by broader political and military considerations. In his estimation, Iran's weakness and the concentration of most of the Iranian army on the border with Afghanistan, where it was burdened with the Turkmen rebellions, created an opportunity to take over parts of Iranian Kurdistan. He intended to use the Iranian areas he would occupy in the first stage as a base from which he would continue the revolt and confront the Ottomans.[22]

British officials in the area were divided as to whether the Ottomans had encouraged 'Ubaydallah to invade Iran or whether his moves ran counter to Ottoman interests and were in fact a continuation of his revolt against the Empire. Western and Turkish scholars claim that 'Ubaydallah received encouragement and weapons from the Ottomans for invading Iran.[23]

Initially, Shaykh 'Ubaydallah's forces succeeded in conquering the city of Sauj Bulak, to the southwest and on the western shore of Lake Urmia; subsequently, they took the city of Miyanduab. Kurdish tribal fighters slaughtered the local urban and rural population, Shi'ites and Christians alike.[24] Shaykh 'Ubaydallah's control of the tribal forces seems to have been limited. In spite of his intention to treat the Christians well, he could not restrain the tribesmen, who were motivated not only by the opportunity for looting but by a desire to slaughter Shi'ites, Christians, and apparently urban Sunnites as well.

The Iranian government dispatched regular military troops, who overcame the Kurdish troops; the latter had mountain guerrilla skills but were not organized as a regular, well-disciplined force. The Iranian army also decimated the civilian Kurdish population. The Qajar shah sent a message to Sultan Abdulhamid II, asking him for the Ottoman army's assistance in suppressing the revolt and keeping it from spreading elsewhere in Kurdistan.[25] The Ottomans began to fear that the unrest and the killing of Christians would either give rise to an Armenian revolt or strengthen the Armenians' demand for Russian protection. The fear that Russia and Britain would intervene drove them to take action against Shaykh 'Ubaydallah. The retreating Kurdish troops encountered Ottoman army forces that blocked their retreat and helped the Iranian troops to annihilate the last vestiges of the Kurdish force.

The encouragement that, according to a number of sources, Shaykh 'Ubaydallah was given by the Ottomans, followed by the military operations launched against him, indicates that the Shaykh and his adherents may have fallen victim to Ottoman manipulation. In fact, in the last stages of his revolt the two regional powers—notwithstanding their rivalry—cooperated in suppressing a Kurdish revolt, which constituted a threat to both of them. This pattern would recur throughout the twentieth century.

The state of Kurdish society and tribal fragmentation also made it harder for Shaykh 'Ubaydallah to incite a broad-scale Kurdish insurrection. Kurdish tribes viewed the invasion of Iran not as an opportunity for Kurdish nationalism (since, after all, they had no national consciousness), but as a raid by rival Kurds, who were perceived as emissaries of the Ottomans. This perception made it easier for Qajar Iran to win the loyalty of Kurdish tribes against Shaykh 'Ubaydallah. The Shaykh himself was arrested in 1881 by the Ottoman authorities. He was transferred to Istanbul, but managed to flee from the capital and return to Nehri. He was captured again, however, and exiled to Hejaz, where he died in 1883.

In the discourse of the Kurdish national movement during the twentieth century, Shaykh 'Ubaydallah's 1879 revolt and his invasion of Iran in 1880 were seen as expressions of Kurdish nationalism. This was the first time that the Kurdish question acquired international significance, while also exposing the Kurds' tragic situation. No international force had any interest in them or any motive for supporting them. The Ottoman Empire sought to exploit the Kurds in order to block the reforms that had been forced on it by the Western powers at the Berlin Conference and to resist the Armenians, whom the Empire perceived as a threat to its integrity. In the end, however, Shaykh 'Ubaydallah's growing power became a threat to the Empire and ran counter to the centralist trends of Abdulhamid's administration, which then sought to eliminate him. Iran viewed the Shaykh as a threat to its lands. Russia suspected that the Empire's attempt to eliminate him was an Ottoman move that had implications for the Kurds in the territories Russia had gained in the war of 1877–1878. Shaykh 'Ubaydallah's religious status worried the Russians, who remembered the difficulty in overcoming the revolt by Shaykh Shamil in the Caucasus during the 1840s and 1850s.[26] The Shah of Iran went so far as to approach Russia and request assistance; Russia, however, refrained from getting involved, preferring not to create tension between itself and Britain.[27] As for Britain, its strategic interest lay in preserving the Ottoman Empire and Iran as barriers to Russian expansion. Britain accordingly favored implementation of the reforms agreed to at the Berlin Conference and was concerned that Shaykh 'Ubaydallah's revolt and invasion would be exploited by Russia to expand Russian influence in Iran and the northeastern part of the Ottoman Empire.

Was Shaykh 'Ubaydallah's revolt the first expression of Kurdish nationalism? Scholars are divided. While some have considered it a first manifestation of Kurdish nationalism, others have viewed him as a traditional religious-tribal leader whose objectives were no different from those of tribal emirates' leaders before him. Still other scholars see Shaykh 'Ubaydallah's revolt as combining traditional Kurdish beliefs and motives with the new elements of a sense of themselves as a distinct collective and a desire to create some kind of Kurdish entity in the framework of the Ottoman Empire.

Wadie Jwaideh, Arshak Safrastian, and Jalile Jalil, important historians of the Kurds, consider Shaykh 'Ubaydallah a new type of Kurdish leader who had a nationalist objective of establishing a Kurdish state.[28] The adoption of a nationalist discourse was reflected in his intention to establish the Kurdish League, which he spoke about at the gathering in 1880, as well as in his discussions with American missionaries and British and Russian consuls. The idea of Shaykh 'Ubaydallah as the first leader to express modern Kurdish nationalism is based on his letter to William Abbott, then the British consul in Tabriz, in which he used the term *milet*, which traditionally meant "religious community" but had sometimes meant "ethnic community," to emphasize that the Kurds were a separate entity. He asked Abbott for his support in making that entity responsible for the management of its own affairs in Kurdistan.[29]

The Soviet Kurdish scholar Jalile Jalil sees Shaykh 'Ubaydallah's moves as preparation for a revolt aimed at the establishment of a Kurdish state that would benefit from British or even Russian protection. Shaykh 'Ubaydallah may have had in mind the example of Bulgaria, which had broken away from the Ottoman Empire. Nevertheless, to date no unequivocal evidence has been found that he intended to formally secede from the Empire. He most probably hoped to establish autonomy—in effect, a state—while continuing to officially recognize the sovereignty of the Ottoman sultan-caliph and the Ottoman state.[30] Shaykh 'Ubaydallah's status as a Muslim clergyman and Sufi shaykh and his particular worldview reinforce the assumption that he sought the protection of Britain in order to effectively establish a state, but within the formal framework of the Ottoman Empire.

Statements by the Shaykh himself, along with the testimony of his interlocutors and the British diplomats with whom he corresponded, indicate that he did in fact subscribe to the concept of ethnic Kurdish distinctiveness and that his intention was political: claiming that the Kurds totaled half a million families, he sought to establish an independent Kurdish state, or an autonomy within the Ottoman Empire, under his own leadership. Corroborative evidence of his thinking is provided by the American missionary Dr. Cochran, who treated the Shaykh and maintained contact with him during his invasion of Iran. In a speech at a gathering of tribal notables in July 1880, 'Ubaydallah used the nationalist term "Kurdistan" and referred to the

Kurds in Iran as "brothers."[31] A further expression of this position was his futile effort to establish the Kurdish League.

At the same time, however, Shaykh 'Ubaydallah expressed his loyalty to the Ottoman sultan, explaining away his attacks on the Ottomans—which were similar to traditional rebel insurrections in the Ottoman Empire—as opposition to corrupt governors. Hakan Ozoglu, an important researcher of the Kurds, adopts a balanced position on this question. As he sees it, Shaykh 'Ubaydallah did indeed want a Kurdish state, under his leadership, in Greater Kurdistan. However, in light of the social and political reality—there was no real chance to withstand the might of the Ottomans—'Ubaydallah's realistic objective was to become the ruler of Kurdistan within the framework of the Ottoman Empire and to accept the sultan's sovereignty. The military force that he succeeded in putting together was supra-tribal, from the standpoint of its objectives and the self-determination of its participants, but not national.[32]

Although Shaykh 'Ubaydallah attributed political significance to Kurdishness and raised a vision of independence for Kurdistan, his actions remained characteristically tribal-Sufi for four reasons: the social conditions in Kurdistan; the political conditions in the Ottoman Empire; the balance of forces between the Empire and the Kurds; and his own traditional worldview. Shaykh 'Ubaydallah expressed ambitions that could be defined as Kurdish nationalist, and his objective—at least for some time—was the establishment of a Kurdish political entity. No one can say with certainty whether he intended that entity to be independent or merely autonomous. He could not, however, rely on a national movement, as no such movement yet existed, and his supporters, the Kurdish tribesmen and peasants, still acted in accordance with their tribal interests and identities and had no national consciousness. Their motives included the preservation of tribal autonomy in the face of what appeared to them to be a weakened central authority; a disinclination to pay taxes to the Ottoman state; their feelings of hostility toward Armenians, other Christians, and Shi'ites; and the prospect of looting. The anti-Armenian and generally anti-Christian positions and motives of at least some of the participants in the July 1880 gathering and the attacks on Christians, especially during the invasion of Iran, ran counter to Shaykh 'Ubaydallah's efforts to maintain good and protective relations with the Christians in Kurdistan and to demonstrate religious tolerance vis-à-vis the West.

Shaykh 'Ubaydallah fell victim not only to Ottoman manipulation but also to the immaturity of the tribal, traditional Kurdish society. Another issue that deserves attention for its importance to understanding the slow and

belated development of Kurdish national consciousness is the similarity between Shaykh 'Ubaydallah's conduct and that of the leaders of the old emirates that had been eliminated during the first half of the nineteenth century.
Owing to the slow pace of modernization and the lack of change in basic socioeconomic conditions in Kurdistan, social patterns in 'Ubaydallah's
world had remained similar to those that prevailed under the emirs. In fact,
the elimination of the emirates—that is, of the supratribal political frameworks—by the Ottomans and the Qajars had created a situation that favored
and strengthened the tribes and Sufi shaykhs.

Shaykh 'Ubaydallah was not a nationalist in the modern sense; his motives and practical conduct were traditional tribal-Sufi. However, his rebellion may be regarded as an early transitional stage in the development of
Kurdish distinctiveness toward modern nationalism.

MUSLIM-CHRISTIAN ANTAGONISMS—
KURDS AND ARMENIANS

During the nineteenth century, the tensions between the Muslim and
Christian communities in the Ottoman Empire escalated. The traditional
pattern of their relations had been undermined by the change in the balance of forces between the Empire and the Western powers; by the Tanzimat reforms, which many Muslims perceived as Western Christian coer-
cion; and by the economic, political, and military infiltration by Western
powers, along with the strengthening of their ties to local Christian communities. The granting (at least at the formal level) of equal civil rights to
Christians as part of the Tanzimat reforms undermined the traditional relationship based on the concept of the Islamic state, in which Muslims were
the superior ruling class and Christians and Jews had a defined, lower status
as protected, tolerated communities with limited political rights. The Ottoman reforms, which were motivated by the desire of Ottoman rulers to
strengthen the Empire against the West, to address its weaknesses, and to
reinforce its central control, were met with incomprehension and objection
on the part of the various groups and sectors whose interests were damaged
by the reforms.

The intensified activity of European consuls and commercial agents, who
forged ties with local Christian communities, and the growing confidence
of local Christians contributed to the rising tensions between ethnic and religious groups. The Christians were increasingly perceived as agents of the
Christian West, which in turn was viewed as a threat to Islam. These tensions often reflected the socioeconomic friction between the generally suc-

cessful urban Christian merchant stratum and the poorer Muslim strata, tribal and otherwise. The growing confidence of Christians was bolstered by the activity of the European merchants, who were assisted by local Christians, and the special status of the Western consuls. The accumulation of wealth by urban Christian merchants and the influence this gave them— which at times amounted to control of certain areas of trade, as well as of exports—under the patronage of Western consuls and merchants augmented the power of a wealthy and Westernizing bourgeois stratum in the cities of the Levant, Lebanon, and Palestine and of Armenians throughout the Empire. In Kurdistan, these tensions were primarily felt, as we have seen, between the Kurds and the Armenians.

In the first half of the nineteenth century, Muslims and Christians clashed mostly in the northeastern part of Kurdistan, between Kurds and Assyrian Christians. To a large degree, those conflicts arose out of the activity of American and British missionaries and the exploitation by Ottoman authorities of the growing strife between ethnic and religious groups: by inhibiting Christian activity, the Ottomans hoped, at the same time, to impose their sovereignty on the autonomous tribal forces and the Kurdish Emirate of Botan. These clashes were limited in scope, however, since the Assyrians represented only a tiny minority in this remote area.

The principal antagonism was in Kurdish-Armenian relations. The Armenians had existed as a distinctive ethnic, linguistic, and religious group since ancient times. Unlike the Kurds, they had evolved their own script, a written language, and a cohesive culture. Following their acceptance of Christianity, Armenians centered their communal life on the Armenian Church and its indigenous ecclesiastical culture. An Armenian state had existed for several centuries and been the strongest and most cohesive political force within and south of the Caucasus. At times it had controlled parts of Kurdistan. These factors gave the Armenian national movement an immense advantage relative to other national movements in the Ottoman Empire and Iran. In addition, Armenians' relatively high level of urbanization and early willingness to absorb elements of modernization and adopt modern Western ideas favored the development of an Armenian national movement.

Over the course of generations, the identities of various social groups and tribes shifted back and forth, from Kurdish to Armenian and from Armenian to Kurdish, according to the prevailing conditions. To this day, some of the Kurdish tribes in northern Kurdistan have traditions that tell of their Armenian roots. At times Armenian tribes and groups accepted Islam and became Kurds. No unequivocal border can be drawn between the areas that were principally populated by Armenians (and that may therefore be referred to as "Armenia") and those whose population mainly consisted of Kurdish Muslims. On numerous maps, the areas to the south and southeast of Lake Van are included within Armenia; on others, they appear as part of Kurdistan. In many places the Kurdish and Armenian populations were intermingled. Significant areas of northern and northwestern Kurdistan were populated by as many Armenians as Kurds, if not more.

Urbanization and the development of a bourgeoisie among the Armenians created a wealthy urban stratum of merchants, moneylenders, and craftsmen and at the same time a settled, nontribal Armenian peasantry. There were also pastoral Armenian tribes. The relationship between urban Armenians and the Muslim population in general—and the Kurdish Muslim population, the majority of whom were pastoral-tribal or settled-rural, in particular—was a complex blend of symbiosis and rivalry, economic interdependence and bitter enmity. The Kurdish tribes and Kurdish rural population needed not only the Armenian merchants and craftsmen but also, in a period characterized by the rising influence of the growing capitalist market economy worldwide, the Armenian moneylenders. The interdependence between the tribal shepherds and farmers and the urban economic groups was accompanied by economic gaps between them that created social tension, which was intensified by their religious differences and by Islamic concepts about the inferior status of Christians in a Muslim state.

Modernization proceeded more quickly among the Armenians, principally the city-dwellers, than among the Kurdish population. The differences in the nature and speed of Armenian modernization, the degree of Armenian exposure to Western influences, and the impact of these on the development of a modern national Armenian identity increased the social tensions with the Kurds and made the latter even more fearful that the area would be taken over by Armenia, under Russian patronage. Kurdish-Armenian enmity escalated dramatically following the Ottoman-Russian War of 1877–1878. During this war, the Armenian Church and many Armenians expressed support for Russia and expected the Russians to assist Armenians in the Ottoman Empire.[33] It is not clear whether this position was shared by the majority of Armenians, many of whom considered themselves loyal Ottoman subjects and shared the Ottomans' anti-Russian suspicions. They objected to identification with Russia for fear of harm to the status of Armenians within the Ottoman Empire.

The pro-Russian position adopted by the Armenians during the war, the strengthening of Armenian nationalist trends, and the increased activity of Armenian national revolutionary movements intensified the hostility of the Ottoman authorities toward the Armenians. Ottoman suspicions were further heightened by the detachment of the Christian Slavic regions in the Balkans from the Empire and by the resolutions adopted at the Berlin Conference of 1878; these resolutions admittedly had an adverse effect on Russia, but they also led to the Armenian issue acquiring an international dimension by legitimating the intervention of the great powers on behalf of the Armenians. The Ottomans feared that the outcome would be a loss of Ottoman control in Kurdistan and southwest of the Black Sea.

Armenian support for Russia during the war and Russian and British support of Armenia, along with Armenians' increasing nationalist activity and expressions of their ambition for national independence (as happened with the Balkan peoples), caused the Kurds to fear the establishment of an Armenian state in Kurdistan. The socioeconomic antagonism was fomented by the destruction, famine, and difficulties in the wake of the war. Against this background, Sultan Abdulhamid's regime began to foster its connections with Kurdish tribal leaders and to build up tribal forces as a counterweight to the Armenians and a means of reinforcing Ottoman control in the area. The Ottomans encouraged tensions between ethnic and religious groups; at times, local authorities even incited hostility to the Armenians. During the war, incidents of physical damage to Armenians and their property became more common, but at the same time Armenians who had served in the Russian army or its auxiliary forces launched murderous attacks against Kurds in particular and against Muslims in general.

In short, the picture of Kurdish-Armenian relations was a complex one. At times, Kurds and Armenians cooperated locally—for example, in the Dersim area—against the Ottoman regime and its army, which cruelly oppressed both groups. The serious and sometimes violent tension in Kurdish-Armenian relations also had a socioeconomic dimension based in changes in agrarian relations and increased land values. These transformations were an outcome of the Empire's Tanzimat reforms between 1839 and 1876, especially the Land Registration Law of 1858, as well as of the growing impact of the global capitalist market economy. Landownership was transformed from a means of survival into a means of production for the export market. Wheat could be grown in Kurdistan—primarily in the Erzurum and Diyarbakir areas—for export to western Anatolia and, in the years when the Tigris and Euphrates Valleys were affected by drought, to Baghdad and Mosul as well.[34]

One of the profound and long-term social consequences of these agrarian changes was the development of a stratum of large landowners drawn from the tribal and rural leaders and notables and urban merchants—those who registered the lands of the villages and tribes in their own names. The members of this stratum were the first to receive a modern Western education and to find positions at various levels in the Ottoman administration. They simultaneously underwent processes that were both complementary and contradictory: Ottomanization fostered integration into and identification with the Ottoman Empire, while localization led to the growth of both collective and territorial identities—such as "Egyptians" or "Syrians"—and supraterritorial identities, principally "Arabs" and "Kurds." Ottomanization and localization among this stratum had far-ranging implications for the social conditions and political transformations in the Middle East up to the second half of the twentieth century.

The severe economic distress from which the population suffered as a result of the war of 1877–1878, along with the direct and indirect implications of a market economy and production for export, led to increased land values, which stoked the strife between Armenian peasants and Kurdish tribal notables. These tribal leaders and rural *aghawat* had strong reasons to take over the lands of their tribes and of Armenian peasants, including the incentive created by the appreciating value of land to own large tracts.[35] The social tensions that arose from the economic changes and the fears about Armenian national ambitions erupted in clashes of various kinds: Muslim Kurds versus Armenian Christians and tribesmen (primarily Kurdish) versus Armenian peasants, and also against nontribal Kurds and the *aghawat*. The Kurdish-Armenian tension led to serious acts of violence and riots by Muslim Kurds against Christian Armenians. These events, as well as the desire to prevent Russia from exploiting the situation in order to reinforce its status as the sole protector of the Armenians, led Britain and France, which had hastened to the aid of the Ottoman Empire, to extend their protection to the Christians and to demand that the Empire protect them against the Kurds.

In 1895–1896, with the Hamidiye cavalry raids on Armenian settlements (as discussed in the next section) and news of the massacre of the Armenians, an Armenian revolt broke out in the city of Zeitun on Lake Van. The rebels, who were organized by an Armenian nationalist-revolutionary party, sought to defend the city, hoping that Russia would hasten to their aid. However, the Ottoman army cruelly suppressed the resistance. One of the Armenian units tried to retreat to Iran toward the Caucasus through territories controlled by the Shikak, the strongest Kurdish tribe in northeastern Kurdistan. The tribesmen attacked the Armenians and pushed them back into the hands of the Ottoman army.

In sum, while educated Kurdish nationalists expressed a desire for Kurdish-Armenian cooperation and coexistence—which was accomplished in some parts of Kurdistan—Ottoman policy exploited and escalated Kurdish-Armenian tensions, leading to outbreaks of violence on both sides.[36]

THE HAMIDIYE CAVALRY

In 1891 the Ottoman administration established tribal cavalry units known as the Hamidiye Light Cavalry Regiments (Hamidiye Hafif Suvari Alay-lari). Recruitment to this force was by agreement with tribal leaders, some of whom were commissioned as officers. The tribes that joined Hamidiye were mainly located along the borders with Iran and Russia, especially the Hakkari area and the lands adjoining Russia to the north of Lake Van. Another area in which many regiments were established lay to the north of the Syrian Desert, where Kurdish tribes competed with Bedouin tribes. By contrast, relatively few regiments were recruited in the Bitlis and Diyarbakir areas, and almost none came from Dersim in western Kurdistan.

The Ottomans' central objective in creating the Hamidiye force was to ensure control of eastern Anatolia, in light of the growing threats posed to the Empire both by Russia and by Armenian nationalist trends. Another, more immediate factor was the revolt by Shaykh 'Ubaydallah. The force was meant to bolster Ottoman control of the areas in which the Empire had difficulty imposing effective sovereignty and to ensure the loyalty of the region's Muslim tribes, the overwhelming majority of whom were Kurds.

Armenian nationalist groups, some of them revolutionary and violent, had been increasingly active since the Ottoman-Russian War of 1877–1878. During the 1880s, three Armenian nationalist parties were established. Armenian ties with Russia and Britain, both of which provided some protection, increased Ottoman fears of loss of control in eastern Anatolia—in the same way that, not long before, Russian-supported nationalist trends in the Balkans had led to the establishment of Romania and Bulgaria on lands that had belonged to the Empire. By setting up the new military units and encouraging the loyalty of Kurdish tribes, Sultan Abdulhamid hoped to create a counterweight to the rising strength of the Armenian national movements.

Another motive for establishing the Hamidiye cavalry was to respond to the efforts by the descendants of the last emir of Botan, Bedir Khan, to reestablish the emirate by forging a bond of loyalty to the Sultan on a tribal basis. In the early 1890s, nearly two decades after the failure of such an attempt by Bedir's sons Osman and Husayn during the Ottoman-Russian War, 'Abd al-Razzaq Bey Bedir Khan explored the possibility of gaining the support of

Kurdish tribes for the renewal of the emirate under Russian or British protection. The establishment of tribal military frameworks strengthened the tribal leadership and its loyalty to the Sultan, forming a kind of alliance between them against the nationalist-oppositionist groups of educated urban Kurds that had sprung up in the towns of Kurdistan.[37]

The Hamidiye force was officially established in Istanbul in 1891 in a ceremony attended by tribal chieftains and notables. Generally speaking, each tribe that enlisted had a separate regiment; sometimes several small tribes would be combined into a single regiment under the command of the strongest tribal leader. The tribal leaders appointed as regimental commanders were given the rank of colonel. Lesser leaders became captains and majors. The Hamidiye officers were honored in various ways, including visits to Istanbul, where they were splendidly hosted. Tribal leaders who became officers were permitted—with the consent of the authorities—to do whatever they pleased to members of the tribes that did not join the Hamidiye cavalry, as well as to nontribal peasants and Christians. The tribes that enlisted and their leaders received payment for their services and were exempted from taxes. Simple tribesmen who joined up were given weapons (generally new rifles), uniforms, and horses.[38] An ordinary Kurd did not have the means to buy a horse. The horses, salaries, and uniforms were clearly instrumental in persuading tribesmen to join the regiments.

As far as is known, 64 or 65 regiments were established, each numbering between 512 and 1,150 men, depending on the size of the tribe on which it was based. All in all, the force comprised some 50,000 fighters.[39] In practice, it might have been that only 150 or 200 men actually served in a tribal regiment. Although the original intention was for Arab, Turkmenian, and Qarapapakh tribes to be included, almost all of the tribes that joined the Hamidiye cavalry were Kurds.

The founder and supreme commander of the Hamidiye was Zeki Pasha, a Circassian officer who was married to Sultan Abdulhamid's sister. He commanded the Fourth Army, which was in charge of eastern Anatolia and the Russian border and was headquartered in the city of Erzincan. The most senior tribal commander in the Hamidiye until 1902 was Mustafa Pasha, the head of the Miran tribe. Miran was one of the stronger tribes in the Emirate of Botan, and Emir Bedir Khan throughout his reign and until 1847 had difficulty exerting his control over it. The exile of most of the members of the Bedir Khan family enabled the Miran tribe to emerge as the central Kurdish force in the Botan area. Although Mustafa Pasha had held neither status nor prestige beyond his tribe, his status as senior commander of the Hamidiye gave him the authority to become the strongest person in the Botan area and to present a counterweight to the Bedir Khan family, whose influence was diminished by their exile.

The exiled activists, especially those from the Bedir Khan family, objected to the founding of the Hamidiye cavalry.[40] The Bedir Khans supported the protests that arose against Mustafa Pasha, and the Hamidiye in general, following a series of acts of violence and destruction against Armenian and Yazidi villages, nontribal Kurdish peasants, and tribes that had not enlisted in the Hamidiye. In 1902, Mustafa Pasha was assassinated by rivals from among his many enemies, including another branch of the Miran tribe.[41] Following this, Ibrahim Pasha, the head of the Milli tribal confederation, became a senior commander of the Hamidiye.[42]

The tribal leaders used their power to promote their personal and tribal interests, in particular by taking over lands or asserting their protection over nontribal peasants and villages. Joining the Hamidiye enabled a tribe to enjoy relative autonomy, achieve dominance over the surrounding population, and possibly take over lands. The Hamidiye became a means by which the state controlled its tribal-pastoral nomad population. Although its establishment strengthened the tribes and tribalism, the Hamidiye also promoted a process that undermined tribal relations over the long term: tribal leaders became transformed into landowners who benefited from the development of agrarian capitalism while retaining their tribal powers and prestige. The expanding market economy, especially the increasing volume and profits from sheepherding products—mainly wool, but also cotton and meat and dairy products—drove up the value of pastureland and fueled tribal leaders' motives for taking it over.[43]

The change in land values and the growth of a capitalist-agrarian market economy in a tribally organized society, as well as the significant transformation under these socioeconomic conditions of tribal leaders—and sometimes of shaykhs—into landowners who produced for market needs, led to serious acts of violence against Armenians, Christians, nontribal Muslim peasants, and weak Kurdish tribes.[44]

In contrast to the Kurdish emirates, in which each emir controlled a number of tribes and enjoyed prestige and a certain capacity for supratribal mediation, the leadership reinforced by service in the Hamidiye was unmistakably tribal in nature. Such leadership was generally based on violence rather than conventions, and it undermined the stability of the region by exacerbating relations with other tribes. The Kurdish tribes that did not join the Hamidiye suffered at the hands of neighboring tribes that had enlisted and acquired both arms and power, which they used to settle intertribal disputes and even to displace weaker tribes. Thus, for example, the Cibran tribe, from which four regiments were recruited, exploited its power and status in the Hamidiye against its rival, the Hormek tribe, which did not join the cavalry—probably because the cavalry was Alewite and not orthodox Sunnite.[45] Having tribal regiments commanded by tribal leaders, coupled with the rising value of their land, strengthened both tribalism and intertribal strife.

The Hamidiye cavalry, the high status of its commanders, and the violence of its regiments aroused opposition and criticism from various directions. Regular Ottoman army officers envied the superior conditions and lightning-fast promotion of the tribal leaders who became regimental commanders. Civilian Ottoman officials were uncomfortable with the actions of the Hamidiye commanders because they exceeded their authority and at times refused to obey the officials. Enlistment in the Hamidiye also elevated the status of the Kurds vis-à-vis the Ottoman bureaucracy.[46] With their position as cavalry officers reinforcing their self-confidence, tribal leaders were now among the intimates of the Sultan and no longer subordinate to the Ottoman administration and to local governors.

The unrest and dissatisfaction of officers in the regular Ottoman army led them to organize the Young Turks movement in opposition to the regime. Eventually joined by reformers, Turkish nationalists, and Western-oriented secularists, in 1908, they overthrew Sultan Abdulhamid and restored the Parliament and the Constitution of 1876, which he had suspended (see chapter 5). Meanwhile, the Hamidiye officers remained loyal to the Sultan. This may well have been important to him in light of the unrest among regular army officers and the urban residents of the Diyarbakir area.[47] The Hamidiye cavalrymen took part in the persecution of the Armenians between 1894 and 1896; in the suppression of protests by Kurdish villages and tribes against the oppressive collection of taxes and the arbitrariness of the Ottoman officials; and in retaliation against nontribal Kurds and tribes that did not have their own Hamidiye regiments.

Following the Young Turks revolution, the Hamidiye units were disbanded because of their loyalty to the Sultan. While tribal leaders who had enjoyed their status as Hamidiye officers sought to uphold Sultan Abdulhamid's rule, previously exiled Kurdish activists now held positions on the Committee of Union and Progress (CUP) and in the Young Turks regime. The difficulty of establishing effective control of its territory, however, led the Young Turks regime to reinstate the tribal units in 1910 under a new name: the Tribal Cavalry Regiments (Asiret Suvari Alaylari).[48] The renamed tribal units fought alongside the Turks against the Greek invasion of Anatolia in 1919–1922. In a battle that took place amid the last remnants of the Ottoman Empire, after the end of World War I, some of the former Hamidiye units remained loyal to the Sultan; others cooperated with Mustafa Kemal Atatürk. In the absence of a recognized national leadership and faced with the weak Kurdish national consciousness, the Hamidiye and the Kurdish tribes followed their own tribal interests and local circumstances.

The establishment of the Hamidiye marked both a continuation of the status quo and a turning point in Ottoman policy toward the Kurds. During the period of the reforms and up to the end of the nineteenth century, the Ottoman state developed channels that enabled the modernized, "Ottomanized" Kurds who repudiated Kurdish distinctiveness to find places in its administration and its military. At the same time, the Ottoman state strove to eliminate collective Kurdish entities—the emirates and strong tribes. In establishing the Hamidiye, the Ottoman state hoped to integrate Kurdish tribal collective entities into the wider Ottoman society. This took the form of an alliance between the tribal leaders, who were becoming landowners, and the Sultan, who sought through them to secure control of the Ottoman state in eastern Anatolia (central and western Kurdistan) and to create a counterweight to the threat of separatist Christian Armenian nationalism.

The Hamidiye cavalry units thus played a complex role in the development of Kurdish national identity. On the one hand, they strengthened the ties between their Kurdish fighters and the Sultan and the Empire. Enlistment in the Hamidiye, and the salary and economic benefits that came with it, created a sense of identity and a common economic interest with the Empire. At the same time, the Ottoman regime was contradicting its own centralist policies in creating the Hamidiye. Recruitment on a tribal basis not only reinforced tribal identities but sometimes also fueled tensions between those tribes that participated and those that did not. The format of tribal recruitment and organization strengthened Kurdish tribalism, which resisted any concept of Kurdish unity and of a collective, supratribal Kurdish identity. In addition, the empowerment of the tribes and their leaders hampered the emergence in eastern Anatolia of an urban middle class, which, generally speaking, is the basis for the development of a national movement.

On the other hand, a consciousness of Kurdish distinctiveness and identity was reinforced by the concentration of Kurds in the Hamidiye units, their separation from the Ottoman army (which was principally Turkish), and the population's perception of the Hamidiye cavalry units as Kurdish. Moreover, the officers of the regiments that participated in the Ottoman Empire's Balkan wars were exposed to the ideas of the Turkish and various Balkan national movements.[49] Some of the activists and commanders in

Kurdish revolts against the Turkish government during the 1920s came from the Hamidiye units.

HARBINGERS OF MODERN NATIONALISM

In April 1898, the first issue of the first Kurdish newspaper, *Kurdistan*, came out in Cairo. Its sponsor and publisher was Mikdad Midhat Bedir Khan, the son of the last ruling emir of Botan. It was very difficult to publish a newspaper in Kurdish because of the absence of a standard language, or even a dominant dialect, so eventually the newspaper was bilingual, written partly in the Kurmanji dialect of Kurdish—a subdialect of Botan—and partly in Turkish. Speakers of other Kurdish dialects, and even of other strands of Kurmanji, could understand it only with difficulty or not at all.

The languages used by literate Kurds at the time were Ottoman Turkish and Arabic. Kurdish students studied in schools where instruction was in Turkish, Arabic, or Persian because of the weakness of the "high" Kurdish language and the lack of books in Kurdish and of any standardization of the language. Kurds who became literate did so in the dominant languages of the region, not in Kurdish. A modern literary Kurdish language was only in its infancy, and so terms and concepts that had matured in modern languages were missing in Kurdish. Accordingly, those parts of the newspaper written in Kurdish were very hard to understand, even for those who knew Kurmanji. After three issues of being written in the Botani-Kurmanji dialect, the paper became officially bilingual (Kurdish-Turkish), but the percentage in Turkish gradually increased.[50]

The newspaper's principal purpose was to foster modern education in Kurdistan as well as a consciousness of a Kurdish collective identity. Its articles reflected an awareness of Kurdish ethnic and cultural distinctiveness within the framework of the Ottoman Empire and Kurdish regionalism. The paper emphasized Kurdish history and inculcated a Kurdish national identity. The first issue, for instance, featured a portrait of Salah al-Din al-Ayyubi (Saladin) as a great Kurdish Islamic hero.

Subsequent issues published, for the first time, the poem *Mam u Zin*, which is considered the cornerstone of Kurdish nationalism.[51] Its publication at that time was of definitive nationalist significance: national movements had been burgeoning throughout the world since the nineteenth century. Not only was the poem a milestone in the development of Kurdish national consciousness and a harbinger of the Kurdish national movement, but its publication was a step forward in the organization of the Ottoman opposition. According to one Turkish scholar, the newspaper benefited from the support of the Ottoman opposition to Abdulhamid's dictatorship.[52]

The paper published appeals to the Sultan as it expressed pro-Ottoman objectives: the promotion of reforms in the Empire, the fostering of Kurdish education and historical and social consciousness, and the improvement of the economic situation of Kurds and Kurdistan within the Ottoman Empire.[53] Various articles severely criticized the corruption in the Empire, and even the Sultan himself, and expressed concern for the Empire's future. The paper emphasized the Kurds' contributions to Ottoman history and argued that the Kurds' future depended on the Empire's destiny.[54] Well-known Kurds connected to the paper, including 'Abd al-Rahman Bedir Khan, were also active in the Ottoman opposition movements and Young Turks organizations.

The paper considered the role of the Kurdish language and called for its modernization, but it also published articles advocating education in Turkish for the Kurds. First of all (as these articles emphasized), Turkish was the language of the Ottoman state, and fluency in it was the key to advancement for the Kurds. Second, the various Kurdish dialects were not sufficiently developed to form the basis of modern education.[55]

The newspaper's readership apparently included not only exiled activists but also notables from the provincial towns of Kurdistan who had already been exposed to Ottoman modernization. It was distributed among educated Kurds in Istanbul and Izmir. An unknown number of issues were sent to the cities of Kurdistan.

In 1901 the newspaper published an acutely critical article denouncing the Hamidiye cavalry as a corrupt institution intended to prevent a joint Armenian-Kurdish uprising against Abdulhamid's tyranny.[56] Members of the Bedir Khan family and other Westernized, educated nationalists were hostile to the Hamidiye regiments, which had succeeded, as intended by the Empire, in strengthening rival tribal forces and encouraging Islamic and tribal support of Sultan Abdulhamid. Some issues of *Kurdistan* also featured articles calling for Kurdish-Armenian cooperation and claiming that only a few Kurds had been involved in the violent incidents against Armenians, just as the ostensible Armenian hostility toward the Kurds was supported by only a minority of Armenians. These articles represented a Kurdish protest against the conduct of the Hamidiye units toward the Armenians.[57]

The emergence of *Kurdistan* and its publication of *Mam u Zin* were important milestones in transforming the consciousness of Kurdish distinctiveness into a national linguistic, ethnic, and cultural identity.

CHAPTER 5

THE BEGINNINGS OF
MODERN KURDISH POLITICS

OPPOSITION TO SULTAN ABDULHAMID II

Abdulhamid II ('Abd al-Hamid) (1876–1908) ascended to the throne in 1876, in an alliance with reformist-liberal circles in the Ottoman establishment and political system. Within a short time, however, he changed his position. In 1877 he suspended the liberal constitution that had been his allies' principal achievement; instituted a rigid, centralist, personal dictatorship; violently persecuted the supporters of reforms; and suppressed any political expression that diverged from his centralist views. Admittedly, he continued to promote modernization and sped up the introduction of modern infrastructure for transportation, communications, and administration. In the political sphere, however, his policies were authoritarian and repressive. He favored a pan-Islamic worldview and began to emphasize his status as a caliph.

Under Abdulhamid II, the political position of both Arabs and Kurds became more complex. Abdulhamid increased the integration of Arab and Kurdish Muslim notables into the Ottoman army and administration, thereby accelerating the process of Ottomanization of the elites among the notables in the Empire's provinces. His policy favored Muslims over non-Muslims and perpetuated the changes brought in by the Tanzimat reforms, which made it easier for tribal leaders and notable urban families to reinforce their status as landowners with connections to the Ottoman administration. However, his suppression and tyranny were at odds with the political concepts being developed by Westernizing, educated liberals and proponents of modernization. Under Abdulhamid's rule, the contradiction intensified between a centralist regime and the reinforcement of local territorial interests and identities, as did the awareness of a collective identity among Arabs and Kurds.

An opposition movement began to be organized, seeking to restore the Constitution of 1876. The activists were educated Westernizers—students, army officers, administrators, and others. Many of them came from families with members working for and supporting Abdulhamid's regime. In the 1880s, educated, Westernizing Kurds began to join the Society of Ottoman Unity, an opposition group; during the 1890s, its name was changed to the Committee of Union and Progress (CUP). Members of the oppositionist organizations included Turks, Arabs, Kurds, and others. On the one hand, the modern, educated elites of the various linguistic and ethnic national groups within the Empire, including the Kurds, were moving toward Ottomanization. On the other hand, the Turkish oppositionists increasingly emphasized their own cultural and linguistic distinctiveness, Turkish national and linguistic predominance, and the development of modern Turkish nationalism.

Among the founders of the CUP were two Kurds, Abdullah Jawdat (Cevdet) and Ishak Sukuti, officer cadets at the Military School of Medicine in Istanbul. Both were involved in the unsuccessful plot against Abdulhamid in 1892. In 1895, Cevdet was exiled to Tripoli in Libya, and Sukuti to Rhodes. However, they escaped to Europe, where they continued their opposition to Abdulhamid. Around 1900, they reconciled with the Ottoman authorities and were given junior positions in Ottoman embassies in Europe. Sukuti subsequently worked as an editor and translator and was a proponent of adopting the Latin alphabet for the Turkish language. Neither of the two is known to have favored Kurdish nationalism.[1]

Other prominent Kurdish activists in the opposition to Abdulhamid came from the aristocratic families of Bedir Khan and Baban and a'ayan (rich notable families) such as Cemilpasha from Diyarbakir; some of them held positions, including senior ones, in the Ottoman bureaucracy.[2] In addition to the exiled family members of former emirs, the activists included Kurdish Sufi shaykhs, especially the sons of Shaykh 'Ubaydallah of Nehri, who, like their father, had been exiled in the 1880s and 1890s and were later given jobs in the Ottoman bureaucracy. One of them, Sayyid 'Abd al-Qadir, had been exiled to Istanbul after he was involved in the failed plot of 1892 against Abdulhamid and was forced to flee. He later held central positions in the Young Turks regime after the 1908 revolution, including that of speaker of the Ottoman Parliament. Attendees at a conference of the Ottoman Union and Progress movement, held in Paris in February 1902, included 'Abd al-Rahman Bedir Khan and Hikmat Sulayman Baban.[3] They did not participate as Kurdish representatives but were present on the basis of their activity and reputation in the opposition to Abdulhamid.

The conference was extensively covered in the newspaper *Kurdistan*, which had relocated from Cairo to Europe.[4] Kurdish activists, especially those associated with the paper, were at first divided between those who believed that their demands to promote the Kurdish language and to develop Kurdistan could be fulfilled within the framework of the Ottoman Empire, and those—primarily members of the Bedir Khan family—who were examining the possibility of complete independence. The predominant approach among Kurdish activists, however, was "Ottomanist"—seeking reform, modernization, and improvement of conditions in Kurdistan and Kurdish autonomy within the framework of the Empire. Following the Young Turks revolution of 1908, separatist trends would develop gradually, alongside the increased sense of Turkish identity in the Empire, and would accelerate after World War I as a result of secularization, the abolition of the Caliphate, and the spread of authoritative Turkish nationalism under Atatürk.

In July 1908, members of CUP, including army officers, government officials, and young educated people, launched the Young Turks revolution. The leaders of the Young Turks forced Sultan Abdulhamid II to restore the Constitution, deprived him of his powers except for a few symbolic ones, and effectively put an end to his tyranny. In April 1909, the Sultan's conservative supporters, backed by social groups that had been harmed or had lost their status as a result of the revolution, attempted a counterrevolt against the Young Turks government, hoping to restore the Sultan's powers and block what they viewed as the new regime's liberal secular trends. The counterrevolt was defeated, notwithstanding the support of conservative forces among the clergy, the masses under their influence, and many who had lost their jobs as a result of the revolution. Following the failed counterrevolt, Abdulhamid was ousted and Abdulwahid ('Abd al-Wahid) was appointed to replace him as sultan.[5]

There were Kurds in both camps, among the conservatives and among the revolutionaries. The divisions between them were to a great degree sector- and class-related. The Westernizing nationalist activists and the few members of the middle class, the *effendiyya*, wished to preserve the distinctiveness of the Kurds, but viewed integration into the Ottoman Empire and involvement in Ottoman politics as the best way to modernize Kurdistan and advance the Kurds as a people. The supporters of the Sultan essentially clung to the old tribal ways. They saw integration into the Ottoman Empire from the perspective of their particular interests—the preservation of their status and landownership, which had been reinforced and legitimized under Abdulhamid.

Most of the Hamidiye cavalry units supported the Sultan and even fought against the supporters of the revolution. Zeki Pasha, the supreme commander of the Hamidiye appointed by the Sultan, was dismissed immediately after the revolution. The news of the counterrevolt in Istanbul in April 1909 encouraged the Sultan's conservative supporters in Kurdistan to oppose the CUP regime. The Hamidiye cavalry units, led by Ibrahim Pasha, the head of the Milli tribal confederation, took over the streets of Damascus. However, after the enlistment of the Arab Shamar tribes, who backed the new regime, the pro-Abdulhamid Kurds retreated and Ibrahim Pasha was killed.[6]

By contrast, the modern, Westernizing political activists, who were mostly from Kurdish notable families who had been exiled to Istanbul, held central positions in the Young Turks administration. Sayyid 'Abd al-Qadir (the son of Shaykh 'Ubaydallah) was elected speaker of Parliament, Isma'il Haqi Baban served as minister of public works, and Sulayman Nadef was appointed the *vali* of Baghdad. As they saw it, Kurdishness and Kurdish identity had become an integral part of the modernizing Ottoman state and it was pointless to strive for political realization in a separate state.

KURDISH ORGANIZATIONS IN ISTANBUL AFTER THE YOUNG TURKS REVOLUTION

Following the overthrow of Abdulhamid's despotic regime, groups of modernized, educated Arabs and Kurds, among them army officers, intensified their political and cultural activities in Istanbul and founded political organizations. These were ethnic and regional in nature (representing Kurdistan and the Arabic-speaking *vilayets*) but Ottomanist in substance; in other words, they aimed to improve the status of Kurdistan and the Arabic-speaking *vilayets* within the framework of the Ottoman Empire. Although these organizations were not yet asking for Kurdish independence, they expressed awareness of Kurdish distinctiveness and interests and sought to introduce far-ranging reforms and modernization. Some of the founders of Kurdish organizations had been active in the CUP when it was still in opposition to Abdulhamid. Others had held positions in Abdulhamid's government but lost them when they supported him during the revolution.

Most of the leaders and activists in the Kurdish organizations came from the aristocracy—the families of emirs who had been exiled from Kurdistan and posted to jobs in the Ottoman bureaucracy in other lands. These included the Baban and Bedir Khan families, relatives of Sufi shaykhs such as Sayyid 'Abd al-Qadir and Shaykh Taha of Nehri, Shaykh 'Ubaydallah's son and nephew, who lived in Kurdistan.[7] Individuals who became more prominent in Kurdistan itself included Shaykh ʿAbd al-Salam Barzani in Bahdinan, Shaykh Mahmud Barzinji in the Sulaymaniyya area, and other tribal leaders who became landowners and benefited from Sultan Abdulhamid's policies.

Between the Young Turks revolution and the outbreak of World War I, a number of prominent Kurdish organizations were established in Istanbul. The first, the Kurdish Society for Mutual Help and Progress (*Kurd Teʿavun ve Terakki Jemʿiyati*, KTTJ), also known as the Society for the Rise and Progress of Kurdistan (*Komeley Taraqi u Taʿali Kurdistan*), was founded in October 1908. Although it was mainly active in Istanbul, it was also active in Bitlis, Diyarbakir, and Mosul. The KTTJ put out a newspaper in Turkish, *Kurd Teʿavun ve Terakki Gazetesi*. The KTTJ and its paper were clearly Ottomanist in nature and presented the Kurds as loyal to the Empire and the Sultan.[8] The KTTJ's declared objectives were to improve the situation in Kurdistan and among the Kurds and to strengthen ties between the Kurds and the Ottoman state, and between the Kurds and the Armenians and Nestorians. The KTTJ did not seek an independent Kurdish state. It emphasized education, economic improvement, and the encouragement of commerce and agriculture in Kurdistan, all within the framework of the Ottoman Empire.[9]

The founders and a great many of the activists in the Kurdish organizations and on the staffs of the Kurdish newspapers were members of exiled aristocratic Kurdish families who held positions in the Ottoman establishment, bureaucracy, and armed forces, including Emir ʿAli Amin Bedir Khan; Ahmad Naʿim Babanzade, and Sayyid ʿAbd al-Qadir of Nehri. The younger, junior activists were members of the middle stratum—officials, army officers, and intellectuals who also held positions within the Ottoman state apparatus. Among the activists in Kurdish organizations was General Sharif Pasha, who served under Abdulhamid as the Ottoman ambassador to Sweden and supported the Sultan during the conflict of 1908–1909. There were also supporters of a separate Kurdish nation-state. The most prominent supporter of an independent Kurdish state was ʿAbd al-Razzaq Bedir Khan.

In 1910 a number of Kurdish activists, members, and affiliates of the KTTJ established the Kurdish Society for the Dissemination of Education (*Kurd Neshr-i Maʿaruf i Jemʿiyati*), which was headed by ʿAbd al-Rahman Bedir Khan and Miktat Midhat Bedir Khan. Notwithstanding their positive attitude toward the CUP, both of the Kurdish organizations were closed down by the government and the publication of the newspaper was stopped in 1909, reflecting the growing Turkish nationalist trends in the Ottoman government. Sentenced to death, Emir ʿAli Amin Bedir Khan and General Sharif Pasha were forced to flee the Empire.

In 1908 Kurdish students in Istanbul established the Kurdish Society of Hope (*Hevi Kurdi Jemʿiyati*), also known as the Kurdish Society of Student Hope (*Kurd Talaba Hevi Jemʿiyati*).[10] The organization operated in Istanbul until the outbreak of World War I and even attempted to establish branches in European cities. It published a newspaper, *Kurdish Day* (*Roja Kurd*) in the Kurmanji dialect; the name was changed to *Kurdish Sun* (*Hetave Kurd*) in 1912. The founders of this organization were the sons of tribal notables and landowners (*aʿayan*) who had sent their sons to study in Istanbul in order to improve their chances of employment in the Ottoman administration. It was not a separatist organization but rather one devoted to expressing moderate Kurdish nationalist aspirations in the framework of the Ottoman Empire. Another publication, the Kurdish-Turkish weekly *Bangi Kurd* (*Kurdish Call*, or *Kurdish Voice*), was founded shortly before the outbreak of World War I by Jamaluddin Baban in Baghdad. This periodical emphasized the importance of education and called for more schools and organizations in Kurdistan. It featured nationalistic articles on Kurdish history.[11]

Until World War I (and even afterward), these Kurdish organizations were small in scope and elitist in social composition, and their ties with the Kurds and Kurdistan were quite weak. Although Sayyid ʿAbd al-Qadir and members of the Bedir Khan family had achieved honor among the Kurds in their native areas, their real connections to and influence in Kurdistan were limited. Among the tribal and rural population, tribal and familial identities were far stronger than Kurdish identity. Even among most of the Westernizing, modern, educated activists, Kurdish identity still lagged behind Islamic, Ottoman, and tribal identities. Kurdish organizations and newspapers expressed the Ottomanist view that was then dominant among Kurdish activists and educated people.[12] In fact, it was the emphasis placed by the Young Turks on the Turkish identity of the Ottoman state in 1912–1913 that accelerated the consciousness of Kurdish distinctiveness, in contrast to Turkish nationalism.

The activity of educated Kurds in Istanbul and other urban centers, such as Baghdad and Cairo, on behalf of modernizing the Kurdish language, fostering Kurdish culture, overcoming illiteracy, and strengthening Kurdistan's economy laid the foundation for modern Kurdish nationalism, even when those involved still believed that their objectives could be accomplished within the framework of the Ottoman Empire. Many Kurdish nationalist activists in Turkey did not become active in the post-1908 organizations until after World War I. In spite of the inherent limitations of tribalism and the geographical and mental remoteness of the great majority of Kurds, these organizations and the recognition of the Kurds as a territorial, linguistic ethnic group that had rights of its own and that might even establish a state in an alliance with a foreign power represented the first shoots of the Kurdish national movement.

OTTOMAN KURDISTAN BEFORE WORLD WAR I

Following the Young Turks revolution, clubs and organizations with links to the KTTJ were established in Kurdistan's provincial towns, but these groups were quite different from those in Istanbul. In the branches of the national organizations in Kurdish towns, a central role was played by officials and teachers, as well as by landowners, tribal leaders, clergymen, and a few modern educated merchants. In Istanbul, KTTJ activists supported and even held positions in the CUP government, which the organizations in Kurdistan regarded with suspicion. The conservative Kurdish elements—religious, tribal, landowning notables who were becoming major landowners—felt alienated from what appeared to be moves toward secularization in the Young Turks regime.

Whereas the founders of the KTTJ in Istanbul were Western-educated and supported social modernization and education, the organizations in the provincial towns arose as a response by conservative landowners and tribal leaders to the ouster of the Sultan, whom they perceived as having been good for them. Also participating in some of these organizations were local clergy, who protested, on behalf of *shari'a* law, against the Young Turks' new, modernist, and seemingly secular regime. The ties between the various organizations were weak, and the organizers were largely motivated by local unrest and anxieties. The variations in point of view, social status, mind-set, and interests formed the background for profound differences between the Kurdish organizations in Istanbul and the provincial Kurdish groups—including those that were supposed to be branches of the Istanbul organizations.[13]

Following the 1908 revolution, anarchy prevailed in Kurdistan. Tribes and tribal leaders-turned-landowners imposed their sovereignty on weaker neighbors or took over the lands of Armenian peasants and nontribal Kurds, ignoring the weak and corrupt Ottoman authorities. The fear of changes and reforms led the tribes to support Abdulhamid and to oppose the new regime, which they regarded as a heretical rebellion against the Sultan. To them, Abdulhamid was also the personification of the Muslim state. Members of the Bedir Khan family strengthened their ties with tribes and tribal leaders who were hostile to the CUP and the Young Turks regime. There was no coordination among various family members, and their activism did not mature into a supratribal national leadership. Members of other aristocratic families, especially Shaykh 'Ubaydallah's, some of whom held senior positions in the Young Turks administration, also held meetings with tribal notables and national societies in the provincial towns.

In the Young Turks revolution, the Union and Progress movement succeeded in ousting the Sultan, restoring the Constitution, and holding elections for Parliament. Nonetheless, it was faced with the fundamental problems of the Ottoman Empire, which was embroiled in a protracted political and economic crisis and torn by separatist trends among its subpopulations—such as the Balkan peoples, who had developed a national consciousness of their own. Given the immediate need to prevent collapse, and despite the internal debates and clashes on the subject, the CUP regime adopted a policy aimed at reinforcing the centralism of the Ottoman government, thereby making ethnic Turkishness the central axis around which the Ottoman state revolved. This policy of centralization reinforced the alienation between the Arab and Kurdish populations of the *vilayets* and the Ottoman state. Nevertheless, even as this policy aroused resistance in the provinces and spurred the growth of ethnic consciousness into expressions of Arab and Kurdish nationalism, the vast majority of Muslims in the Empire remained loyal.

THE RISE OF TWO BARZINJI SHAYKHS IN SULAYMANIYYA

To the north and northwest of the city of Sulaymaniyya, a complex relationship prevailed between the Ottoman authorities and the Qadiri Sufi shaykhs of the Barzinji family, which had become a powerful clan. Families of Qadiri shaykhs began to achieve prominence in Sulaymaniyya as early as the eighteenth century. The strengthening of the Barzinji tribe under the leadership of Shaykh Sa'id Barzinji in the last quarter of the nineteenth century grew out of the vacuum created by the overthrow of the emirate controlled by the House of Baban earlier in the century as well as the increased status of the Sufi shaykhs.[14]

A complex mosaic of social and political forces held sway in the area. These included the Talabani tribe, who were the families of the shaykhs from the Qadiri Sufi order that had established a presence in Kirkuk during the nineteenth century and enjoyed the support of the Sulaymani, who had also gradually become a tribe; the Jaf tribe, to the south and west of Sulaymaniyya; the Hamawand tribe, whose leaders controlled many nontribal villages in the area; and an urban population of merchants and craftsmen in the city itself. Also living in Sulaymaniyya were some family members of the emirs of Baban; until the midnineteenth century, the city had been the capital of their emirate. The descendants of the Baban family enjoyed distinction and a high economic status, but lacked any real political influence.

The relationships between the various populations in the city and its environs combined cooperation, interdependency, and social and political rivalry, which at times spilled over into violence. The rivalry between the Barzinji and Talabani tribes led on numerous occasions to murders and raids by one tribe in villages subordinate to the other. Such rivalries played out against the backdrop of the Ottoman reforms and the development of a market economy, which had motivated tribal leaders and Sufi shaykhs to take over lands, especially pasturage and orchards. Moreover, in the vacuum after the disappearance of the emirates, the Hamawand tribe, a small, militant tribe of shepherds and farmers, countered Ottoman weakness by becoming stronger after the war of 1877–1878. The local rival of the Hamawand tribe was the Barzinji tribe, under the leadership of Shaykh Sa'id. All of these factors combined after the 1877–1878 war to make Kirkuk and Sulaymaniyya lawless areas where the Talabanis and the Barzinjis killed and raided in each other's territory and the Hamawands carried out raids on villages and highway robberies. Under these conditions, the Ottoman authorities were able to make an ally of Shaykh Sa'id, who began a series of moves intended to restore Ottoman control of the area and to suppress the rebellious Hamawand tribe.[15]

According to a British traveler, the intelligence officer Ely Banister Soane, who visited Kurdistan in 1909, Shaykh Sa'id had taken control of territory in the Sulaymaniyya area in 1881 and since then, in coordination with the Ottoman governors, had levied heavy taxes on the city's merchants. The merchants had sought the aid of the Hamawand tribe, which besieged the offices of the Ottoman governor and the headquarters of Ottoman army units in Sulaymaniyya in an attempt to oust the governor.[16] With the assistance of an Ottoman military force, however, Shaykh Sa'id had regained control of the area and continued—now abetted by the Sultan himself—to oppress the city-dwellers and the Hamawand tribesmen.[17]

In 1894 a violent intratribal conflict developed between Shaykh Sa'id and his supporters and another branch of the Barzinjis, headed by Sayyid Mahmud Effendi, who sought to undermine Shaykh Sa'id's authority.[18] The conflict was related to power struggles in the central government in Istanbul and to the maneuvers by Sultan Abdulhamid among various people and powers in his administration. The local Ottoman authorities, who wanted to keep the peace and ensure the regular collection of taxes, exploited the struggle in order to weaken the Barzinjis and pacify the area.

The *vali* of Mosul, who was supported by the Council of Ministers in Istanbul, demanded the dispatch of a strong military force to Kirkuk and Sulaymaniyya in order to forcibly suppress the tribes and local militias. However, the Sultan, wishing to preserve his direct relationship with the shaykhs and tribes in Kurdistan, denied the request. The Barzinji tribe—or, more precisely, the branch headed by Shaykh Sa'id Barzinji—had the support of Sultan Abdulhamid and his court; the Ottoman governors of Mosul and the Council of Ministers in Istanbul, however, were hostile toward the Barzinjis. Abdulhamid held a grudge against the Hamawand tribe for its revolts during the 1890s, which had demonstrated the tribe's opposition to the Ottoman authorities' endorsement of Shaykh Sa'id's takeover of their lands, a move backed by Abdulhamid. The Sultan's conciliatory attitude toward the ferment among the Kurds resulted from his desire for their support in light of the Armenian revolts that had broken out at the time and that the Sultan perceived as a severe threat should they be backed by Britain and Russia.

The continued raids by the Shaykh's men on the Hamawand tribe gave the local Ottoman authorities grounds to restrain him by direct force. Their decision to do so was supported by the Council of Ministers in Istanbul, but was again rejected by Abdulhamid, who in 1901 had invited Shaykh Sa'id to Istanbul and given him a splendid reception.[19] As long as the Sultan remained in power, he continued to back Shaykh Sa'id against the Hamawand tribe and the Ottoman administration in the area.[20]

With the weakening of Abdulhamid's power following the Young Turks revolution and his eventual ouster in 1909, Shaykh Sa'id's own status was damaged. In 1908 and 1909, a certain rapprochement took place between the Hamawands and Shaykh Sa'id. They began to cooperate against the new regime, and apparently also against the merchants of Sulaymaniyya. The antagonism between Shaykh Sa'id's men and the merchants led the latter to request assistance from the Ottoman government. When the Shaykh, accompanied by a small group of supporters, went to Mosul in 1908, he was arrested by the Ottoman authorities and detained for some time. Following his release a few weeks later, he was murdered by an urban mob, with the support of the local Ottoman governor, in a house that he owned in Mosul. In reprisal, a force loyal to Shaykh Sa'id's son and heir, Shaykh Mahmud Barzinji, terrorized Sulaymaniyya. Hamawand tribesmen also carried out raids in the environs of Mosul, and Nadim Vali, the governor of Baghdad, intervened in an effort to restore calm. In 1910 he reached an understanding with Shaykh Mahmud. At the end of Nadim Vali's term in office, however, the area was again reduced to anarchy, with no effective Ottoman control. This situation continued until the outbreak of World War I.

The robberies, land takeovers, raids by militant tribesmen on the roads and in the towns, and their activity against representatives of the Ottoman authorities appeared to be acts of opposition to the new government and at times were accompanied by expressions of support for the Sultan. In fact, however, they were outbreaks of tribal anarchy, facilitated by the weakness of the regime.

After World War I, when Kurdistan's future was unclear (it would eventually be integrated into the new state of Iraq), Shaykh Mahmud Barzinji, who had a broader and more modern point of view than his father, would become the most prominent Kurdish figure in Iraq and in Kurdish-British relations. Eventually he would declare himself King of Kurdistan. Many of his utterances, and those of some of his supporters, reflected nationalist concepts.[21]

THE BITLIS REVOLT AND SHAYKH ʿABD AL-SALAM BARZANI'S CLAIMS TO AUTONOMY

Immediately before World War I, two Kurdish revolts took place in the Empire: one led by Shaykh ʿAbd al-Salam Barzani in the Bahdinan area and the other in the city of Bitlis. Although these were local events and did not become broad-scale supratribal revolts, they displayed elements of Kurdish nationalism.

The Barzanis—a family of Naqshbandi Sufi shaykhs—developed into a tribe following the weakening of the old Emirate of Bahdinan, which was conquered by Muhammad Kor, the emir of Soran, in the early 1830s and then entirely wiped out by the Ottomans at the end of that decade. Families of nontribal peasants and nomads from small tribes coalesced around the Naqshbandi Sufi shaykhs from the Barzani family. The strengthening of this family and its development into a tribe took place amid social tensions with the Zibari tribe, a dominant group of landowners to whom many villages north of Mosul and south of Hakkari were subordinate.

The most prominent leader of the Barzanis after 1908 was Shaykh ʿAbd al-Salam Barzani, who unified a number of tribes and factions into a sort of tribal confederation around himself. According to a source sympathetic to the Barzanis—a book by a family member, Massoud Barzani—ʿAbd al-Salam attempted to promote social reforms, some of which were far-ranging, such as the distribution of land to peasants, the abolition of landownership (apparently an attempt to harm the major landowners), the abolition of the customs of dowry and forced marriage, the construction of mosques as social centers in villages, and the establishment of village committees to manage local affairs. It is difficult to determine whether his intention to institute broad-based reforms received any significant support. He did, however, forge ties with Kurdish organizations in Istanbul.

Although 'Abd al-Salam Barzani was a traditionally tribal-quasi-feudal and religious-Sufi leader, his actions and statements had a nationalistic tone as well. In 1907 he participated in a conference of tribal leaders in the home of a shaykh of the Qadiri Sufi order, Nur Mohammad Brivkani. The participants sent the Istanbul government a telegram containing demands of national as well as religious significance: that Kurdish be recognized as an official language in Kurdish areas; that Kurdish be established as the language of instruction in the schools in those areas; that Kurdish speakers be appointed as regional and district governors (*kaymakams* and *mudirs*); that the courts be subjected to Islamic law; and that resources be directed to the construction of mosques and schools.[22] As far as the available documents reveal, this was the first time that concrete Kurdish demands of national significance were made.

Starting in 1907 and at intervals until 1914, a struggle went on between the Ottoman authorities and the supporters of Shaykh 'Abd al-Salam Barzani, who was twice forced into exile from his village by the Ottoman army, returning only after its retreat. In 1913 he visited Tbilisi in the Caucasus, where he met with Russian representatives. Against the background of the corrupt Ottoman administration and the weakness of the Ottoman governor in Mosul, rivals of the Barzanis attempted on various occasions, starting in 1909, to take over a number of villages that were subordinate to them.[23] The *aghawat* (tribal landowners) from the Zibari tribe and their allies among the notables of Mosul, who wanted some of the Barzani lands, pressured the Ottoman authorities to act against Shaykh 'Abd al-Salam.[24]

Following a conference of shaykhs and tribal leaders led by 'Abd al-Salam in Dohuk in 1909, a list of demands was sent by telegram to the national activists in Istanbul. Most of these demands were nationalist in nature, and some were Islamic:

(1) Kurdish had to be the official language in the five Kurdish subdistricts.
(2) Instruction in schools had to be given in Kurdish.
(3) Administrative positions in Kurdish areas (*kaymakams* and *mudirs*) were to be filled by officials conversant with Kurdish.
(4) The courts in the area had to operate according to *shari'a* law.

(5) The positions of *mufti* judges (adjudicators of religious legal doc-
trine) had to be filled by members of the *al-madhab al-shaafi'i* school
of law. (The great majority of Kurds belonged to the Shafa'i school of
law, whereas the Turks and the Ottoman state generally adhered to the
Hanafite school of law [*al-madhab al-hanafi*].)

(6) Taxes were to be collected in the area in accordance with *shari'a* law.

(7) Taxes were to be dedicated to the development of the area.[25]

The demands in the telegram were based in the ethnic-linguistic-cultural
and religious-judicial distinctiveness of the Kurds and amounted to a demand for autonomy within the framework of the Empire. The demands regarding the legal system and taxes may be interpreted as an expression of
the Kurds' religious distinctiveness, within the context of Islam, as a distinct
proto-national ethnic group.[26]

A previous conference, in 1907, had presented similar demands. Shaykh
'Abd al-Salam's contacts with Kurdish national activists in Istanbul (Amin
Bedir Khan, Shaykh 'Abd al-Qadir, General Sharif Pasha) and the nationalist
nature of the demands reflected for the first time a Kurdish national point
of view—albeit one with tribal and Islamic foundations. The letter sent by
'Abd al-Salam to Kurdish activists in Istanbul reinforces the assumption that
their purpose was autonomy within the Empire, not independence or secession. The shaykhs and tribal leaders may have been attracted by the example
of the protection and assistance granted by the Western powers to Christian
communities within the Empire, or by Russian assistance to those who had
rebelled against the Ottomans in the Balkans.

When the Ottomans, who feared a Russian invasion of Kurdistan, heard
the news about the organizing of Kurdish tribes, the developing ties between Shaykh 'Abd al-Salam Barzani and the Russians, and the meetings
with a representative in Tbilisi and with the Russian consul in Erzurum, they
took sharp military action against him. Although the Kurds were victorious
against an Ottoman unit in the first clash, 'Abd al-Salam's forces were unable to resist the regular Ottoman army. In spite of his Sufi religious status,
'Abd al-Salam was unable to recruit Kurdish forces beyond loyal members
of his own tribe and did not have the time to organize a multitribal force.
Isolated by the splits between the tribes and the Ottomans' ability to retain the loyalty of other Kurdish tribes, 'Abd al-Salam was defeated and fled
to Iran. From there he went on to Baku, where he was hosted by the Russian authorities. In the autumn, he returned to Iran, where he attempted
to organize a tribal alliance against the Ottomans. He also met there with
another prominent person who maintained ties with the Russians—Isma'il

Agha Simko, a tribal-feudal leader whose sovereignty extended over the majority of the Shikak, a strong tribal federation, and whose influence prevailed in the areas south and west of Lake Urmia. Apparently motivated by tribal considerations, Simko, who would become infamous as a traitor, ordered his Shikak fighters to seize 'Abd al-Salam Barzani and turn him over to the Ottomans. The governor of Mosul, Sulayman Nadhif, who was a Yazidi Kurd, had Barzani executed hastily, in December 1914, to avoid having to pardon him under pressure by Istanbul.[27]

Between 1911 and 1914, petitions were composed in Bitlis calling on the Ottoman authorities to appoint Kurdish officials, to implement *shari'a* law, and to establish territorial army units that could impose order. In March 1914, an uprising broke out in Bitlis after the arrest by the Ottoman authorities of a local leader and *'alim*, Mullah Salim. Residents of the city freed him by force and took over the city and its environs. The rebels' demands included the expulsion of Ottoman officials and the implementation of *shari'a* law. The Ottoman administration was perceived as a Turkish government that was attempting to weaken the Kurds and to sell their homeland to foreigners.[28] This uprising resulted from the deterioration of local relations between the government and the populace, as well as from resistance to what was perceived, from a conservative Islamic viewpoint, as the secular and anti-Kurdish tendencies of the Young Turks regime.

The outbreak of the uprising in March anticipated and frustrated the preparations for a revolt, with Russian support, that had been scheduled for April. That revolt was planned by 'Abd al-Razzaq Bedir Khan and Mullah Salim. The uprising, based in a confused mix of nationalist, religious, and local concepts and perceptions, broke out with no planning or preparations and was suppressed in a short time; its local leaders found shelter in the Russian consulate.

SIMKO FROM THE SHIKAK TRIBE IN IRANIAN KURDISTAN

In 1906 a constitutional revolution took place in Iran, after which a conflict broke out between its more conservative opponents and its supporters, who were largely modernist. Pro- and anti-revolutionaries in Iranian society were divided along sector and class lines, and their differences transcended the boundaries of ethnic communities. A small number of urban Kurds supported the revolution, but the tribal population, among whom the great majority of Kurds were numbered, was in the conservative camp. With confusion and uncertainty prevailing in Iranian Kurdistan, the weakness of the Qajar state raised the status of the tribes and tribal leaders.

In 1907 Britain and Russia came to an agreement on the division of Iran into zones of influence, while preserving the Iranian state and the rule of the Qajar Dynasty. Most of Iranian Kurdistan was included in the Russian zone of influence. Between 1906 and 1914, the central Iranian administration became extremely weak and was beset, like other parts of Iran, by a struggle between the forces of the constitutional revolution and their conservative opponents. During that period, Russia and Britain emerged as the principal Western powers in the area. The Ottoman Empire, fearing a Russian takeover of Iranian Kurdistan, attempted to block Russia by military occupation of the area and through efforts to attract Iranian Kurdish tribes to its side. The Ottomans sought not only to exploit Russia's weakness following its defeat in the Russo-Japanese War, the attempted revolution of 1905, and the violent sociopolitical unrest within the country but also to take advantage of the decline of the Qajar government in Iran after the constitutional revolution. Accordingly, beginning in 1906, the Ottomans increased their activity in Kurdistan.[29] Early in that year, Ottoman forces, with the assistance of Kurdish tribes from within the Ottoman Empire, occupied most of Iranian Kurdistan. Ottoman commanders pressured the local Kurdish tribes to swear loyalty to the Sunnite Ottoman sultan rather than the Shi'ite shah.

With confusion and uncertainty prevailing, and fearing an Ottoman takeover, several tribal leaders sought to strengthen their ties with Russia. Under these conditions, the Shikak leader Isma'il Agha Simko, whose conduct and ambitions were tribal in nature, saw his power and status increase.[30] He became the leader of tribes in an extensive area of Iranian Kurdistan, southwest of the city of Khoy, west of Lake Urmia and as far as the periphery of the city of Banne in the south, which was known for its refusal to comply with any government whatsoever.

In 1911 Britain and Russia agreed to cooperate in order to protect their commercial interests in Iran. According to this understanding, Iranian Azerbaijan—which was considered by both Iran and Russia to include Kurdistan—was designated a Russian zone of influence. Pursuant to this agreement, the Russians pressured the Ottomans to withdraw from their position along the Ottoman-Iranian border, which they had taken up in 1905. In light of the stance adopted by both Britain and Russia, the Ottomans were forced to withdraw. All of Iranian Kurdistan was occupied in 1911 by the Russians, who controlled it until 1917, although rather ineffectively in most areas.

The weakness of the Iranian and Russian control of Iranian Kurdistan created a governmental vacuum that was exploited by Simko to boost his own status. Although his actions were clearly tribal in nature, he began to reveal modern nationalist elements as well. As his power increased, he forged ties with Kurdistan activists in the Ottoman Empire. He married the sister of Shaykh Sayyid Taha, the grandson of Shaykh 'Ubaydallah. He also established ties with 'Abd al-Razzaq Bedir Khan, who spent some time in 1911–1912 in the city of Urmia, where he published a Kurdish-language newspaper, with Simko's support.[31] 'Abd al-Razzaq Bedir Khan was the most active supporter of a Kurdish national independent state. However, because almost all the Kurdish population identified with their tribe or with their religious or local affiliation, Kurdish nationalism and the Kurdish "imagined community" was meaningless to most of them. The Kurdish national movement in Iran came later, in response to Iranian state- and nation-building policy, the destruction of the tribal social structures, and the suppression of Kurdish identity under the regime of Pahlevi Riza Shah, beginning in the 1920s.

BETWEEN OTTOMAN LOYALTY AND OVERTURES TO RUSSIA

Kurdish tribes and Russia continued to try to cooperate throughout the nineteenth century, against the background of Russian pressure on the Ottoman Empire and Iran and efforts by the latter to extend its sovereignty over the Kurdish tribes, which were attempting to preserve their autonomy and perceived the centralist trends and reforms of both states as a threat.

From the earliest stirrings of a national identity, some Kurds viewed Russia as a potential ally against the Ottomans. As early as 1889, 'Abd al-Razzaq Bedir Khan and Ja'far Agha Shikak (the tribal leader of one of the most powerful Kurdish tribes in southern Kurdistan—Iranian Kurdistan, west of Lake Urmia) visited Russia and proposed Kurdish-Russian cooperation.[32] Between 1908 and the outbreak of World War I, prominent Kurdish activists and tribal leaders were in frequent contact with Russia. Although the majority of Kurds remained loyal to the Ottoman Empire, a number of leading Kurdish activists and certain tribal leaders began to look for a diplomatic mainstay among the Empire's Western rivals. They were aware that the Ottoman Empire might crumble, and they feared the Armenians' national ambitions. Notwithstanding their different approaches and rivalries, such as the rivalry between the Bedir Khan family and the descendants of Shaykh 'Ubaydallah, the common goal was to establish Kurdish independence or autonomy under Russian protection in the framework of a decentralized Ottoman Empire. Among the prominent pro-Russians were 'Abd al-Razzaq Bedir Khan, Kamel Bedir Khan, Shaykh Muhammad Sadiq, and his son, Shaykh Sayyid Taha (the son and grandson of Shaykh ʿUbaydallah); also in this camp were Simko and Shaykh ʿAbd al-Salam Barzani.

ʿAbd al-Razzaq Bedir Khan was clearly—indeed, extremely—pro-Russian. He had received a modern education and was familiar with diplomatic and political realities outside Kurdistan. After serving as third secretary of the Ottoman embassy in St. Petersburg, during which time he became familiar with the Russian language and culture, he concluded that only with Russia's help could the Kurds achieve independence. As early as 1894, he met with Russian representatives in Tbilisi and proposed the organization of a Kurdish revolt with Russian assistance.[33] From 1909, he strengthened his ties with the Russians and attempted to convince them that their support of the Kurds would significantly increase Russia's influence and status in the Ottoman Empire and in Iran. In 1910 he traveled to St. Petersburg in an attempt to obtain Russian support for either a Kurdish state or Kurdish autonomy under Russian protection.

The relationship between ʿAbd al-Razzaq Bedir Khan and Russia was complex. The Russians sought to exploit him against the Ottomans, but were suspicious of his plans to establish a Kurdish state under Russian protection. At a certain point, he began to receive the modest salary of 300 rubles per month from Russia for his activities. In 1913 ʿAbd al-Razzaq met with the Russian consul in Khoy in western Azerbaijan—in Iranian territory (north of Lake Urmia)—and asked to have the Russian Orientalist Joseph Abgarovich Orbeli (1887–1961), a specialist in the history of the southern Caucasus, sent to Kurdistan to formulate modern rules of grammar for the Kurdish language. ʿAbd al-Razzaq also proposed the translation of Russian literary works into Kurdish, and of Kurdish poetry into Russian. In his conversations with Russian experts, he expressed the desire to establish a center of Kurdish studies in St. Petersburg. He was interested in founding a network of national Kurdish schools in which Russian would be taught as a foreign language. Immediately prior to World War I, he did succeed in establishing a Kurdish school in Khoy at which the Western language of study was Russian.[34] In addition, ʿAbd al-Razzaq held talks with tribal leaders in Iranian and Ottoman Kurdistan with a view to convincing them to take Russia's side and to establish ties with its consuls.[35]

In 1913, ʿAbd al-Razzaq Bedir Khan established Irshad, an organization that operated for a short time in Van, Diyarbakir, and Urfa and whose objective was to organize a revolt against the Ottomans. After it was exposed by the Ottomans, ʿAbd al-Razzaq founded another organization, *Jihandani*. It is not clear how large these organizations were or whether they had a real chance of arousing a broad-based revolt. Any chance of success disappeared with the unplanned outbreak of the uprising in Bitlis.[36]

Like Bedir Khan, Shaykh Sayyid Taha adopted a pro-Russian line and maintained relations with Russian representatives. Surprisingly, his uncle, Sayyid 'Abd al-Qadir, was one of the Kurdish activists who had been successful in the Union and Progress movement, and although the views he expressed were clearly pro-Ottoman, he also kept in contact with the Russians. He even sent an emissary to Grand Duke Nicholas, then viceroy, heir to the Russian throne, and chief commander of the Russian front in the Caucasus. 'Abd al-Qadir continued to support the Ottoman sultanate and caliphate, but strove to reinforce the status of the Kurds and favored Kurdish autonomy under Russian protection within the Ottoman state.

Another leader who approached the Russians was 'Abd al-Salam Barzani, who had a grasp of modern politics. He was not as pro-Russian as 'Abd al-Razzaq Bedir Khan; even as he made contact with the Russians, he expressed a willingness to cooperate with the British. He suggested to British travelers that Britain should establish schools in Kurdistan.[37] Although relations between the authorities and 'Abd al-Salam became more relaxed between 1911 and 1913, they soon deteriorated again. It seems that during that time 'Abd al-Salam initiated contacts with Russia in the hope of obtaining Russian assistance for the Kurds who, under his leadership, were supposed to revolt against the Ottomans.[38]

Shaykh Muhammad Sadiq of Shemdinan, Shaykh 'Ubaydallah's son, maintained contacts with the Russians through the villages under his sovereignty in an area under Russian control in Iran. His son, Shaykh Taha, who inherited his father's position, made efforts to strengthen those ties with a view to enlisting Russian support. These contacts with the Russians reflected the beginning of Russia's adoption of a more active policy toward the Kurds. Shaykh Mahmud Barzinji was also in communication with the Russians and asked their consul in Mosul for clarification of Russia's policy in Kurdistan.[39]

In 1908 a group of tribal and local khans and beys in Iranian Kurdistan approached the Russian consulate in Urmia and asked it to open a network of vice consulates throughout the area.[40] The main reason for this request lay in the aggressiveness of the Ottoman Empire, which had conquered the city of Sauj Bulak (Mahabad) in 1906, with the assistance of Kurds loyal to the Empire, and was demanding that the Kurds in Iran swear loyalty to the Ottoman sultan as a Sunnite caliph. The request was motivated, however, not only by Ottoman aggression, which was intended to damage both Russia and Iran, but also by the weakness of the Qajar Iranian state and the inclusion of Iranian Kurdistan in the Russian zone of influence, in accordance with Russia and Britain's 1907 agreement on zones of influence in Iran.

The most prominent individual in the group of Iranian Kurds who approached the Russian consulate was Simko, whose status was threatened by the 1906 invasion of Iranian Kurdistan by Ottoman and pro-Ottoman Kurdish forces. Simko again contacted the Russian consulate in Urmia in 1911 and visited Russia in 1912.[41] In 1911, as mentioned earlier, Russian forces chased the Ottomans out of western Iran and occupied it, although very loosely, and there was no permanent Russian presence in the territory of the Shikak tribal confederation. The response by the majority of the Russian officials, diplomats, and experts with whom Simko met was positive. Apparently, a limited degree of cooperation ensued, as expressed in the pressure that the Russians exerted on junior tribal leaders to swear loyalty to Simko, in exchange for handing over to the Russians, in 1913, an Azeri-Azerbaijani anti-Russian activist who had found asylum with Simko—who had supported the anti-Russians prior to 1911.[42]

Russian policymakers refrained, however, from adopting a clear position, and Russia did not officially bend to Kurdish nationalist ambitions for an active policy toward the Ottoman Empire and Iran. Russia was willing to exploit the Kurdish tribes tactically in order to increase its own influence, but never agreed to support the Kurds as a collective and never forged an alliance with them.

THE WEAKNESS OF KURDISH NATIONALISM BEFORE WORLD WAR I

Prior to World War I, some of the tribal leaders in Kurdistan began to prepare themselves for the possibility that the Ottoman Empire, and possibly Iran as well, would collapse and that, as a result, Russia would become the dominant Western power in the area. Kurdish autonomy would benefit from Russian protection within the Ottoman Empire, which would be decentralized. These tribal-feudal leaders felt that such an option should be prepared for by strengthening ties, or even forming an alliance, with Russia. Their goal of securing their own status should Russia become the dominant power gave Kurdishness a new political significance.

The unrest and riots in both Ottoman and Iranian Kurdistan were tribal and local; they lacked any common vision that could have coalesced into a national strategy or some kind of supratribal leadership coordinated with local power brokers. Nevertheless, Kurdish self-awareness increased. Several exiled intellectuals and activists began to conceptualize ethnic Kurdish existence as a political entity. The feeling that the Ottoman Empire was likely to collapse and the examples provided by the Balkan peoples, who had detached themselves from the Empire and become independent states, provided activists with a diplomatic and political horizon. One way they responded was by searching for an ally outside the Ottoman Empire. The belief that Russia had a chance of becoming the dominant power was more forcefully expressed during World War I, when Kurdish activists and tribal leaders cooperated with Russia and Shaykh Muhammad Barzinji offered Sharif Husayn of Mecca Kurdish-Arab cooperation in the revolt against the Ottomans.

Nevertheless, Kurdish national development in the Ottoman Empire prior to World War I was hampered by a series of factors relating to the social structure in Kurdistan, the virtual nonexistence of a cohesive, influential modern stratum, and the tribal and Sufi Islamic character of the dominant discourse:

1. *Primary identity:* The poor, illiterate Kurdish masses were mainly motivated by personal economic survival and identified primarily with their tribes, their families, or Sufi shaykhs. The collective Kurdish identity did not play a major role in their day-to-day experience, but was only one of a series of collective identities. Islamic and tribal identities, and sometimes the Ottoman identity, took precedence. Kurdish tribesmen and nontribal peasants felt, identified as, and behaved like tribesmen and nontribal peasants and like Muslims who identified with their Sufi shaykhs.

2. *The personal or tribal interests of the landowners and Sufi shaykhs:* Tribal leaders, some of them Sufi shaykhs around whom tribes had developed, became tribal landowners and used the concept of Kurdish tribes to promote their own and their tribes' conservative interests. Insofar as they believed that control of their tribal lands, control of the lands of expelled Armenians, and recognition of their status would serve their interests, they were willing to cooperate with the Ottoman authorities, the supporters of the sultan, and even their national rivals, the Young Turks.

3. *The strength of intertribal rivalries:* Strong intertribal rivalries hindered the growth of any supratribal leadership.

4. *The weakness of the Kurdish modern middle class and bourgeoisie:* Most Kurds with a modern education considered Kurdish distinctiveness an antimodern anachronism and preferred to identify with Ottomanism or Turkish nationalism. Generally speaking, the few who had had the privilege of studying in a modern Ottoman school, even if they acknowledged their Kurdish origins, viewed themselves as Muslim Ottomans loyal to

the sultan caliph. Some of them even attempted to deny their Kurdish origin and to attach themselves to an imaginary Turkish community or nationality.

5. *The absence of a clear nationalist vision:* Even the Kurdish activists in Istanbul had no clear nationalist vision; many of them clung to promoting Kurdish interests in Kurdistan as a regional and ethnic issue, within the confines of the Ottoman Empire. Among the Kurdish activists were those who dreamed of heading a Kurdish state; nevertheless, the separatist vision—that is, secession from the Ottoman Empire and an independent Kurdish state—was shared by only a few.

CHAPTER 6

THE KURDS AND KURDISTAN
DURING WORLD WAR I

BETWEEN RUSSIA, BRITAIN, AND THE OTTOMAN EMPIRE

During World War I, Kurdistan and eastern Anatolia suffered an appalling human tragedy: hundreds of thousands of Kurds and Armenians—perhaps more than 1.5 million people in all—died as a result of the deportation and mass slaughter of the Armenians and the deportation and starvation of vast numbers of Kurds.

Over the course of the war, northwestern Ottoman Kurdistan became a battlefield between the Ottoman and Russian armies, and belligerent operations extended into the Khanaqin area. Between October 1914 and January 1915, the Russian army reinforced its control of northwestern Iran and the major part of Iranian Kurdistan. In the face of Ottoman weakness and the loss of Iranian control, many Kurdish tribes and notables in eastern and northeastern Kurdistan chose to cooperate with the Russians. Various parts of Ottoman Kurdistan, such as Sulaymaniyya and Khanaqin, were passed around between the Ottomans, the Russians, and the British.

In the secret negotiations conducted by Britain, France, and Russia in 1915–1916 on the postwar division of the Ottoman Empire's territory, the Russian foreign minister, Sergey (Serge) Sazonov (1860–1926), demanded that the Russian zone of control extend to the south of Lake Van and include Bitlis.[1] Because the Russians had already taken over most of Iranian Kurdistan, acceding to this demand would have put most of Kurdistan, and most of the Kurds, under Russian rule.

During the war, Kurdish nationalist activists and prominent tribal leaders in the Ottoman Empire and in Iran attempted to forge ties with Russia and Britain, hoping that such cooperation would either assist in establishing a Kurdish state under their leadership or secure their status should the Ottoman state and Iran become protectorates under Russian or British control.

As a British intelligence officer, Major E.W.C. Noel, recalled, Shaykh Taha went to Russia and represented himself as the leader of Kurdistan under Russian patronage. Basile Nikitine, who served as Russian consul in Urmia at the time, reported on a letter written by Shaykh Taha in 1917 in which he proposed Russo-Kurdish cooperation.[2] Shaykh Taha's uncle, Sayyid ʿAbd al-Qadir, who was employed in the Young Turks regime, also approached Russian diplomats in Tehran and Russian officials in Tbilisi early in 1917.

Members of the Bedir Khan family were likewise working to achieve Russian support. In 1916 Kamel Bedir Khan met with Grand Duke Nicholas, then viceroy and chief commander of Russian forces in the Caucasus.[3] The conquest of Khanaqin by the Russian army in April 1917 and Russia's control of the area until June of that year encouraged the local tribal notables to approach the Russians and promise them the support of their tribes against the Ottomans.

Among the Russians, several officials who had served as consuls in the cities of Ottoman and Iranian Kurdistan before the war, as well as some intelligence officers who were familiar with Kurdistan, favored fostering ties with the Kurds as being in line with Russian interests. Prominent among them were Vladimir Minorsky (1877–1966) and Basile Nikitine, both of whom, after the end of World War I, became important scholars of Kurdish history. Boris Shakhnovski, formerly the Russian consul in Damascus, was placed in charge of the liaison between the Russian command and the Kurds. To this end, Shakhnovski exploited his good connections with the Bedir Khan family.[4] Perhaps the most conspicuous Russian act of rapprochement with the Kurds was the appointment of ʿAbd al-Razzaq Bedir Khan as *vali* of Bitlis and of his brother Kamel Bedir Khan as *vali* of Erzurum, following the conquest of those cities by the Russian army in 1917.

In contrast to the recommendations by those supporting an alliance with the Kurds, most Russian commanders displayed a suspicious, reserved attitude toward them and showed a clear preference for cooperation with the Armenians. The Russian officials and officers who favored ties with the Kurds did not succeed in achieving widespread Russian support for this or for a Kurdish state, or even for formulating a clear policy toward the Kurds.[5] The efforts by the proponents of Russian support for the Kurds—which would also ensure that Russia was not dependent on the Armenians alone, in light of the suspicions of Armenian ties with Britain—did not find a sympathetic response from the commanding officers of the Russian army. The Russian commanders in the field (including high-ranking ones, some of whom were of Armenian origin) generally had more in common with Armenian Christians than with Muslim Kurdish tribesmen. Some field commanders even took brutal measures against the Kurds, including arresting and exiling tribal leaders and notables, and frustrated attempts at dialogue with them. In a number of incidents, Armenians who collaborated with and were protected by the Russian army carried out cruel acts of vengeance against the Kurds.

Kurdish nationalist activists with a pro-Russian orientation did not succeed in formulating a national vision or program attractive enough to appeal to either educated, Westernizing Kurds or tribal notables. The tribal shaykhs who forged ties with the Russians could not put together a significant Kurdish force that would appeal to the Russians as a possible basis for building their influence in the area. Russia's avoidance of adopting a clear pro-Kurdish position had the effect of limiting the influence of the pro-Russian activists. The appointment of two members of the Bedir Khan family as *valis* and the recruitment of several Kurdish tribes as auxiliary forces were tactical moves intended to exploit local forces, not expressions of an overall policy designed to win Kurdish support. The British intelligence officer Major Noel recalled that the British suspected that Russia was conducting a policy of winning over the Kurds. However, according to Basile Nikitine, the Russians did not formulate a policy toward the Kurds.[6] In spite of the attempts at dialogue by Kurdish nationalist activists, some of whom took Russia's side, most of the Kurds continued to view Russia as a Christian power and a supporter of the Armenians, whom a considerable portion of the Kurds viewed as their local rivals.

In April 1917, the Russians conquered Khanaqin and Sulaymaniyya. Because of Ottoman weakness and the collapse of the Iranian government, many Kurdish tribes and notables in eastern and northeastern Kurdistan chose to cooperate with the Russians. The Russians apparently allowed their control of the area to be weak because it was considered marginal relative to the central front against the Ottomans to the northwest, in the areas of Kars and Erzurum.[7] Against the background of the February and October 1917 revolutions in St. Petersburg, Russia's status as a great power competing with Britain declined and its involvement in Kurdistan disappeared.[8] In June of that year, the Russian forces retreated from the Khanaqin area and from Iranian Kurdistan, and the Ottomans took it over again.

The British forces landed at Basra in December 1914 and gradually conquered the plains of Mesopotamia over the next four years. In September and October 1917, they began to take control of southern Kurdistan. In December 1918, they took Khanaqin, Sulaymaniyya, and Kirkuk, forcing direct Russian influence out of Kurdistan. From that point onward, the developments concerning the Kurds and opportunities to establish a Kurdish state took place in the context of British-Turkish-Arab-Kurdish relations. Nevertheless, the shadow of the Russian threat continued to be a British consideration with respect to the future of Kurdistan.

DESTRUCTION AND SUFFERING IN WARTIME KURDISTAN

Although Kurdistan was only a marginal front in World War I, the Kurdish and Armenian populations of the area suffered greatly. Hundreds of thousands of Kurds and Armenians died of hunger and cold or were murdered in inter-ethnic clashes. Many more thousands were expelled from their homes by the Ottoman army or in clashes between ethnic communities. For example, in dozens of villages in northern Kurdistan, nearly two-thirds of the population starved to death. Even in areas farther away from the worst of the fighting between the Russians and Ottomans, such as Sulaymaniyya, the population was reduced to about one-third of its prewar number.

In the same way, cities and villages in other areas of Kurdistan whose populations had numbered in the tens of thousands before the war were left with only a few thousand residents. Several factors gave rise to terrible famine and starvation: the confiscation of food by the Ottoman army; the mass conscription of men, who had made up most of the agricultural and pastoral labor force; and the destruction of settlements and of means of subsistence in the areas that passed between the Ottomans, the Russians, and the British.[9] In a planned Ottoman campaign, some 700,000 Kurds were driven from their homes into western Anatolia, where they were scattered among the Turkish population so as not to constitute a threat.[10]

Although most of the battles on the Caucasus front took place north of Kurdistan itself, many Kurdish recruits were attached to Ottoman units on that front. Some of the tribal units (the former Hamidiye) were sent to the Balkan front. Kurdish units in the regular Ottoman army received fewer supplies and were considered inferior to those staffed by Turks. The Third Brigade of the Ottoman army, which fought against the Russians on the Caucasian front and into which most of the Kurds were drafted, suffered a crushing defeat in the winter of 1914–1915 and actually fell apart. Tens of thousands of Kurdish soldiers—possibly more than 150,000—perished in the battles, under conditions of starvation and freezing cold in the high mountains.[11]

It was not surprising that under the dreadful conditions of famine, cold, and epidemic disease to which the Ottoman troops were exposed, desertion was extremely common. Also contributing to the extensive desertions by Kurdish troops—many more of whom deserted than did troops of other na-

tionalities—may have been their relative closeness to Kurdistan; their famil-
iarity with conditions in the mountainous areas; and their physical and mental ability, as mountaineers and shepherds before they joined the fighting, to
withstand the dangers and difficulties of desertion. Yet, despite the terrible
suffering of the Kurdish population and the growing disappointment with
Ottoman weakness and failures at the front, a considerable proportion of
the Kurds remained loyal to the Ottoman Empire as an Islamic state headed
by a sultan-caliph. That loyalty derived from a number of sources:

1. *Fear of the Armenians:* The Kurds perceived the Armenians as local rivals
   and competitors supported by the Western Christian powers. This fear facilitated the Ottoman effort to enlist the support of the Kurds as Muslims, against the background of the long-standing tensions and clashes
   between the Muslim Kurds and the Christian Armenians and Assyrians,
   conflicts that were at times encouraged by the Ottoman authorities. The
   developing Armenian national movement aroused Kurdish fears that the
   Armenians would establish a Christian state of their own, under Western
   protection, that would engulf the Kurds. Another element of the Kurds'
   fear of the Armenians derived from the socioeconomic gaps and divisions between the tribal Kurdish population and the Armenians, most of
   whom were urban residents or settled farmers.

2. *Tribal loyalty:* The tribes whose members served in the Hamidiye cavalry,
   especially the tribal notables, had a tribal economic interest in the continuation of Ottoman rule and the sociopolitical status quo from which they
   benefited.

3. *The socioeconomic interests of tribal and religious leaders:* Tribal leaders
   and notables, under the protection of the Ottoman state, had established
   themselves as landowners and had a socioeconomic interest in maintain-
   ing the status quo.

4. *Lack of choice:* The superiority of the Ottoman army and its unrestrained
   cruelty to the civilian population gave most Kurds little choice but to
   obey the authorities and join the Ottoman army or the auxiliary forces.

CHAPTER 7

THE KURDS AND THE NEW MIDDLE EAST
AFTER THE OTTOMANS

SHAYKH MAHMUD BARZINJI'S FAILURE
TO ESTABLISH A KURDISH STATE

The British forces took over the city of Mosul on November 3, 1918, after the armistice with the Ottoman Empire was signed in Modrus on October 30 and became effective the following day.[1] The Turkish nationalists, who, led by Mustafa Kemal Atatürk, had coalesced in 1919–1920 into the strongest force in the Ottoman state, claimed that the British occupation of Mosul was illegal and constituted a breach of the armistice agreement. Starting in 1919, the Turkish nationalists, or Kemalists, who included many Kurds, were active among the Kurdish tribes in the Mosul area with a view to harming the British and ensuring that the region was included in the territory of Turkey. At the Turkish National Congress in Sivas in September 1919, the majority called for the inclusion of Kurdistan within Turkey, and the Kurds within the Turkish nation. Kurdish anti-Kemalist activists were opposed to Turkish nationalist trends, however, and found refuge in the Mosul area under British control; they were even exploited by the British, who sought to bolster their control of the area.

In ruined, starved southern Kurdistan, shattered and devoid of any supra-tribal leadership, the British found a complex tribal reality. In Sulaymaniyya, once the proud capital of the Emirate of Baban, and in Istanbul, some notables of the House of Baban still remained, but their influence and ability to lead the residents of Sulaymaniyya and the surrounding area were quite limited. The only person whose status appeared to extend beyond his own tribe was Shaykh Mahmud Barzinji, who was both a Qadiri Sufi shaykh and a tribal leader and thus had the support of his tribe as well as influence among other tribes in Sulaymaniyya, Khanaqin, Dohuk, and adjacent areas in Iran.[2] To the British officers familiar with the practice of "Indian" colonialism—the model of administration used in India, especially in tribal border areas—Shaykh Mahmud seemed suitable to fill the role of an "authentic" leader whose influence on the local population would help them retain control of Sulaymaniyya.

A desire to block the activity of the Kemalist-nationalist Turks among the Kurds was one priority guiding British choices in regard to the Kurds, especially at the tactical level. However, the support of (and the objections to) Shaykh Mahmud Barzinji presented the British with the strategic question of whether to annex the Mosul region to a state with an Arab majority, which would be established in the former Ottoman districts of Baghdad and Basra, or to create a Kurdish state. Should southern Kurdistan (the *vilayet* of Mosul) be integrated into the Iraqi state, or should a British-dependent Kurdish protectorate with limited independence be established to serve as a buffer between Turkey and British-controlled Arab Iraq? The British strategic considerations included preserving Britain's own national interests; fortifying its status in Iraq and the Persian Gulf; and managing its relationship with Turkey, which was essential for blocking what was now an ideologically Communist Russian threat.

Shaykh Mahmud Barzinji's attempt after World War I to establish a Kurdish state under British protection, as part of the reshaping of the map of the Middle East, was the most important such attempt. His efforts were frustrated by the British, who decided to annex southern Kurdistan to the state of Iraq, which they established in 1920. In this way, they decided in favor of a policy that prevented the establishment of a Kurdish state, preferring to support Arab national ambitions in Iraq. The profound tribal splits and the strenuous objection to Shaykh Mahmud of rival tribes, and of part of the urban Kurdish population of Sulaymaniyya, Kirkuk, and other towns, reduced his influence and his ability to maneuver successfully vis-à-vis the British. Because of his weaknesses and his limited understanding of the British, Shaykh Mahmud failed in his political maneuvers, and the British easily suppressed his attempts to revolt against them.

Shaykh Mahmud exploited the British military takeovers of most of southern Kurdistan in the early spring of 1918 and the departure of the Ottoman regime to gather support for himself as ruler of Kurdistan under British protection. On his initiative, a group of tribal notables, urban notables, and members of the *effendiyya*—officials, teachers, and retired army officers—met in Sulaymaniyya and decided to establish a temporary Kurdish government, headed by the Shaykh, and to express their support of Britain, hoping that the British would assist them in developing a Kurdish sovereign entity. Shaykh Mahmud, who did not consider Kurdistan a part of Iraq, sent a letter to the British high commissioner and asked to form a Kurdish government under British auspices.[3]

To the Kurds' disappointment, the British decided in May 1918 to make a tactical retreat from the Kirkuk area; they abandoned the Kurdish notables, leaving them at the mercy of the Ottomans, who had retaken Kurdistan. This was a blow for the shaykhs and tribes who had chosen to favor the British. Shaykh Mahmud and his supporters were arrested by the Ottoman authorities, but released shortly afterward. In October 1918, the Ottoman governor of Sulaymaniyya surrendered to Shaykh Mahmud and transferred his executive powers to him. Shaykh Mahmud was now the strongest man in southern Kurdistan; in practice, however, his influence could only be exerted through the tribes that accepted his sovereignty or the tribal notables who believed that alliance with him would serve their interests.

In November of that year, Major E.W.C. Noel, who had been appointed political officer in the Kirkuk area, arrived in Sulaymaniyya and was assigned the task of organizing the administration in southern Kurdistan. He appointed Shaykh Mahmud as *hukumdar* (governor) of the Sulaymaniyya division, between the Diyala and Great Zab Rivers. Tribal notables and shaykhs were recognized and empowered by the British authorities and submitted to Shaykh Mahmud.[4] On December 1, 1918, Sir Arnold Wilson, the acting civil commissioner of Iraq, came to Sulaymaniyya and met with sixty tribal leaders and shaykhs. In his discussions with them, he officially confirmed Shaykh Mahmud's position. Some of his interlocutors, however, told him that they consented to a British administration but objected to the appointment of Shaykh Mahmud.

Britain's policy in Kurdistan was similar to its policy in southern and central Iraq, where the status of tribal heads and notables, some of whom owned tribal lands, was reinforced. Adopting this approach in Kurdistan, and especially recognizing tribal law as part of the legal system—a recognition that in 1925 was written into the Iraqi Constitution—created conditions for an Iraqi regime that was socially conservative and repressive toward *fellahin* (peasants) and women. However, the implications of this system for the Shi'ite and Sunnite areas of southern and central Iraq differed from its implications for Kurdistan. In parts of southern and central Iraq, tribalism had been on the wane as a consequence of the socioeconomic changes flowing from the takeover of tribal lands by tribal notables. These takeovers had relegated the tribesmen to the status of landless, or nearly landless, peasants and agricultural laborers. Thus, in those areas, granting legal powers to the tribal notables and recognizing their landowner status accelerated two contradictory developments. On the one hand, these measures legitimized and encouraged the takeover of tribal lands; on the other hand, by recognizing the legal powers of tribal notables who were large landowners, they reinforced (and in many cases, revived) tribal identities that had been receding or even disappearing in practical terms.

In Kurdistan, the tribal frameworks were better preserved than in other parts of Iraq. Admittedly, the development of a market economy and the transformation of tribal notables into landowners had been taking place since the midnineteenth century; nevertheless, these changes moved more slowly in tribal society, and their implications for tribal society were different. The establishment of the Hamidiye cavalry by Sultan Abdulhamid and the Ottoman interest in reinforcing the powerful tribal frameworks as a counterweight to the Armenians and a border force against the Russian threat helped to preserve tribalism. The tribes also retained their relevance owing to the distinctive religious status of some tribal leaders who were also Sufi shaykhs. The tension between Kurds and Armenians had a religious dimension, but it was socioeconomic as well. Most of the Kurds were tribal and pastoral, whereas most Armenians were city-dwellers or (usually nontribal) farmers. The conflicts between them, which at times reflected the struggle for control of lands, enhanced the power and relevance of tribal frameworks.

Shaykh Mahmud Barzinji began to establish a government, recruiting members of his tribe and loyal supporters to serve in it. At the same time, he approached the *effendiyya* with the idea of fostering Kurdish nationalism as an additional basis for the legitimacy of his government. A national flag was even selected. Under Barzinji's sponsorship, members of the *effendiyya* in Sulaymaniyya began to publish a newspaper, *Roji Kurdistan* (*Day of Kurdistan*), which became Barzinji's journal.[5]

There was also tension between Barzinji and the city-dwellers. The taxes he imposed and the entry of his tribal supporters into the city aroused objections among the merchants. Although he enjoyed the support of his own and several other tribes, primarily the Hamawand, some strong tribes in the area did not accept his sovereignty, including most of the Jaf tribe; the Bajalan tribe, headed by influential Naqshbandi shaykhs; and the Talabani tribe, headed by Qadiri shaykhs. Merchants and Kurds in the cities of Kirkuk and Kifri, to which he sought to extend his rule, also objected to Shaykh Mahmud. The urban social stratum did not want to be under the sovereignty of a tribal Sufi shaykh. Shaykh Mahmud's language had some nationalist aspects but also frequently featured the *jihad* motif and had Sufi religious overtones. His objectives also ran counter to those of the British.

It was Shaykh Mahmud's ambition to establish a large Kurdish state, encompassing all of southern Kurdistan and beyond, under his control. This ambition ran counter, of course, to Britain's practice of "Indian" colonialism; to the British, Shaykh Mahmud was a traditional tribal leader whose control of a limited area around Sulaymaniyya, defined by them, would make it easier for them to keep the peace in Kurdistan. Accordingly, his activity beyond the confines of the British-designated area caused tension.

In March 1919, Major Noel, who had supported cooperation with Shaykh Mahmud, was replaced by Major Ely Banister Soane, who was hostile toward the Shaykh. Soane strenuously objected to the British policy of encouraging tribalism; he considered the fostering of tribal leaders to be retribalization, which impeded modernization and development. Soane's attitude toward Shaykh Mahmud had been extremely negative since his previous tour of Kurdistan in 1909, and he immediately took measures to prevent the Shaykh from acting beyond the area allocated to him. According to Soane, Shaykh Mahmud had become a nuisance and needed to be got rid of. Major Soane's attitude stemmed from his belief that Shaykh Mahmud did not represent Kurdish nationalism but rather his own ambitions as a tribal leader exploiting nationalist expressions for his own interests. Soane therefore took strong measures against the Shaykh's supporters, including an attempt to co-opt those members of the Barzinji tribe who disputed or opposed the Shaykh's activities. The British policy to confine his influence to Sulaymaniyya and to undermine his rule pushed him to revolt. On April 20, Shaykh Mahmud's forces took control of the city, arrested the British officers and administrative staff in Sulaymaniyya, and raised the Kurdish flag. The government formed by him designed symbols of sovereignty, issued stamps, and adopted a national emblem.

A number of Kurdish tribes, some of which were in Iranian territory, came to the Shaykh's assistance. Even so, the troops at his disposal numbered only a few hundred fighters, with limited quantities of weapons and ammunition. The British forces defeated Shaykh Mahmud's supporters, suppressed his revolt and effort to set up Kurdish rule, and captured and wounded the Shaykh in Barda Qaraman on June 9. Taken prisoner, he was court-martialed and sentenced to death, but then pardoned and exiled to the Andaman Islands. During his trial, *Barzi Willat*, a small organization of Kurdish nationalist intelligentsia, called on the British to leave Kurdistan, "the fatherland of the Kurds," and to release the Shaykh. Soane, however, in accordance with his view that Kurdish autonomy should be promoted within the framework of an Iraqi state but without encouraging tribal leaders and loyalties, intensified his efforts to encourage individuals and groups in Sulaymaniyya who were opposed to Shaykh Mahmud. As part of this effort, he facilitated the publication of a Kurdish newspaper directed toward the local urban Kurdish *effendiyya*.

The internal British debate centered on two main issues: the building of the Iraqi state under the official kingship of Faysal bin Husayn, and relations with the nationalist regime under Mustafa Kemal Atatürk in Turkey. Both issues were overshadowed by Britain's concern about how it could prevent Bolshevik Russia from taking over the Caucasus. It had long been traditional British policy to block any possibility of Russian penetration of the Middle East through the Caucasus because of its impact on British interests in potential oil-producing areas.

While the internal British debate continued, tension grew between Britain and the government in Ankara established by Mustafa Kemal's nationalists. Although this government had admittedly relinquished control of the Arabic-speaking areas that had been under Ottoman sovereignty, the Kemalists perceived the Kurds as Turks, and Kurdistan as part of Turkey. Accordingly, they viewed southern Kurdistan (the Mosul area) as part of the Turkish state—which, in 1919, was still Ottoman.

In the summer of 1919, Major Noel, who enthusiastically supported the establishment of a Kurdish state, visited Turkish-controlled Kurdistan. He was accompanied by prominent Kurdish activists—the brothers Jaladat and Kamuran 'Ali Bedir Khan and Ekrem Chemil.[6] During his visit, Noel met with Khalil Bedir Khan, a local Ottoman governor who supported the Sultan and was assembling Kurdish cavalry forces in an attempt to attack the participants in the nationalist conference in Sivas. Major Noel's tour aroused fear and suspicion among the Turkish nationalists, who thought that Britain, in cooperation with the Sultan and the Armenians, was acting against the nationalist forces. Noel did support activism among the Kurds in Turkey, but his attitude was not based on any strategic decision by Britain, which had not yet reached a decision about the Kurdish revolts. Following the organization of nationalist forces under Mustafa Kemal, who succeeded in winning the support of some of the Kurdish tribes, Noel and his Kurdish followers were forced to cut short their consultations in the area and move on to Syria.

In contrast to the complex—and at times chaotic and inconsistent—policy conducted by the British and Shaykh Mahmud in Kurdistan, which was a direct result of differences of opinion among the British themselves, the policy formulated by Britain in 1921 in regard to Iraq at the regional level was cohesive. In March 1921, a conference of senior British officials and officers in the Middle East and a number of leading Arabs met in Cairo, with a view to reaching a decision on the British-controlled areas in the Fertile

Crescent.[7] The Cairo Conference decided to establish two sovereign entities in the British-controlled areas: Iraq and Transjordan. In so doing, Britain chose the so-called Hashimite solution: that is, to reinforce its status in the Fertile Crescent by appointing two members of the Hashim family of Hejaz—who had been allied with Britain in World War I and carried the banner of Arab nationalism—as rulers of the two new states. It was decided that the Iraqi state would be established on the former Ottoman *vilayets* of Baghdad and Basra. The Hashimite Faysal bin Husayn, who had been the military leader of the Arab revolt against the Ottomans during World War I, now became King of Iraq. The British decision to establish a state on the *vilayets* populated by Arabs, principally Shi'ites with a Sunnite minority, would eventually strengthen those who supported the addition of the Mosul region (southern Kurdistan, populated by Sunnite Kurds) to the Iraqi state in order to create a Sunnite-Shi'ite balance. At the Cairo Conference, however, those who supported the establishment of a separate Kurdish state prevailed, at least for a short time.

The fourth session of the Cairo Conference on March 15 was dedicated to Kurdistan. Major H. Young of the Colonial Office's Middle East Department (and later the acting high commissioner of Iraq) and Major Noel spoke in favor of a Kurdish state that would constitute a buffer between Turkey and Iraq. They were opposed by the British high commissioner in Iraq, Sir Percy Cox, and his highly influential secretary, Gertrude Bell—the two strong personalities who in effect managed British policy in Iraq and demanded the addition of Mosul to the Iraqi state.[8] They recognized the need to give the Kurds a degree of autonomy, but insisted on including them in Iraq. Winston Churchill, then secretary of state for the colonies, supported Young's and Noel's position.[9] (Noel's position was also supported by Edwin Montagu, the secretary of state for India who favored the creation of a Kurdish state that would include southern and western Kurdistan.)

The grounds for including the *vilayet* of Mosul in Iraq were varied. Its annexation, with its majority-Sunnite Kurdish population, was intended to strengthen the Sunnite element in Iraq and was favored by both the British and Faysal bin Husayn. The absolute majority of the population in the Arab *vilayets* of Baghdad and Basra was Shi'ite, but the British had decided to appoint a Sunnite, Faysal, as King of Iraq. It was also strategically important to ensure that the Iraqi state, under British protection, would maintain control of the mountain ranges north of the Tigris and Euphrates Valleys, which separated the plains of Iraq from the two strong states of Turkey and Iran. Economically speaking, the annexation of the Mosul and Kirkuk areas to Iraq was intended to secure British control of the Kirkuk oilfields. The inclusion of an oil-rich area in the new Iraqi state was meant to ensure that it would have a source of income, so that the British Treasury would not be forced to subsidize its budget. Cox also argued that Kurdistan should not be separated from Iraq for economic reasons.

With regard to Kurdistan's future, the Cairo Conference supported Churchill's and Noel's belief that southern Kurdistan should not be made part of Iraq, but rather that measures should be taken to establish a separate political entity.[10] Nevertheless, the key decisions at the Cairo Conference—which gave precedence to the British encouragement of the Arab national movement, that is, the Hashimite dynasty—also signaled a victory for the policy supported by Cox and Bell. The conference's strategic decision to rely on the Hashimite royal house ran counter to the decision in favor of the separation of southern Kurdistan. Notwithstanding the victory for the supporters of a Kurdish state, the adoption of the Hashimite policy of reliance on the Arab national movement, along with the political strength of those on the ground who supported the inclusion of southern Kurdistan in Iraq, eventually frustrated the possibility of a Kurdish state. Cox and Bell, who worked in close cooperation with Faysal and the Hashimite royal house, continued to promote the inclusion of southern Kurdistan in Arab Iraq and to frustrate the creation of a Kurdish state.[11]

In accordance with the decisions adopted at the Cairo Conference, Faysal bin Husayn was crowned King of Iraq in August 1921. Shoring up the Hashimite Arab monarchy became one of the basic elements of British policy in the Middle East. In the context of the future of southern Kurdistan, the creation of the monarchy reinforced the position of those who objected to a separate Kurdish state. Faysal himself emphasized to Cox the importance of joining Sunnite Kurdistan with Iraq, in light of the large numerical advantage of the Shi'ite population in Iraq's Arab regions. The position held by Faysal was exploited by Cox in order to reinforce his claim that Britain should favor including southern Kurdistan in the Iraqi state.[12]

LOST OPPORTUNITIES: FROM THE TREATY OF SÈVRES TO THE TREATY OF LAUSANNE

After World War I, the victorious states met at a peace conference in the Palace of Versailles near Paris. The yearlong Paris Peace Conference, from January 18, 1919, to January 20, 1920, was led by Britain, the United States, and France. It deliberated on the shaping of the new world order, forged international arrangements that were intended to prevent the outbreak of war in the future, and drew new maps—primarily of the territories of the defeated states: Austria-Hungary, Germany, and the Ottoman Empire. The spirit of the principles laid down by US president Woodrow Wilson concerning the right of self-determination of peoples gave hope to many national movements, which initially believed that their objectives of independence or autonomy could be achieved.

Wilson's withdrawal from the conference for reasons unrelated to foreign policy gave the upper hand to the old colonial powers, Britain and France. As they saw it, the top priority was to reach arrangements in Europe that would prevent any renewal of the German threat. In regard to the future of the conquered Middle Eastern territories, internal debates arose among officials and decision-makers. At times, these reflected different worldviews about the future of the colonial British Empire, or even about modernization in general. At other times, however, differences of opinion on the best way to serve British interests in the future were more tactical.

There was heated activity on the sidelines of the Versailles Conference among delegations and individuals representing the stateless national movements that were attempting to achieve their objectives within the newly coalescing world order. General Sharif Pasha, who headed a delegation on behalf of the Society for the Advancement of Kurdistan (*Kurdistan Teali Cemiyeti* [*Jem'iyati*], also known as SAK or KTC), which was organized in Istanbul in 1918 and officially founded in December of that year, was the most prominent Kurdish activist at the conference. Several members of his family, which was related to a branch of the House of Baban living in exile in Istanbul, had found positions in the Ottoman administration. Like his father, Sa'id Pasha Kurd, who had been the Ottoman foreign minister in 1881 and in 1885, Sharif Pasha served in the Ottoman army and then joined the Ottoman foreign service. Following the Young Turks revolution, he lost his position and became critical of the new regime. He left the Empire for Europe, no later than 1909 from what is known. His loss of status was apparently the reason he turned toward Kurdishness and Kurdish nationalist activity—even though he did not speak Kurdish and had apparently never visited Kurdistan. In 1914, early in World War I, Sharif Pasha attempted to reach an understanding with the British, in the hope of achieving overall Kurdish-British cooperation. In June 1918, he attempted to persuade Sir Percy Cox that Britain should establish an autonomous Kurdish area, under British protection, in southern Kurdistan.[13]

After the end of the war in November 1918, Sharif Pasha, then living in Paris, established connections with Shaykh Mahmud Barzinji, Shaykh Taha, and Simko (the strong tribal leader in Iran) with a view to promoting an independent Kurdistan.[14] His diplomatic experience and place of residence made Sharif Pasha aware that, after the crumbling of the Ottoman Empire, the victorious powers would have to draw new borders in the Middle East and take into account the principle of self-determination of peoples that had been put forward by President Wilson. When the SAK was organized in 1918, the dynamic Sharif Pasha became, for all intents and purposes, its international representative and the principal spokesperson of the Kurdish nationalists on the sidelines of the peace conference.

On March 19, 1919, he distributed a document, accompanied by a map, among conference participants that set forth Kurdish demands for a state. In late July, and again on October 9, he submitted additional letters to the British embassy in Paris in which he elaborated on the Kurdish demands for statehood, asking that they be presented to Foreign Secretary Lord Balfour. At the same time, Sharif Pasha took measures aimed at establishing cooperation with the Armenians. He claimed that the hostility and violence between the Kurds and the Armenians had resulted from Turkish incitement, and that Kurdish and Armenian interests called for mutual cooperation. He presented a proposal—which, in the end, did not come to fruition—for a permanent Kurdish-Armenian commission. The outcome was that Sharif Pasha and the head of the Armenian delegation, Bogos Nubar Pasha, came to an understanding about the border between the future states of Armenia and Kurdistan. According to this, the area of Lake Van was included within Armenia. Sharif Pasha's sober political pragmatism, coupled with his long years of diplomatic experience in the Ottoman foreign service, prompted him to submit a final map that did not include any Kurdish areas within Iran.

The agreement between Sharif Pasha and Bogos Nubar Pasha was encouraged by the British, who feared not only Turkish nationalists but, even more, the expansion of Russian Bolshevik rule into and south of the Caucasus. Armenian-Kurdish cooperation and an Armenian state, as Britain saw it, would act as a barrier against the spread of Bolshevik influence.[15] In line with the agreement with the Armenians, Sharif Pasha submitted a new map of Kurdistan to Richard Webb, the British high commissioner in Istanbul, on March 1, 1920. Sharif Pasha's compromises provoked a severe response from Emir Amin 'Ali Bedir Khan, vice president of the Society for the Advancement of Kurdistan. The map showed Kurdistan including the area of Lake Van, areas of Iranian Kurdistan, and an outlet to the Mediterranean Sea near the Bay of Alexandretta.[16]

On August 10, 1920, the Ottoman state signed the Treaty of Sèvres with Britain. It reduced the Ottoman state to a modest part of northwestern Anatolia and a small area in Europe. The treaty was forced upon the de-

feated, crumbling Ottoman Empire. Articles 62, 63, and 64 included recommendations for the establishment of an Armenian state and for Kurdish
autonomy; the Kurds would have the option of approaching the League of
Nations within one year and petitioning for independence. Also mentioned
was the possibility that the Kurds in southern Kurdistan—the Mosul area,
now under British control—would be joined with the Kurds in Turkey in a
Kurdish state. The Treaty of Sèvres gave the Kurds, for the first time, an international assurance of a future Kurdish state. This window of opportunity,
however, was short-lived. The strengthening of the Turkish national movement headed by Mustafa Kemal Atatürk changed conditions in the region,
and British strategic considerations prevented implementation of the Treaty
of Sèvres. In 1923 it would be replaced by the Treaty of Lausanne, which
omitted the promises to the Kurds and the Armenians.

In May 1919, Greece invaded western Anatolia and conquered vast areas
along the Aegean Sea, around and to the east of Izmir. The Greek invasion
aroused objections and anxiety among the Turkish public and hope among
the Armenian Christians, who stepped up their activity aimed at creating a
large Armenian state in all of eastern Anatolia. The Greek invasion, the Armenian activity and revolt, and the anxiety among Turkish Muslims created a tailwind that added momentum to the Turkish national movement.
As the Turks saw it, the nationalists were the only force capable of blocking
the Greeks and preventing the total collapse of the state and its takeover by
Christians.

From May 1919, a national movement arose in eastern Anatolia that rejected the absolute surrender of Sultan Abdulhamid and sought to preserve
the independence and most of the territory of the Ottoman Turkish state.
The rapidly organizing Turkish nationalist forces, known as the Kemalists, defined their objectives in two congresses that took place in the eastern Anatolian cities of Erzurum (July 23–August 7, 1919) and Sivas (September 4–11, 1919).[17] As long as the conflict between the nationalists and the
supporters of the Sultan continued, both sides attempted to win the support of the Kurds. Some of the Kurdish tribes remained loyal to the Sultan,
on the basis of Islam and the interests of the tribal landowners. The followers of the Sultan and opponents of the Turkish nationalists succeeded in enlisting the support of some Kurdish tribes, which went so far as to threaten
the nationalist forces. The heads of the SAK attempted to exploit the opportunity in order to obtain from the Sultan a promise of Kurdish autonomy (which, in practical terms, would amount to Kurdish independence
with nominal recognition of the Sultan) in exchange for the support of the
Kurdish tribes against the Kemalists.

In July 1919, representatives of the Ottoman government, which remained loyal to the Sultan, met with several key figures in the SAK, including 'Abd al-Qadir and Emin 'Ali Bedir Khan. The Sultan and his government sought to exploit the Kurdish organization in order to frustrate the threatened establishment of an Armenian state and to secure the loyalty of the Kurds against the Kemalist forces. The Ottoman authorities were also concerned about the activity of General Sharif Pasha in Paris and tried to exert pressure on the Kurdish activists in Istanbul. At the meeting, it was hinted to the Kurds that the Ottoman government and Sultan Abdulhamid were willing to consider granting them a certain degree of autonomy.

The SAK's objective, however, was independence, or at least a broad-based autonomy, in line with Woodrow Wilson's principle of self-determination. On this basis, the scholar Hakan Ozoglu has defined the SAK as the first "national" Kurdish organization.[18] However, owing to the rivalry between the Bedir Khan and Shemdinan families and their contradictory visions about Kurdish national aims, the SAK was plagued by conflicts among its leaders. 'Abd al-Qadir, the SAK president, strove for the integration of Kurds into Turkey and for Kurdish autonomy in the framework of the Turkish state. Vice President Emin 'Ali's vision was of an independent Kurdish state. Faced with 'Abd al-Qadir's prominence in the SAK, Emin 'Ali and his supporters split off in 1920 and established a new organization that campaigned for the full independence of Kurdistan.

At the same time, Kemal Atatürk and the Turkish nationalists made tremendous efforts to attract the Kurds to their side in 1919 and 1920. From the standpoint of the Kurdish landowners and tribal notables, who were now taking over the lands abandoned by the Armenians, supporting the Turkish authorities was based on the same interests that motivated other Kurdish landowners and notables to support the Sultan: they wanted to strengthen their control and obtain official confirmation of their ownership of the lands in question.[19]

Many Kurdish delegates were invited to the Sivas and Erzurum congresses, where the Kurds were promised equal rights. The orientation of the national movement was basically Turkish. At first its leaders viewed the Kurds as partners and sought to enlist popular Kurdish support by using Islamic arguments and asking the Kurds to help them save the Sultan. The secular nationalist trend promulgated by Mustafa Kemal and his followers would develop gradually after 1929, parallel to the shaping and maturing of the concept of Turkish nationalism. The background was the conflict with the Ottoman Sultan, which led to the abolition of the sultanate and the caliphate.

The Greek invasion, the increased Armenian activity, and the Treaty of Sèvres gave some of the Kurdish nationalist activists, tribes, and tribal notables reason to hope that a historic opportunity had arisen for an alliance between the Kurds and the Greeks that, with British backing, would allow the Kurds to establish a state of their own. Because the Sultan's status was on the wane and the power of the Turkish nationalists who rejected the Treaty of Sèvres was on the rise, the heads of the SAK approached Britain in 1921 to ask for its support. Also involved in this attempt to achieve autonomy (in effect, Kurdish independence), under British protection and legitimated by a weak and symbolic Ottoman sultan, were members of the old aristocratic Bedir Khan and Baban families, as well as their rivals Sayyid ʿAbd al-Qadir and Shaykh Taha, both from the Shemdinan family and both descendants of Shaykh ʿUbaydallah. In the summer of 1921, a delegation of SAK Kurdish nationalists from Istanbul, led by Amin ʿAli Bedir Khan, visited Baghdad and asked Britain for assistance in establishing an autonomous state. The delegates offered to organize a broad-based Kurdish revolt against the Turkish nationalist government.[20]

Kurdish activists also met with the prime minister of Greece. British High Commissioner in Iraq Sir Percy Cox supported the idea of a Kurdish revolt in Turkey in order to block the Kemalists and enable implementation of the Treaty of Sèvres.[21] However, Winston Churchill, as secretary of state for the colonies, was opposed to any backing of a Kurdish revolt and did not wish Britain to become directly embroiled in the struggle in Turkey. The key British considerations were based on their fear of the expansion of Bolshevik–Soviet Russian influence in the Caucasus, as well as fear of an alliance between the Kemalist nationalists and Russia. To block Bolshevik Russia, engaging in dialogue with the Kemalist nationalists and preserving the existence of Turkey were more important to the British than supporting Kurdish revolts. Moreover, the British themselves had not yet decided what they preferred: an independent Kurdish state under British protection as a buffer to the north of Iraq, or the addition of the Mosul region to the Iraqi state.

This debate became moot when the Turkish nationalist forces, during August and September 1921, defeated the Greeks and overcame an Armenian offensive. In October 1922, the Kemalists took over Istanbul. On November 1, the Turkish Grand National Assembly resolved to abolish the sultanate and to leave the caliph as the spiritual head of the Turkish state. (The caliphate was later abolished in 1924.) The rise of Turkish nationalist forces, the defeat of the Greek invasion, and the organization of the Turkish state headed by Mustafa Kemal precluded any realization of the Treaty of Sèvres in the absence of broad-scale British military intervention, which Britain was not prepared to make. Accordingly, on November 20, 1922, an international commission gathered in Lausanne, with the participation of Britain, France, Italy, Japan, Yugoslavia, and Romania; representatives of both the Sultan's government and the Turkish nationalist government were also invited. The abolition of the sultanate had left the nationalist government and its representatives as the only political entity with which the great powers could effectively negotiate. Britain was now consistently striving to reach an understanding with Turkey. Its policy vis-à-vis the Kurds depended on this principal objective.

The decisive blow to the separation of Kurdistan from Iraq came with the fall of the Lloyd George government in Britain at the end of October 1922 and the establishment of a new government headed by Bonar Law. Winston Churchill, the most senior supporter of separating Kurdistan from Iraq, was replaced by William Cavendish, who had no clear-cut position on the issue but tended to favor the integration of southern Kurdistan into Iraq. Moreover, the understandings with the nationalist regime in Turkey had reduced the fears of a rapprochement between Turkey and Russia.

The Treaty of Lausanne was signed on July 24, 1923. Turkey now had to relinquish territories in the east of the Ottoman Empire—territories that had been controlled by Britain and (in the case of Syria) by France since the war. Among Turkey's achievements under the nationalist regime was the absence of any mention of autonomy for the Kurds or independence for the Armenians. Admittedly, the future of southern Kurdistan remained in dispute, and the Kemalist government would continue to demand its annexation to Turkey until 1926, when it was forced by British and French pressure to waive that demand.

The Kurds had no influence on the Treaty of Lausanne, which ignored the articles of the Treaty of Sèvres concerning the possibility of Kurdish and Armenian states. From that point on, the chance of establishing a Kurdish state through the international negotiations shaping the new map of the Middle East was lost. In the absence of influential Kurdish leadership, the Kurds were too politically weak after the Treaty of Sèvres to take any further significant steps toward preparing for establishing a Kurdish state. The Kurds in the areas added to Iraq had no supratribal leadership that the British could have built on as a basis for a state that would be allied with Britain and serve British interests in the Middle East. Shaykh Mahmud Barzinji had no understanding of the political arena in general or of British policy in particular and was supported by only some of the tribes and part of the urban population of Sulaymaniyya.

Now directed toward achieving a political arrangement with Kemalist Turkey, British policy had led to the Treaty of Lausanne, which changed the international conditions under which the Kurds had any chance of obtaining autonomy or independence. The decision-makers in London and the representatives of the British administration in Iraq decided not to support a Kurdish revolt in Turkey and to oppose the establishment of a Kurdish state in southern Kurdistan (northern Iraq). When Churchill left the Colonial Office in October 1922, the supporters of a Kurdish state in the British administration lost their most senior and influential political proponent. His departure amounted to a decision in favor of integrating southern Kurdistan into the Iraqi state.

THE REBELLIONS OF SHAYKH MAHMUD: TRIBAL INSURRECTION COMBINED WITH NASCENT KURDISH NATIONALISM

The struggle between Britain and Turkey for control of southern Kurdistan from 1921 to 1923 created conditions that Shaykh Mahmud Barzinji attempted to exploit in order to establish a Kurdish state under his leadership.

In 1921 the Turks continued their activity in the Mosul region, with a view to including it in the Turkish state. Turkish army units were encamped in the cities of Rawanduz, Raniya, Qala Diza, Koy Sanjaq, and Kifri. The strong Turkish commander and governor Özdemir Pasha, whose headquarters were in Rawanduz, worked hard to gain influence among those tribes that opposed British rule and integration into the Iraqi state under Arab rule. His efforts were facilitated in part by the weakness of the British. The unrest and revolts among the Zibari, Hamawand, Barzani, Sorchi, and other tribes had greatly undermined British control of a considerable portion of southern Kurdistan.[22] In April the leaders of Zibari, Surchi, and Harki had arrived in Rawanduz to negotiate with Özdemir. These talks, combined with the Turkish activity in Kirkuk and Sulaymaniyya in 1921–1922, were viewed with alarm by the British, who had considered the Turks the principal threat. They dreaded an extensive Kurdish revolt supported by the Turks, which would require the involvement of large British military forces. The British in Iraq did not have the available ground forces to take control of Kurdistan, and their Mandatory Government in Baghdad was suffering from budgetary problems.

In October 1921, the Royal Air Force planes struck Turkish forces, forcing their retreat from Qala Diza and Koy Sanjaq.[23] Even so, the Turkish activity among the Kurdish tribes in the area continued to cause anxiety to the

Mandatory Government. In the summer of 1922, Özdemir Pasha's renewed efforts to secure Turkish control of Kirkuk and Sulaymaniyya were treated as an emergency by the British and the Iraqi state.

The British dilemma was deciding whether to integrate the Sulaymaniyya and Kirkuk areas into the Iraqi state, without taking the Kurdish residents' wishes into account, or establish autonomous rule under a Kurdish governor, who would be influential but loyal to the British. Unilateral integration would have constituted a breach of the promises given to the Kurds and a deviation from the intentions of the Cairo Conference. However, the British had difficulty locating a strong Kurdish individual with supratribal status and the ability to lead the Kurds in the area. No descendant of the old notable families could do it. Members of the Baban family of Sulaymaniyya had lost their influence and offered no one who could take on a leadership role.

In August 1922, the British appointed Shaykh Taha of Shemdinan, the grandson of Shaykh 'Ubaydallah who enjoyed a certain degree of influence in the Rawanduz area, as governor of the city. They intended that he would put together a Kurdish force to help drive the Turks from the city, which he would govern under British protection. This move, which was orchestrated by Sir Percy Cox, was also meant to build a local leader in addition to Shaykh Mahmud, who, even after his defeat and exile, enjoyed prestige within and beyond Sulaymaniyya. Another objective was to reinforce the separation between various parts of southern Kurdistan and thereby prevent the coalescence of Kurdish resistance throughout Kurdistan. In addition to helping the British contend with the Turkish threat, Shaykh Taha's appointment was a move by which those wanting to bring southern Kurdistan into Iraq could exploit intra-Kurdish divisiveness and the absence of a universally accepted Kurdish leadership.[24]

Shaykh Taha of Shemdinan had relatively little support among the tribal and urban population of the Sulaymaniyya area; even in Rawanduz his influence was limited. In November 1922, he began to attempt to organize the tribes that supported him and even received a supply of weapons from the British. Until the winter of 1923, however, he had no credible ability to drive the Turks and their Kurdish supporters out of the Rawanduz and Raniya areas.

In Sulaymaniyya and among some of the tribes, Shaykh Mahmud's supporters were the active and influential faction. The exile of Shaykh Mahmud and the absence of support for Shaykh Taha had created a political vacuum in the Sulaymaniyya area, and the British were concerned that it would be exploited by the Turks. Major H. A. Goldsmith, who had replaced Major

Soane as Britain's political officer in Sulaymaniyya, supported the return of Shaykh Mahmud, who appeared to be the only person capable of leading the Kurds and blocking Turkish activity. In light of the situation, High Commissioner Sir Percy Cox decided to bring Shaykh Mahmud out of exile in Kuwait and back to Sulaymaniyya.[25]

The Shaykh returned on September 30, 1922, accompanied by Major Noel, and was reappointed to the post of *hukumdar* (governor) on October 10. The city's residents welcomed him with mixed feelings. Back in July 1922, a group of educated notables headed by a retired Ottoman army officer had established the Kurdish Society (*Jamiyʿati Kurdistan*), a national society that published a periodical, *Bangi Kurdistan* (*Voice of Kurdistan*). The society's active members belonged to the *effendiyya* and were not subject to the authority of religious tribal shaykhs. Notwithstanding the Islamic and tribal characteristics of Shaykh Mahmud's government, their support of him was based on nationalist motives. His return aroused suspicions among urban notables and merchants, who feared taxation and tribal dominance and preferred arrangements with the British, by which they could maintain the status quo, under British protection, in the framework of the Iraqi state.[26]

Within a few days, the profound differences between Shaykh Mahmud and the British flared up again. Whereas the British viewed him as a local leader operating with limited powers, within the Iraqi state, and under British protection, the Shaykh continued to strive for a Kurdish state, under his own leadership, that would control all of Kurdistan. Immediately on his return, he began a series of measures aimed at establishing an independent state. He formed a government of eight ministers. Apart from members of his family and tribe, it included educated members of the *effendiyya* from Sulaymaniyya, mostly from notable families. In November, Shaykh Mahmud Barzinji appointed himself King of Kurdistan and approached the British high commissioner with a demand that a Kurdish state embracing the entire territory of Kurdistan be established and that the border between that state and Iraq be determined. In addition to *Roji Kurdistan* (*Day of Kurdistan*), Shaykh Mahmud's official journal, a new periodical, *Bangi Haqq* (*Voice of Truth*) began publication the following March.[27]

A short time after his return, it seems that Shaykh Mahmud initiated contact with the commander of the Turkish forces in Rawanduz, Ozdemir Pasha, and with Shiʿite leaders in southern Iraq. These moves again led the Shaykh into direct conflict with the British, who were imposing political and military conditions that, from his point of view, were hopeless. Although the new British secretary of state for the colonies, William Cavendish, was uncertain on the subject, Lord Curzon, the foreign minister in the new government, supported the position held by Cox and by his replacement as high commissioner of Iraq, Sir Henry Dobbs.[28]

Under the threat of losing Iraqi-British control in southern Kurdistan, the British, starting in the spring of 1923, activated all the military forces at their disposal in Iraq, primarily the Royal Air Force. In March 1923, in a combined ground and aerial operation, the British defeated the Turks at Rawanduz, causing a general Turkish retreat from all of southern Kurdistan. Following this expulsion, Dobbs appointed Shaykh Taha as the *kaymakam* of Rawanduz, hoping that the Shaykh's connections with tribes in the area would help to block Turkish influence. He also hoped to nurture another local leader so as to make it more difficult for Shaykh Mahmud to harbor any pretensions of exclusive leadership of the Kurds.

As part of the effort to restore control of the area, British aircraft bombed the Kurdish government buildings in Sulaymaniyya on March 3, 1923. Shaykh Mahmud left the city, after which the British attempted to put together a temporary council. Shaykh Qadir Barzinji, Shaykh Mahmud's brother, whose connections with the British were strong, was placed in charge of defense and security.[29] In June, the prime minister of Iraq, 'Abd al-Muhsin al-Sa'adun, visited Kurdistan and together with a number of British consultants met with members of the Kurdish temporary council. The meeting was not successful, however, owing to the Iraqi prime minister's rigid position and his unwillingness to grant some degree of autonomy to the Kurds.[30] Thus, the attempt to establish a local government that was not headed by Shaykh Mahmud failed. Between Iraqi intransigence and the lack of a permanent British military force in the city, the temporary administration could not contend with Shaykh Mahmud's supporters. In July 1923, Shaykh Mahmud resumed control of Sulaymaniyya. The urban population was divided between those who resented the tribal domination, were afraid of his rule, and preferred British protection and those, some of them educated and holding Kurdish nationalist views, who supported his rule. Following his return, in what was perceived as a retreat by the British and the Iraqi government, approximately 2,000 people, most of them the merchants and craftsmen who feared him, left the city.[31]

In August 1923, the British again launched airstrikes against Shaykh Mahmud's government because of his refusal to accept British proposals that would limit his powers and the areas under his control. In December 1923 and again in May 1924, the British launched much stronger bombing attacks against Shaykh Mahmud's centers of control, forcing him to flee to Iran. In July 1924, large Iraqi army ground forces, accompanied by British troops, entered Sulaymaniyya. Many of the city's residents, including most of the merchants and craftsmen who had fled during Shaykh Mahmud's rule and the clashes with the British, returned to the city at that time.

Shaykh Mahmud continued to enjoy support and prestige in Sulaymaniyya, especially among educated Kurdish nationalists, members of the Barzinji tribes, and loyalists from other tribes. His supporters among the *effendiyya* in Sulaymaniyya continued their Kurdish nationalist activity throughout the 1920s, but were harassed by his rivals, who wanted to improve the lot of the Kurds within the Iraqi state. In spite of the nationalist activity of his urban supporters at this time, the British considered Shaykh Mahmud's rebellion a tribal insurrection.

In 1930 Shaykh Mahmud returned to Sulaymaniyya, seeking to bolster his status and to raise a revolt. Following the unrest and riots that broke out in the city and deteriorated into a conflict with the Iraqi army, which slaughtered Kurdish demonstrators on September 6, 1930, Shaykh Mahmud was arrested by the Iraqi and British authorities and permanently banned from reentering Kurdistan.[32]

Although the British viewed the Shaykh Mahmud rebellion as tribal, in fact it expressed a nascent Kurdish nationalism, as reflected in its support by small nationalistic organizations of Kurdish intellectuals, such as *Barzi Willat*, *Fidakarani Kurd*, *Kurdistan Gizing*, and *Wetenparwaran*. After the capture of Shaykh Mahmud by the British, *Barzi Willat* called for his release and declared, in nationalistic language, that "the British are aliens here" and "Kurdistan is the homeland of the Kurds."[33]

The primary reasons for Shaykh Mahmud's failure were his inability to understand the international system and British policy and his hasty moves, which brought him into direct conflict with the British. Unlike various members of the Hashimite family—who, notwithstanding their status as proponents of Arabism, had a certain level of modern education and had acquired political experience in Istanbul—Shaykh Mahmud was devoid of any modern political experience, and his worldview was essentially traditional-tribal and Islamic.

The British preferred to keep the Arab Iraqi state as their mainstay in the area and abandoned the idea of establishing independent Kurdish rule in southern Kurdistan. Shaykh Mahmud's British supporters, who favored conservative "Indian" colonialism, had sought to set him up as a local feudal-tribal leader, but did not want him to be King of Kurdistan. Their rivals, primarily senior officials in the Foreign Office who were inclined toward the concept of a British Commonwealth and preferred alliances with national movements and pro-modernization forces, preferred the Arab national movement led by the Hashimites and pursued a dialogue with the Kemalist Turkish national movement. The outcome of the debates and maneuvering among British officials and politicians was the policy that favored preserving Arab Iraq and Turkey, as well as the Arab and Turkish national movements, which ruled out Kurdish independence. Iraq, under Hashimite rule, was a cornerstone of Britain's policy, strategic outlook, and economic interests in the Middle East. Nationalist Turkey under Atatürk played another important role for the British by blocking Russian access to the Middle East and the Mediterranean Sea.

Shaykh Mahmud Barzinji's failure was also directly related to the conditions of Kurdish society. In addition to intertribal rivalry and the prevailing historical circumstances, the Kurds had to contend with the Arab and Turkish national movements, which Britain preferred to support while abandoning the Kurds and abrogating the Treaty of Sèvres. The intertribal rivalry, the tensions between tribes and nontribal peasants—as well as between landowners and peasants, Muslims and Christians, Kurds and Arabs—and the weakness of a Kurdish collective identity relative to the tribal, religious, and local identities claimed by the Kurds made it difficult to develop a national leadership and precluded conducting a policy with national objectives. Additional obstacles were presented by the weakness and limited scope of the educated modern middle class and the lack of leadership among the old-time notables, some of whom lived in far-off Istanbul.

Like the emirs of the House of Hashim in Hejaz, who adopted modern nationalism and raised the banner of Arab nationalism, Shaykh Mahmud, who remained active until the early 1930s, took over Kurdish nationalist slogans and discourse as a means of realizing his ambitions and establishing a Kurdish state under his leadership. However, many tribes and sections of tribes resisted his efforts, which were also opposed by urban merchants and craftsmen. In contrast, the Hashimite emirs maintained complete control of Hejaz and had the support of the Bedouin tribes in the area, as well as of the urban populations of Mecca and Medina. The House of Hashim also enjoyed unique prestige among the Muslims as heirs of the Prophet Muhammad. Despite Mahmud Barzinji's standing as a Qadiri shaykh, his religious status was inferior to that of the Hashimites.

Throughout the 1920s and until his death in 1933, King Faysal of Iraq made efforts to integrate Kurdish notables into the Iraqi state. Unlike Turkey and Iran, which denied the existence of Kurdish nationalism and adopted a policy combining suppression and assimilation, Iraq recognized the national distinctiveness of the Kurds. Unlike Turkish nationalism, Arab nationalism did not seek to assimilate the Kurds into the Arab nation. Economically, however, Kurdistan and the Kurds suffered discrimination and neglect, stemming from the Arab view of the Kurds, not as equal partners, but as a minority in an Arab national state. Much as it did with Shi'ite Arab landowners and notables in southern and central Iraq, the Hashimite regime found government positions for Kurdish tribal landowners and others who supported the social and political status quo and the conservative regime in Iraq. Nonetheless, given the general neglect and deprivation of Kurdistan and the growing nationalism among educated Kurds, the Iraqi government's policy failed to respond to the discrimination and alienation felt by most of the Kurdish population, from traditional tribesmen and peasants who lived in abject poverty to the Westernized, educated Kurdish *effendiyya* and some tribal notables, such as the Barzanis.

In 1930 the uprising in Sulaymaniyya of the Kurdish urban population led by educated and merchant elements was suppressed by the Iraqi army, with British assistance. This restored the leadership and political initiative to the tribal-clannish leaders and the tribal and rural sectors of Kurdish society—and especially to the Barzani tribe, whose leadership held Sufi religious status and combined tribal-clannish conduct and leadership with demands of Kurdish nationalist significance. The activity and motives of Shaykh Ahmad Barzani, the dominant figure in the family in the early 1930s, were Sufi and tribal in nature. His younger brother, Mullah Mustafa Barzani, who began to play a significant part in Kurdish nationalist activity in Kurdistan, combined essentially tribal behavior with what were clearly Kurdish nationalist demands. Once Mullah Mustafa Barzani succeeded in becoming a supratribal leader, it was under his leadership that the protracted Kurdish struggles in Iraq became explicitly nationalistic.

Two events at the end of World War II marked the beginning of a new stage in the Kurdish national movement: the establishment of a Kurdish republic in Mahabad in western Iran in 1946, and the founding of the Kurdish Democratic Party (KDP) in Iraq in the same year (in 1952 its name was changed to the Kurdistan Democratic Party) and the Kurdish Democratic Party in Iran in August 1945. Mullah Mustafa Barzani was commander of the armed forces of the short-lived Republic of Mahabad and was elected president of the Kurdish Democratic Party. Educated urban activists, whose status was only slightly related to their tribal and family origin (and sometimes not at all), were also involved in Kurdish political life. The tensions between the Kurdish Sufi-tribal heritage and modern politics—with its party- and class-related ideological aspects and regional differences between Kurmanji-dialect speakers in the northern regions of Iraqi Kurdistan and Sorani-dialect speakers in the southern regions—would characterize Kurdish politics in general and the central Kurdish national political party, the KDP, in particular.[34] During the late twentieth and early twenty-first centuries, these tensions would be reflected in the struggles between the KDP led by Massoud Barzani and the Patriotic Union of Kurdistan (PUK) led by Jalal Talabani, as well as in the political and administrative system of the Kurdistani Region of Iraq.

FROM DISTINCTIVENESS TO NATIONALISM— CONTINUING ISSUES OF KURDISH COLLECTIVE IDENTITY

THE GROWTH OF NATIONAL MOVEMENTS is interwoven with national histories. Against a background of particular social, political, cultural, and economic circumstances, national movements spring up in response to events and developments that take place over generations. Although national movements are sometimes a response to more sudden events and developments, the political, social, economic, and ideological circumstances that provide fertile soil for the growth of national movements and modern nations nevertheless develop over much longer periods of time.

The Kurdish national movement did not contrive the development of Kurdistan or the events that occurred involving speakers of Kurdish dialects; rather, it invested historical events—whether they actually took place or were invented or were woven into the tales and myths of the local populace—with national significance. This is why the historical continuity of the people now known as Kurds can be traced back at least as far as the beginnings of Islam. Thus, the past events and narratives of Kurds—that is, a distinctive group within human society long regarded as distinctive— must be considered Kurdish history in the modern discourse of identity and nationalism.

Before the modern era, tribal, pastoral-agrarian Kurdish society did not give rise to a supratribal political entity within which a collective Kurdish identity could develop. There were four principal reasons why such an entity never developed:

1. *The geographical and political conditions of Kurdistan:* The proximity of large, powerful states on the heights of Iran, in the Tigris and Euphrates Valleys, and in Anatolia prevented the growth of a strong political force in Kurdistan, even as these powerful states had difficulty imposing a stable sovereignty that could unite the area under their control. For a much

longer time than surrounding areas, such as the Levant, Egypt, Istanbul, and western Anatolia, landlocked Kurdistan was kept from experiencing the direct effects of modernization, Western influences, and the global changes that accompanied the emergence of the modern world and capitalism. In the twentieth century, the lack of an outlet to the sea and the scant interest shown by world powers in the creation of a Kurdish state made it difficult for the Kurds to obtain outside support for their nationalist ambitions and uprisings.

2. *The slow and limited development of the bourgeoisie and the modern middle class:* Many Kurds were integrated into the Iranian, Ottoman, and Turkish state bureaucracies. Also limiting the development of a Kurdish bourgeoisie was the assimilation of some Kurds into the Turkish and Iranian national movements.

3. *The dominance of tribal and emirate social and political patterns:* Not all of the Kurds were tribal and pastoral; some of them were always nontribal peasants. The tribes and tribalism gained or lost strength with changes in the conditions for physical survival: the political circumstances, the Kurds' relations with ruling states, and the prevailing economic conditions. Nonetheless, all political activity in Kurdistan was based in Kurdish tribes, tribal loyalties, and the Kurdish emirates.

4. *The historical development of the Kurdish language:* The linguistic weakness of the Kurdish language relative to the dominant languages of the region (Arabic, Turkish, and Persian), and especially the lack of a standardized high language, hindered the coalescence of a supratribal political entity in Kurdistan.

The political and administrative changes in Kurdistan in the first half of the nineteenth century, the elimination of the Kurdish emirates, and the imposition of the centralist Ottoman administration were not accompanied by economic upheavals, but neither did these moves accelerate development and modernization among the Kurds. Kurdistan's economy continued to be agrarian and pastoral. What did change were patterns of landownership and the nature of agrarian relations. The Ottoman reforms, in particular the Land Registration Law of 1858, and the development of a global market economy that made production for export more profitable led to tribal lands being taken over by tribal notables. These takeovers were accompanied by an expansion of trade and an increasing number of merchants in the cities of Kurdistan, as well as by increases in the number of openings for Kurdish employees in the Ottoman administration. Still, until World War I, no strong bourgeoisie with its own significant interests developed in Kurdistan. Most of the merchants in the towns were Armenians, and some were Jews. Many of the educated Kurdish officials and merchants became "Turkified" or "Iranized"—they considered their Kurdishness nothing more than a cultural signifier and also a sign of backwardness—and they sought to become integrated, as individuals of Kurdish origin, within the Ottoman Empire or the Iranian state. After World War I, these more educated Kurds turned to Turkey, Iran, and Iraq and even identified with the Turkish, Iranian, and Arab national movements.

In the absence of a high Kurdish language and modern Kurdish schools, Turkish, Persian, or Arabic was the language of literacy and modern education—for those Kurds who became literate and educated. The Kurds' awareness of linguistic, ethnic, and (at times) social distinctiveness developed only slowly, and the conditions for a national movement based on a defined Kurdish identity were by no means as compelling as those for the Turkish, Iranian, and Arab national movements.

At the end of World War I, political circumstances provided a brief opportunity for the establishment of a Kurdish state. Within a short time, however, the international and domestic conditions in Turkey and Iraq changed, as did British policies and the British decision-makers and officials in the Middle East. Those opportunities faded away following the Treaty of Lausanne in 1923, the British decision to favor those who opposed a Kurdish state, the suppression of Shaykh Mahmud Barzinji's attempt to establish a state in 1920–1924, and the determined resistance of the Turkish nationalist, anti-Kurdish Atatürk regime.

The British decision to include southern Kurdistan within the Iraqi state and the weakness of the Kurdish national movement and Kurdish political forces were the direct reasons why a Kurdish state was not established after World War I. However, the situation of the Kurds after World War I cannot be completely understood without examining the social, political, and cultural developments among them and in Kurdistan, as well as the geopolitical conditions that had prevailed in Kurdistan at least since the beginning of Islam. This examination is essential to an understanding of the forces that affected Kurdistan and its people during the nineteenth and early twentieth centuries, when the Arab, Iranian, Turkish, and Armenian national movements began to develop in the area, and after World War I, when the map of the modern Middle East was drawn.

Following the war, Kurdistan was again divided among states that denied the existence of a Kurdish collective entity and sought either to assimilate the Kurds into the Turkish or Iranian nationality or to preserve them as a minority subject to the Arab majorities in Iraq and Syria. Admittedly, Iraq recognized the distinctiveness of the Kurds, who could not be integrated into the Arab national movement and Arab nationality primarily because of the centrality of the Arabic language to both the movement and the nationality. Despite this recognition, the exclusion of the Kurds from the privileged status of Iraqi Arab nationality, the significance of Arabism to Iraqi identity, and the economic and political deprivation of Kurdistan made it harder for the Kurds to become integrated into the Iraqi state and to perceive themselves as equals within the Iraqi identity. In Turkey and Iran, individual Kurds could advance socially, but only if they identified with the Turkish or Iranian nationality, served the Turkish or Iranian state, or accumulated sufficient wealth and status to take their place among the Turkish or Iranian elite. Turkey and Iran either denied the existence of a national and cultural Kurdish collective or perceived it as hostile to the Turkish or Iranian nation-state and culture. Kurdistan was the poorest, most deprived, and most neglected area in both Turkey and Iran. The great majority of Kurds belonged to the impoverished and exploited classes of Turkish, Iranian, and Iraqi society. Nevertheless, it was precisely the exclusion of the Kurds in Iraq and the denial of their existence as an ethnic or national entity in Turkey and Iran that empowered the Kurdish national movement.

At the same time, social change and modernization were gradually expanding the social stratum that supported the growth of consciousness of a collective Kurdish identity. Even as many Kurds who had obtained a modern education and many Kurdish religious and tribal leaders viewed themselves as part of the Turkish or Iranian nationality, the trend toward Kurdish nationalism gradually gained strength. The events that followed World War I would highlight the dichotomy between the agrarian-pastoral tribal nature of Kurdish society and the tribal (and sometimes Sufi-religious) motives for the Kurdish uprisings, on the one hand, and the very small but gradually expanding class of modern, educated, nationally and politically conscious city-dwellers, on the other.

In Turkey, expressions of Kurdish nationalism began with the activity of the Society for the Advancement of Kurdistan (SAK) in Istanbul after World War I. The conflicting national visions of 'Abd al-Qadir, Emin 'Ali Bedir Khan, and the latter's sons and the old rivalry between the Bedir Khan and Shemindan families eventually tore apart the SAK. Emin 'Ali Bedir Khan's vision was of an independent Kurdish state, but 'Abd al-Qadir and the majority in SAK strove for Kurdish autonomy and recognition of Kurdish rights in the framework of the Turkish state. Some of the Kurdish rebellions in Turkey after World War I had Kurdish nationalist motives; for instance, the military mutiny of Kurdish officers and soldiers organized by Kurdish nationalists in military barracks in Beit Shebab in September 1924. The most important rebellion was that of Shaykh Sa'id from Palu in 1925. Although the rebellion was mainly a tribal one, with Naqshbandi Islamic motives, it was supported by the Kurdish nationalist SAK activists, who had become frustrated by the Kemalists' Turkish nationalism, which denied Kurdish national rights and foiled hopes for Kurdish autonomy. A great majority of the Kurds supported the Ottoman state on the basis of their Islamic faith and the Islamic legitimation of the Ottoman sultan-caliph. The abolition of the caliphate and the secularization of the Turkish state initiated by Mustafa Kemal Atatürk reinforced the alienation of the tribal, rural Kurdish population from the growing Turkish national state. The Kemalist regime's policy of making Turkish nation-building the core of the Turkish nation-state, combined with its efforts to deny Kurdish identity and assimilate the Kurds into the Turkish nation, pushed some modernized and educated Kurds toward Kurdish nationalism as a response to the regime's enforced Turkification.

Shaykh Sa'id had contacts with the Kurdish nationalists and was aware to some degree of their modern nationalist discourse about Kurdish distinctiveness and ethnic identity versus Turks and the Turkish state. However, the Sufi Naqshbandi and tribal leaders and militants in the rebellion had their own grievances: the abolition of the Islamic caliphate by Atatürk in 1924, which annulled the Islamic legitimization of Turkish rule, and the steps taken by the Kemalist regime toward secularization intermingled with Turkification. The rebellion was both a tribal revolt led by a Sufi shaykh and an expression of Kurdish nationalism.

The modern, urban, educated, nationalist activists prepared for a national revolt while pursuing a dialogue with Shaykh Sa'id. The revolt broke out locally, however, before these plans could be completed. The composition of the revolt reflected the antagonisms and splits within Kurdish society: the participants were tribesmen from the Dersim area who spoke the Zaza dialect and whose motives were primarily tribal and religious; their leader was Shaykh Sa'id, and they were joined by only a few speakers of the Kurmanji dialect.[1] The Alawite Kurds disapproved of this primarily Sunnite revolt, headed by a Naqshbandi Sunnite Sufi shaykh. There was deep distrust between Naqshbandi and non-Naqshbandi Kurds, and many Kurdish landowners, intent on preserving their status with the assistance of the state, opposed the revolt.[2]

The Kemalist regime perceived the rebellion as conservative, obscurantist-religious opposition to the modernization, Westernization, and development of the new Turkish state. In suppressing the rebellion, the Kemalists intensified their policy, in the name of Turkish nationalism and modernization, of denying not only the national rights of the Kurds but even their existence as an identifiable ethnic, cultural, and linguistic group. Kemal Atatürk used Shaykh Saʿid's rebellion as a pretext for overcoming opposition in the Turkish political arena, coming mainly from the Progressive Republican Party. The suppression of Shaykh Saʿid's rebellion (1925), the Ararat rebellion (1928–1931), and, later, the Dersim insurrection (1936–1937) and the ongoing threat of Kurdish nationalism played important roles in the Kemalists' consolidation of the Turkish national state, in how they defined the role of the army, and in the strengthening of their regime. After the rebellions were quelled, the Kurds and the Kurdish national movement were suppressed by the nationalist Turkish state until the founding in 1978 of the Kurdistan Workers' Party (PKK), against the background of radical leftist opposition to Turkey's authoritarian regime.

In Iraq, the Kurds were recognized as a linguistic and ethnic minority in an Arabic-speaking state whose policies nevertheless discriminated toward Kurdistan and marginalized the Kurds. The promotion of the Arab identity of Iraq and of pan-Arab ideology created conditions for the development of a Kurdish national movement in Iraq. The founding of the Kurdish Democratic Party (KDP) in 1946 in Iraq and of its counterpart in Iran, the Democratic Party of Iranian Kurdistan (KDPI), in August 1945 marked a turning point in the historical development of the Kurdish national movement. The KDP, which became a leading player in the Kurdish national movement, was led by Mullah Mustafa Barzani, who combined tribal conduct with nationalism, and by educated nationalists with a leftist world outlook, some of whom were influenced by the Communists. The (sometimes radical) leftist trend of the Kurdish nationalist activists who established the Kurdish Democratic Party was fostered by several conditions, including: the poverty and deprivation of Kurdistan as a whole; the urbanization that caused Kurds to migrate to the cities, where, for the most part, they constituted an abjectly poor and rejected minority; and the growth of a modern, educated stratum whose members were aware of the double discrimination—national and economic—practiced against the Kurds.

In Iran, the growth of modern Kurdish nationalism was accelerated after the 1920s by the denial of Kurdish distinctiveness, the suppression of the Kurds, and their forced inclusion in the Iranian nation-building project by Pahlevi Riza Shah, who based his regime on an alliance with the large landowning tribal leaders.

Tribal, religious, and class-related splits and rivalries, as well as linguistic differences, enabled the ruling states to organize elements within the Kurdish population to assist in putting down the revolts, which were also national in character. The strength of tribalism and the landowning tribal lead-ers' class-related fears of agrarian reform and Communist influence made it easier for the Iranian authorities to eliminate the Republic of Mahabad in late 1946, once the Soviet Union had withdrawn its support from the Kurds.

During the Kurdish revolt against the Qassim government of Iraq be-tween 1961 and 1963, tribalism enabled the Iraqi regime to recruit members of tribes hostile to the Barzanis into a militia that fought against the Kurd-ish national revolt led by Mullah Mustafa Barzani and the Kurdistan Dem-ocratic Party. Nevertheless, the Kurdish nationalist vision and class-related ideological politics gradually assumed a central role in the power struggles within the Kurdish political arena. Following the end of World War II and up to the last days of the global Cold War in the late 1980s, class-related ide-ological discourse and political patterns became more prevalent in both the regional and international political arenas. Notwithstanding the continued existence of tribalism, nationalism, class issues, and ideology came to domi-nate the discourse and politics among the Kurds as well.

Even since 1975, when modern Kurdish politics began to take shape in the form of two secular national parties—the Kurdistani Democratic Party, led by Mas'ud Barzani, and the Patriotic Union of Kurdistan (PUK), led by Jalal Talabani—tribal and familial loyalties have continued to play a role in Kurdish politics in Iraq. However, these tribal loyalties have been compli-cated by ideological splits. Between 1992 and 1998, a Kurdish civil war was fought between the KDP and the PUK. Only the division of Iraqi Kurdistan into two separate areas, each controlled by a political party, brought an end to the fighting in 1998. Party leaders did not understand the need for unifi-cation of the two Kurdish areas, the coordination of policy, and the forma-tion of a common front until they were confronted by the situation that de-veloped after 2001 as Iraq prepared for the war that led to the fall of Saddam Hussein. The complex and difficult process of unifying the two regions and building a nonviolent Kurdish political arena, which began in 2002–2003, has not been completed to this day, more than a decade later.

Splits and divisions that originated in tribal struggles and rivalries still exist in Kurdish politics; indeed, those divisions have been maintained and even intensified within modern political parties. Nonetheless, in recent years rapid urbanization has transformed most residents of Iraqi Kurdistan from pastoral nomads and peasants into city-dwellers, the educational level has increased dramatically, individualistic bourgeois values have been widely adopted, and the mass media and the Kurdish diaspora in Europe, the United States, and Australia have become very influential.

From the perspective of 2015, the chances for the establishment of an independent Kurdish state or autonomous, self-governing Kurdish regions in the framework of the existing states depend on circumstances and developments in the international arena and on the policies and domestic politics of Iraq, Turkey, and Iran. Nevertheless, the new conditions created by the profound changes in Kurdish society will have an impact not only on Kurdish domestic politics but on the future of Kurdish nationalism and the building of a Kurdish state or Kurdish self-governing regions.

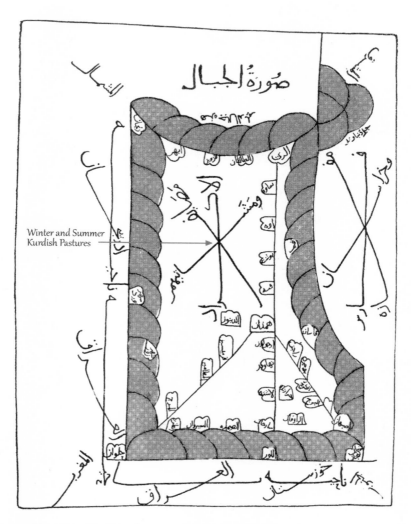

Winter and Summer Kurdish Pastures

MAP 1. Map of the World by Ibn Hawqal (tenth century). From Ibn Hawqal, *Kitab surat al-Ard* (Beirut: Manshurat dar maktabat al-Hayat, 1979), 305.

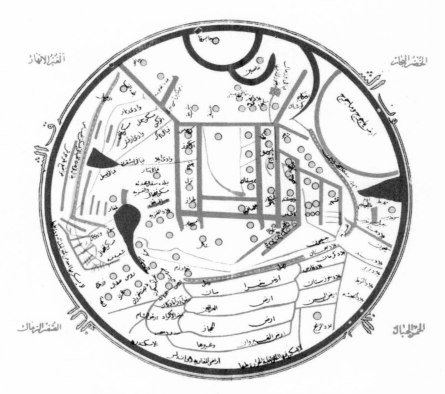

MAP 2. Map from Mohammad al-Kashgari's *Diwan* (eleventh century), *Ard al-Akrad* (*Country of Kurds*), Wikimedia Commons, https://en.wikipedia.org/wiki/File:Kashgari _map.jpg.

OTTOMAN EMPIRE

IRAN

BITLIS (BIDLIS)

L.Van

Amed
Diyarbakir

Bitlis

HAKKARI

L.Urmiah

Cizra (Jazirat bin Omar)

Urmiah

BOTAN
(BHOTAN)

BAHDINAN

Amadiya

Nisibln

Rawannduz

SawjBulak
Mahabad

Irbil

SORAN

Mosul

Sulaymaniyya

Sanandaj

Euphrates River

Tigris River

BABAN
SHAHRIZUR REGION

ARDALAN

Names of main Emirates

Baghdad

MAP 3. Main Kurdish emirates (seventeenth to nineteenth centuries). Map by author.

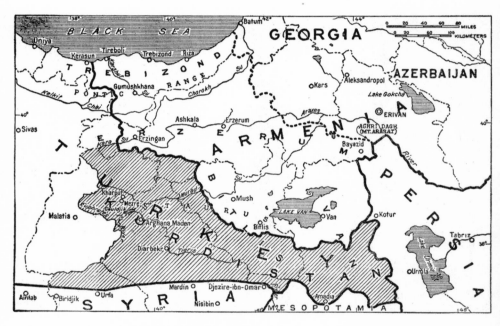

MAP 4. Map of Kurdistan according to the Treaty of Sèvres, 1920 (Articles 62, 64).
Map compiled by Lt. Col. Lawrence Martin, reprinted in *The Treaties of Peace 1919–1923*
(New York: Carnegie Endowment for International Peace, 1924), 814.

INTRODUCTION: THE ORIGINS OF THE KURDS

1. Limbert, "Origins and Appearances," 48.

2. For a comprehensive discussion of the origins of the term "Kurd"—which is beyond the framework of the present book—see Driver, "The Name Kurd"; Nikitine, *Les Kurdes*, 2–16. See also the Arabic translation by Nuri Talabani of Nikitine, *al-Kurd dirasat*, 43–61; MacKenzie, "Origins of the Kurds"; and the important article by Asatrian, "Prolegomena," 22–25.

3. Asatrian, "Prolegomena," 22–25; Limbert, "Origins and Appearances," 48. About premodern distinctiveness and identities, see Smith, "The Nation: Invented, Imagined, Reconstructed?"

4. For myths on the origins of the Kurds, see al-Mas'udi, *Muruj al-Dhahab*, 307–308; Bitlisi, *The Sharafnama*, 28–29, 30–35; al-Bidlisi, *Sharafnameh*; Driver, "Studies in Kurdish History," 491–492.

5. Driver, "The Name Kurd," 393–403.

6. Xenophon, *Anabasis*, 287–325.

7. Ibid., 287.

8. MacKenzie, "Origins of the Kurds," 68–70; Asatrian, "Prolegomena," 25.

9. Strabo, *The Geography of Strabo*, vol. 5, 305; vol.7, 157.

10. Villard, *Il Libro della peregrinazine*, 66; Galleti, "The Italian Contribution to Kurdology," 104.

11. Izady, *The Kurds*, 40.

12. Izady, "Introduction to the Sharafnama."

13. Bedir Khan, "The Case of Kurdistan," 121.

14. James, "Uses and Values of the Term *Kurd*."

15. This is reflected in the apposite title of the book by the American documentary photojournalist Susan Meiseles, *Kurdistan: In the Shadow of History*; see the introduction by Martin van Bruinessen.

16. For an in-depth discussion of the issues of Kurdish identity and its dynamic and elusive boundaries, see van Bruinessen, "Nationalisme kurde."

17. O'Shea, *Trapped between the Map and Reality*, 45.

18. Le Strange, *The Lands of the Eastern Caliphate*, 192; see also Ibn Hawqal, *Kitab Surat al-Ard*, 305 (the map), and 239–241.

19. Ozoglu, *Kurdish Notables*, 61; Kunt, *The Sultan's Servants*, 96, 108, appendix 1, fig. 6. In 1852 the *eyelet* of Kurdistan was dissolved as a result of the Ottoman governors' failure to manage the affairs of the region properly.

20. Bitlisi, *Sharafnama*, 59.

21. O'Shea, *Trapped between the Map and Reality*, 45.

22. Maunsell, "Kurdistan"; Maunsell, "Central Kurdistan."

CHAPTER 1: KURDISH DISTINCTIVENESS UNDER ARAB, PERSIAN, AND TURKISH DOMINANCE

1. Al-Baladhuri, *Futuh al-Buldan*, 464, 467, 538, 548. For the participation of the Kurds in the struggle between the Muslims and the Sassanids, see Parvaneh, *Decline and Fall of the Sassanian Empire*, 237–238.

2. Al-Tabari, *History of Tabari*, vol. 15, 34.

3. Ibid., vol. 14, 73, 78–79.

4. On the socioeconomic meaning of the terms *kurd* and *akrad*, see Asatrian, "Prolegomena," 28; see also Ozoglu, "The Impact of Islam."

5. Kurdo, *Kurdistan*, 55.

6. Important articles and books on the poem *Mam u Zin* include: Shakely, *Kurdish Nationalism in MAM U ZIN*; Hassanpour, "The Making of Kurdish Identity," especially 106–131; van Bruinessen, "Ehmedi Khani's Mem u Zin"; and Mirawdeli, *Love and Existence*.

7. Minorsky, "Kurds."

8. Ibn al-Athir, *Al-Kamil fi al-Ta'rikh*, vol. 6, 506–507.

9. The Buwayhids were a Persian dynasty whose members served as sultans in Baghdad and were the main strength of the Abbasid Empire, in light of the weakening of the Abbasid caliphs, the nominal heads of state. See Ibn Khaldun, "Rizankas," in Ibn Khaldun, *Ta'rikh al-'alamat* vol. 4, 1093; al-Bidlisi, *Sharafnameh*, 77–80.

10. Minorsky, "Annazids."

11. For basic research on the Shadadids, see Minorsky, *Studies in Caucasian History*. Minorsky strongly argues that the Shadadids were a Kurdish dynasty.

12. Amedroz, "The Marwanid Dynasty"; Bidlisi, *Sharafnameh*, 65–77; Ibn Khaldun, *Ta'rikh al-'alamat*, vol. 4, 674–686.

13. Amedroz, "The Marwanid Dynasty," 131.

14. Ibn al-Athir, *Al-Kamil fi al-Ta'rikh*, vol. 9, 384–386.

15. Ibid., vol. 9, 598–599.

16. Ibid., vol. 10, 65–67.

17. Ibid., vol. 10, 144.

18. Ibid., vol. 10, 601.

19. The fortresses of Aqar and Shush were retaken in AH 528 (AD 1133–1134) (ibid., vol. 11, 14–16) and in AH 527 (AD 1142–1143) (ibid., vol. 11, 91).

20. Ibn Khaldun drew a similar picture of Kurdish society in his book *Ta'rikh al-'alamat* and relied, to a great degree, on Ibn al-Athir, *The Chronicle of Ibn al-Athir*, 240, 307, 367. The Kurdish historian Sharaf al-Din al-Bitlisi (al-Bidlisi), at the end of the sixteenth century, wrote his book *The Sharafnama (Sharafnameh), or, The History of the Kurdish Nation* in Persian. It is based on the works of Persian historians. In the first volume, which is devoted to the Kurdish dynasties during the centuries from the rise of Islam to the Ayyubid Dynasty (midthirteenth century), he wrote about the Marwanids, the Fadilwayhids, and the Chiginids (a dynasty of Lorestan in southeast Kurdistan, an area now located in modern-day Iran and inhabited by people who, for the most part, are not considered Kurds) (Bitlisi, *The Sharafnama*, 18–19). Bitlisi's work focuses, however, primarily on the Kurdish dynasties of eastern and southern Kurdistan; he ignores or is unaware of those in northern and western Kurdistan (Izady, "An Introduction," xvii–xxxv).

21. Ibn al-Athir, *The Annals of the Saljuq Turks*, 15, 19, 45, 58, 60–62, 86, 91–92, 97, 156, 181, 208.

22. Ibn al-Athir, *Al-Kamil fi al-Ta'rikh*, vol. 11, 343; Minorsky, *Studies in Caucasian History*, 137.

23. Minorsky, *Studies in Caucasian History*, 136–139, 146–157.

24. James, "Uses and Values of the Term *Kurd*."

25. Amitai-Preiss, "The North Syrian Frontier."

26. Woods, *The Aqqoyunlu*. For a comprehensive article on the Turkmen, see Blaum, "From Steppe to Empire."

27. Woods, *The Aqqoyunlu*, 104.

28. Ibid., 92–93.

29. Ibid., 59, 60.

30. Ibid., 59.

31. Van Bruinessen, *Agha, Shaikh, and State*, 137.

32. Woods, *The Aqqoyunlu*, 81, 111–112, 123; van Bruinessen, *Agha, Shaikh, and State*, 137.

CHAPTER 2: THE ERA OF OTTOMAN AND IRANIAN RULE

1. Van Bruinessen and Boeschoten, *Evliya Celebi* [pronounced "Chelebi"] *in Diyarbekir*, 13–15. The emirs of Bidlis (Bitlis) belonged to the Rojiki (Rozhiki) tribe, which was related to the Marwanid Dynasty (984–1083). Because that dynasty claimed ties with the pre-Islamic Sassanid Persian Empire, the roots of the emirs of Bidlis and the emirs of Ardalan date back to the pre-Islamic period. Mehrdad Izady prefers a different transcription for the name of the tribe: Roshaki or Rozhaki (see al-Bitlisi, *The Sharafnama*, xvii, 255).

2. On the conflict between the Kurds and Qizilbashis and the role of the Qizilbashis in the service of the Safavids, see the pro-Safavid chronicle written by an official in the court of Shah 'Abbas I (1588–1629), Monshi, *History of Shah 'Abbas the Great*, vol. 2, 51.

3. On the ancient origin of the al-Ruzkia (Rojiki / Rozhiki / Roshaki) tribe and the active role of the emirs of Bidlis in the Ottoman-Iranian Safavid struggle, see Bitlisi, *The Sharafnama*, 339–442; Ozoglu, *Kurdish Notables*, 50.

4. Olson, *The Siege of Mosul*, 34–35.

5. Hassanpour, *Nationalism and Language*, 55–56. The patterns of development associated with "feudal nationalism" differ from those of modern nationalism, which began in the nineteenth century mainly in western Europe and the "Atlantic world" in the context of the rise of industrial capitalism, the working class, and the bourgeoisie and the spread of "print capitalism."

6. Kunt, *The Sultan's Servants*, 108; see also fig. 6.

7. Ozoglu, *Kurdish Notables*, 59.

8. Bitlisi, *The Sharafnama*, 20, 47.

9. Dankoff, *Celebi in Bitlis*, 57.

10. On the history of the emirs of Bitlis and the Rojiki tribe, see Izady, "An Introduction to the *Sharafnama*," xxvii–xxix; Dankoff, *Celebi in Bitlis*, 12–13.

11. Ozoglu, *Kurdish Notables*, 33–35.

12. Van Bruinessen, "Kurdistan in the 16th and 17th Centuries," 129–171.

13. Dankoff, *Celebi in Bitlis*, 10–92.

14. Ibid., 283–295. This description of 'Abd al-Khan's library is based exclusively on Celebi's report, which apparently is the only source that describes it. Joseph von Hammer-

Purgstall, an Austrian historian, diplomat, and scholar of Middle Eastern studies who wrote, in the beginning of the nineteenth century, a detailed history of the Ottoman Empire, relies on Celebi in his account of the conquest of the emirate. In his brief description of the palace treasures, based on Celebi, he sees fit to point out only the books in Persian (Hammer-Purgstall, *Histoire de l'Empire Ottoman*, 37–38).

15. Dankoff, *Celebi in Bitlis*, 157.

16. Tavernier, *Les Six voyages*, 28; Dankoff, *Celebi in Bitlis*, 17.

17. See the Arabic translation of chapters of Pietro Della Valle's book, especially the description of the socioeconomic and political conditions in Kurdistan and the independence and military strength of the emir of Bitlis (Valle, *Rihlat Dillavalle*, 94). See also the abridged translation, Valle, *The Pilgrim*, 119–121; and Galleti, "The Italian Contribution," 104–105.

18. Dankoff, *Celebi in Bitlis*, 167, 183.

19. Ibid., 179.

20. Reid, "Rozhiki Revolt," 13–40.

21. Al-Damaluji, *Imarat Bahdinan*.

22. For the most comprehensive study of the Emirates of Baban and Ardalan, see Vasileva, *Yugo-Vostochniy Kurdistan*; see also the chronicles of the principality of Ardalan, written in the nineteenth century, Bani Ardalan, *Khronika*.

23. Bani Ardalan, *Khronika*, 110; Bitlisi, *The Sharafnama*, 117, 255. On the genealogy of the emirs of Ardalan and their roots in the Marwanid Dynasty and the pre-Islamic Iranian Sassanid dynasty, see Izady, "An Introduction to the *Sharafnama*," xxvi–xxvii.

24. Monshi, *History of Shah 'Abbas the Great*, vol. 1, 346–347.

25. Hassanpour, "Dimdim"; Jalilov, *Kurdskij grodicheskij*, 5–26, 37–39; Hassanpour, "Baradost"; McDowall, *Modern History of the Kurds*, 30–34.

26. Monshi, *History of Shah 'Abbas the Great*, vol. 2, 994–1002.

27. Ibid., vol. 2, 1252.

28. Bani Ardalan, *Khronika*, 72.

29. Jwaideh, *The Kurdish National Movement*, 17. Sharaf Khan al-Bitlisi regarded the Lurs as Kurds.

30. Perry, *Karim Khan Zand*, 184–185.

31. Kinneir, *A Geographical Memoir*, 143–144.

32. Edmonds, *Kurds, Turks and Arabs*, 52–53.

33. On Kurdish poetry, see Blau, "Le Développement de la littérature kurde"; Shakely, "Classical and Modern Kurdish Poetry," part 1; Rudenko, "Kurdskaya literatura XVII veka."

34. Blau, "Kurdish Language and Literature."

35. Shakely, "Classical and Modern Kurdish Poetry," part 2.

36. Driver, "Studies in Kurdish History," 508–509.

37. Monshi, *History of Shah 'Abbas the Great*, vol. 1, 227.

38. Al-Bidlisi, *Sharafnameh*; see also the English translation by M. R. Izady in Bitlisi, *Sharafnama*, 28–29, 30–35. On the history of this book, see Pirbal, "*Sharafnama*, the Book."

39. Bajalan, "Sheref Khan's *Sharafnama*," especially note 20 on the different accounts of Bitlisi's shift of allegiances.

40. Al-Bidlisi, *Sharafnameh*, 45.

41. Malcolm, *Sketches of Persia*, 278.

42. In both Arabic and Turkish, *ta'ife* denotes "ethnic or religious community," and even "nation" in its premodern sense.

43. For examples of poetry written in the Gorani dialect from the region of Sinna and from the Mukri tribe, see Soane, *To Mesopotamia and Kurdistan*, 391–392.

44. For a short essay on Ahmad-i Khani, with citations for translations, see Shakely, *Kurdish Nationalism in MAM U ZIN*. See also Hassanpour, "The Making of Kurdish Identity," especially 106–131.

45. Ozoglu, "The Impact of Islam," 28.

46. Hassanpour, "The Making of Kurdish Identity," 118–119; Khani, *Mam i Zin*, 52–53.

47. Hassanpour, "The Making of Kurdish Identity," 109.

48. Reid, "Rozhiki Revolt," 14–16.

49. Khani, *Mam i Zin*, 53.

50. Ibid.

51. Anderson, *Imagined Communities*.

52. Shakely, *Kurdish Nationalism in MAM U ZIN*, 74. For a profound study of *Mem u Zin* written by a Kurdish intellectual, poet, and activist, see Mirawdeli, *Love and Existence*.

53. Mirawdeli, *Love and Existence*, 104–105; Khani, *Mam i Zin*, 54.

54. Hassanpour, "The Making of Kurdish Identity," 129–142. On the role of *Mam u Zin* in modern Kurdish nationalism, see Bruinessen, "Ehmedi Khani's *Mem U Zin*," 40–57.

CHAPTER 3: THE DEMISE OF THE KURDISH EMIRATES IN THE NINETEENTH CENTURY

1. Eppel, "The Demise of the Kurdish Emirates," 243–246.

2. Ceylan, *The Ottoman Origins of Modern Iraq*, 40.

3. Russia's relations with the Kurdish tribes (and in fact with the Kurds in general), against the background of the wars between Russia and the Ottoman Empire starting in 1804, was the subject of a study, based on documents from the Russian military archives, published in 1900 by P. I. Averianov, a staff officer in the Caucasus Command of the Russian army (Averianov, *Kurdi b voinakh Rossii*, 43–78).

4. Monteith, *Kars and Erzeroum*, 154, 221, 262–265, 302; Allen and Muratoff, *Caucasian Battlefields*, 31, 44; Nikitine, *al-kurd dirasat*, 301.

5. Rich, *Narrative of a Residence in Koordistan*.

6. Ceylan, *The Ottoman Origins of Modern Iraq*, 46.

7. Edmonds, *Kurds, Turks, and Arabs*, 52–53.

8. Rich, *Narrative of a Residence in Koordistan*, vol. 1, 55.

9. Ibid., vol. 1, 96–97; Nieuwenhuis, *Politics and Society in Early Modern Iraq*, 97. Stephen Longrigg claims that it was actually the Ottomans who refused to nominate 'Abd al-Rahman as a *vali* rather than 'Abd al-Rahman's rejection of an Ottoman proposal (Longrigg, *Four Centuries*, 226–227).

10. Ceylan, *The Ottoman Origins of Modern Iraq*, 40.

11. Van Bruinessen, *Mullas, Sufis, and Heretics*, 217–218.

12. On Shaykh Mawlana Khalid's escape, see Rich, *Narrative of a Residence in Koordistan*, vol. 2, 320–321. For more information on Shaykh Mawlana Khalid, see Abu Manneh, "The Naqshbandiyya in Ottoman Lands," 5; Abu Manneh, *Studies in Islam*, 17–18; Shakely, "The Naqshbandi Shaiks," 71–74.

13. Ceylan, *The Ottoman Origins of Modern Iraq*, 52; Edmonds, *Kurds, Turks, and Arabs*, 55.

14. Rawlinson, "Notes on a Journey," 32; Amin, *Khulasat ta'rikh al-kurd*, 243.

15. Fraser, *Travels in Koordistan*, vol. 1, 64.

16. Ceylan, *The Ottoman Origins of Modern Iraq*, 45, 51.

17. Jwaideh, *The Kurdish National Movement*, 55–56; Longrigg, *Four Centuries*, 285.

18. Fraser, *Travels in Koordistan*, vol. 1, 102; for the claim that Muhummad Kor could call up 50,000 fighters, see Jalil, *Kurdi osmanskoi imperii*, 96.

19. Jalil, *Kurdi osmanskoi imperii*, 55; Nikitine and Bosworth, "Rawwandiz."

20. Jwaideh, *The Kurdish National Movement*, 59; Amin, *Khulasat ta'rikh al-kurd*, 245.

21. For a detailed description and discussion of the fall of Muhammad Kor, see Jalil, *Kurdi osmanskoi imperii*, 100–102.

22. Wood, *Early Correspondence*, 97. On Wood's attempt to bring about a compromise that would leave Muhammad Kor as the ruler of Rawanduz but subject to Ottoman sovereignty, see also an account by the British traveler William Francis Ainsworth, *Travels and Researches*, vol. 2, 323.

23. Wood, *Early Correspondence*, 105. Colonel J. Shiel, who visited the area in 1836, also recounted the rumor of a battalion of Russian Cossacks organizing in Iran (Shiel, "Notes on a Journey from Tabriz," 55). This may have been a group of Russian deserters. The rumor may also have been false; none of the Russian sources and studies at our disposal make reference to it.

24. Amin, *Khulasat ta'rikh al-kurd*, 247; Fraser, *Travels in Koordistan*, vol. 1, 81–82; Jwaideh, *The Kurdish National Movement*, 60, 319.

25. Ainsworth, *Travels and Researches*, vol. 1, 323; Jwaideh, *The Kurdish National Movement*, 60.

26. Van Bruinessen, *Agha, Shaikh, and State*, 176–177.

27. Safrastian, *Kurds and Kurdistan*, 56.

28. Ozoglu, *Kurdish Notables*, 71.

29. Ceylan, *The Ottoman Origins of Modern Iraq*, 52–53.

30. On the activities of the missionaries from their perspective, see Salibi and Khoury, *The Missionary Herald*. See also Layard, *Discoveries in the Ruins of Nineveh*; Layard, *Popular Account of Discoveries at Nineveh*, 122–170; Layard, *Nineveh and Its Remains*, 173–215; Joseph, *The Nestorians and Their Neighbors*; Taylor, *Fever and Thirst*.

31. Soane, *To Mesopotamia and Kurdistan*, 156.

32. For a detailed discussion of the relations between Bedir Khan and the Nestorians, see Jwaideh, *The Kurdish National Movement*, 62–74.

33. Ainsworth, *Travels and Researches*, vol. 2, 271, 281.

34. Salibi and Khoury, *Missionary Herald*, 474, 483.

35. Layard, *Popular Account of Discoveries at Nineveh*, 122.

36. On Khan Mahmud, who governed a limited region south of Lake Van, see Shiel, "Notes on a Journey from Tabriz," 63–64; Safrastian, *Kurds and Kurdistan*, 105.

37. Ozoglu, "'Nationalism,'" 395.

38. Ozoglu, *Kurdish Notables*, 60–63.

39. For the Russian perspective on the Yezdansher rebellion, see Averianov, *Kurdi b voinakh Rossii*, 80–157; Badem, *The Ottoman Crimean War*, 360–377.

40. Averianov, *Kurdi b voinakh Rossii*, 91.

41. Badem, *The Ottoman Crimean War*, 366; Averianov, *Kurdi b voinakh Rossii*, 93.

42. Averianov, *Kurdi b voinakh Rossii*, 149.

43. Badem, *The Ottoman Crimean War*, 373. On the British involvement, see the memoirs of Dr. Humphrey Sandwith, *A Narrative: The Siege of Kars*, 212–215.

44. Shakely, "Haji Qadir Koyi."

CHAPTER 4: SEEDS OF KURDISH NATIONALISM IN THE DECLINING OTTOMAN EMPIRE

1. Descriptions of the situation in Kurdistan appear in the memoirs of the British physician Dr. Humphrey Sandwith (*A Narrative: The Siege of Kars*), who was in charge of the medical team in the Ottoman corps that fought the Russians in the area of Kars during the Crimean War.

2. Ibid., 181–182.

3. Jwaideh, *The Kurdish National Movement*, 117.

4. Averianov, *Kurdi b voinakh Rossii*, 98; Jalil, *Vosstaniye Kurdov*, 31.

5. See a letter written in 1878 by the Russian consul of Erzurum, cited in Averianov, *Kurdi b voinakh Rossii*, 226; see also Khalfin, *Borba za Kurdistan*, 114–115.

6. Averianov, *Kurdi b voinakh Rossii*, 224; Jalil, *Vosstaniye Kurdov*, 48.

7. Jalil, *Vosstaniye Kurdov*, 48–50; Averianov, *Kurdi b voinakh Rossii*, 224–225; Klein, *The Margins of Empire*, 90–91.

8. Olson, *The Emergence of Kurdish Nationalism*, 1–26.

9. Jalil, *Vosstaniye Kurdov*, 72. Although he was a member of the Naqshbandi order, 'Ubaydallah adopted the title "of Nehri" from a long-standing dynasty of *saadat* (families with noble status as descendants of the Prophet Muhammad) in the village of Nehri, which was also related to 'Abd al-Qadir al-Gaylani, the founder of the Qadiri order.

10. On the *saadat*, see van Bruinessen, "The Sadate Nehri." Dr. Joseph Plumb Cochran, a physician and missionary, treated Shaykh 'Ubaydallah and talked with him. See Speer, *The "Hakim Sahib"*; see also Jwaideh, *The Kurdish National Movement*, 73–101; Ozoglu, *Kurdish Notables*, 72–78.

11. See the letter written by the Russian consul cited in Averianov, *Kurdi b voinakh Rossii*, 226.

12. Ibid., 235; Wilson, *Persian Life and Customs*, 111.

13. See the letters written by the Russian consul in Tabriz and cited in Jalil, *Vosstaniye Kurdov*, appendix. See also the conversation between Shaykh 'Ubaydallah and Dr. Cochran cited in Speer, *The "Hakim Sahib,"* 103–113.

14. Averianov, *Kurdi b voinakh Rossii*, 227; Jwaideh, *The Kurdish National Movement*, 86–88.

15. Averianov, *Kurdi b voinakh Rossii*, 229.

16. Olson, *The Emergence of Kurdish Nationalism*, 6; Safrastian, *Kurds and Kurdistan*, 63.

17. Jwaideh, *The Kurdish National Movement*, 83–86; Wilson, *Persian Life and Customs*, 111; Khalfin, *Borba za Kurdistan*, 124–128.

18. Averianov, *Kurdi b voinakh Rossii*, 228–230.

19. For a detailed study of the invasion, see Kilic, "Sheikh Ubeidallah's Movement," 66–75.

20. Jwaideh, *The Kurdish National Movement*, 91.

21. Kilic, "Sheikh Ubeidallah's Movement," 47–49, 67.

22. Averianov, *Kurdi b voinakh Rossii*, 230; Jalil, *Vosstaniye Kurdov*, 71.

23. Olson, *The Emergence of Kurdish Nationalism*, 6–7.

24. Wilson, *Persian Life and Customs*, 111–117; Jwaideh, *The Kurdish National Movement*, 92–94.

25. Kilic, "Sheikh Ubeidallah's Movement," 130.

26. The Naqshbandi Shaykh Shamil (1797–1871) led the great insurrection by the Muslim tribes, principally Chechens and Avars, against Russian rule during the 1840s and 1850s.

27. Jwaideh, *The Kurdish National Movement*, 96.

28. Safrastian, *Kurds and Kurdistan*, 62–63; Jwaideh, *The Kurdish National Movement*, 80–82; Jalil, *Vosstaniye Kurdov*, 51–72.

29. Olson, *The Emergence of Kurdish Nationalism*, 2. Anja Pistor-Hatam in her article "Sheikh 'Ubaidullah's Revolt and the Kurdish Invasion of Iran," points to the Shaykh's traditional religious views and aims and lack of proto-nationalism.

30. An example of an independent state that continued to accept Ottoman authority and legitimacy was Egypt under Muhammad 'Ali and his heirs.

31. Ozoglu, "'Nationalism,'" 391–392; Jwaideh, *The Kurdish National Movement*, 80–87.

32. Ozoglu, "'Nationalism,'" 391–392.

33. Hovanissian, *Armenia on the Road to Independence*, 26.

34. Owen, *The Middle East in the World Economy*, 274–279.

35. Klein, "Conflict and Collaboration."

36. Bozarslan, "Remarques sur l'histoire des relations kurdo-arméniennes," 55–69; Bozarslan, "Les Relations kurdo-arméniennes, 1894–1896," 23–33.

37. Klein, *The Margins of Empire*, 91.

38. Van Bruinessen, *Agha, Shaikh, and State*, 185–186.

39. According to Olson (*The Emergence of Kurdish Nationalism*, 10), there were fifty-seven Hamidiye regiments in 1893, with a total strength of between 29,000 and 65,000 men.

40. Ahmad, *Kurdistan*, 55.

41. Klein, *The Margins of Empire*, 63–74.

42. Van Bruinessen, *Agha, Shaikh, and State*, 186–189; Klein, *The Margins of Empire*, 97–103.

43. Klein, *The Margins of Empire*, 67, 135.

44. Ibid., 128–169.

45. Olson, *The Emergence of Kurdish Nationalism*, 11.

46. Ibid., 13.

47. Van Bruinessen, *Agha, Shaikh, and State*, 188.

48. Klein, *The Margins of Empire*, 109–112.

49. Olson, *The Emergence of Kurdish Nationalism*, 12.

50. Strohmeier, *Crucial Images*, 21–26.

51. The content of the Kurdish poetry written in the nineteenth century was Islamic and mystical-Sufi, but it also expressed characteristics of Kurdish life experience and the landscapes of Kurdistan. For example, Mewlewi, or Seyid Ebdulrehimi Mela Seidi Tawegozi (1806–1882), a Sufi-Naqshbandi *'alim*, published several books of poetry in a subdialect of the Sorani dialect of Kurdish; see Kerim, "Mewlewi."

52. Hanioglu, *The Young Turks in Opposition*, 117.

53. See examples of translations from *Kurdistan*, April 23, 1899, in Strohmeier, *Crucial Images*, 215–216.

54. Aslan, "Clashes of Agencies," 112.

55. Ibid., 20.

56. Ahmad, *Kurdistan*, 56–57.

57. Ibid., 161. See translated examples of these articles *Kurdistan*, March 13, 1901, in Strohmeier, *Crucial Images*, 217–218.

CHAPTER 5: THE BEGINNINGS OF MODERN KURDISH POLITICS

1. McDowall, *Modern History*, 88–89; Zurcher, *The Unionist Factor*, 13.

2. Aslan, "Clashes of Agencies," 92; Ozoglu, *Kurdish Notables*, 104–105.

3. Jwaideh, *The Kurdish National Movement*, 102–103.

4. Hanioglu, *Young Turks in Opposition*, 184, 188, 197.

5. Zurcher, *Turkey*, 100–105.

6. Jwaideh, *The Kurdish National Movement*, 109.

7. By contrast to the Baban and Bedir Khan families, whom the authorities prevented from returning to the areas that they had controlled in Kurdistan, Sufi shaykhs from the Barzani and Barzinji tribes, as well as Shaykh Muhammad Sadiq—the son of Shaykh ʿUbaydallah and the father of Shaykh Taha, who was permitted to return to Shemdinan—continued to operate in Kurdistan.

8. Olson, *The Emergence of Kurdish Nationalism*, 15; Aslan, "Clashes of Agencies," 113.

9. Strohmeier, *Crucial Images*, 36–42; Ozoglu, *Kurdish Notables*, 78.

10. *Hevi* in Kurmanji dialect (*hiwa* in Sorani dialect) means "hope." On the Kurdish Society of Student Hope as a Kurdish nationalist association of young intelligentsia, see Bajalan, "Between Conformism and Separatism."

11. Ahmad, *Kurdistan*, 62–63.

12. Aslan, "Clashes of Agencies," 116.

13. Klein, "Kurdish Nationalists."

14. Van Bruinessen, "The Qadiriyya."

15. Çetinsaya, *Ottoman Administration*, 77.

16. Soane, *To Mesopotamia and Kurdistan*, 189.

17. Çetinsaya, *Ottoman Administration*, 79.

18. Ibid., 80–81.

19. Soane, *To Mesopotamia and Kurdistan*, 187–188.

20. Çetinsaya, *Ottoman Administration*, 85–86.

21. Bell, *Amurath to Amurath*, 249; Soane, *To Mesopotamia and Kurdistan*, 179–183, 192.

22. Barzani, *Mustafa Barzani*, 18–20.

23. Al-Damaluji, *Imarat Bahdinan*, 80–94, 98–105; Wigram and Wigram, *The Cradle of Mankind*, 139; Jwaideh, *The Kurdish National Movement*, 111–113.

24. Al-Damaluji, *Imarat Bahdinan*, 92, 131–133.

25. Ibid., 86–87; McDowall, *Modern History*, 98.

26. Al-Damaluji, *Imarat Bahdinan*, 84, 87.

27. Ibid., 90–94; Jwaideh, *The Kurdish National Movement*, 110–114.

28. Ahmad, *Kurdistan*, 65–66; see also a work based on Russian sources, Lazarev, *Kurdistan i Kurdskaya Problema*, 215–216.

29. McDowall, *Modern History*, 83.

30. Arfa, *The Kurds*, 48. On the growth of the Kurdish national movement in Iran, mainly under the Pahlevi Dynasty, see Vali, *Kurds and the State in Iran*.

31. Van Bruinessen, "Kurdish Tribes and the State of Iran," 383–384. For a comprehensive and nuanced analysis of the Kurds in Iran, see Natali, *The Kurds and the State*, 117–139.

32. Eagleton, *The Kurdish Republic of 1946*, 7.

33. Reynolds, "Abdurrezak Bedirhan."

34. Lazarev, *Kurdistan i Kurdskaya Problema*, 227–228.

35. Ibid., 238.

36. Reynolds, "Abdurrezak Bedirhan," 431–432, 442–445.

37. Wigram and Wigram, *The Cradle of Mankind*, 145.

38. Nikitine, "Les Kurdes racontés"; Jwaideh, *The Kurdish National Movement*, 113.

39. Lazarev, *Kurdistan i Kurdskaya Problema*, 216–217.

40. Ibid., 169.

41. Ibid., pp. 169–170, 180, 227.

42. Van Bruinessen, "Kurdish Tribes and the State of Iran," 383.

CHAPTER 6: THE KURDS AND KURDISTAN DURING WORLD WAR I

1. Sazonov, *Fateful Years 1909–1916*, 260; Wilson, *Loyalties: Mesopotamia, 1914–1917*, 153.

2. Nikitine, *Les Kurdes*, 195.

3. Jwaideh, *The Kurdish National Movement*, 128–129.

4. Ahmad, *Kurdistan*, 92–93.

5. Jwaideh, *The Kurdish National Movement*, 121.

6. Ibid.

7. Lazarev, *Kurdistan i kurdskaya problema*, 32.

8. In contrast, the conflict actually increased in the nearby Caucasus in 1918. The Bolsheviks were trying to take over all the areas that had previously been controlled by Czarist Russia and to expand their influence to Iran and Turkey.

9. Wilson, *Mesopotamia, 1917–1920*, 32–33. The Kurdish refugees who were driven from their villages by the fighting and the famine that led to mass mortality are the subject of *A Measure of a Man: William A. Shedd of Persia: A Biography*, a book by Mary Lewis Shedd, an American Presbyterian missionary who spent the war years in Urmia, Iran; see pp. 236–237. For a discussion of the horrors of war in Kurdistan, see O'Shea, *Trapped between the Map and Reality*, 102–105.

10. Safrastian, *Kurds and Kurdistan*, 76, 81.

11. Lazarev, *Kurdistan i kurdskaya problema*, 314; Ahmad, *Kurdistan*, 133.

CHAPTER 7: THE KURDS AND THE NEW MIDDLE EAST AFTER THE OTTOMANS

1. Edmonds, *Kurds, Turks, and Arabs*, 25.

2. Shaykhs of the Qadiriyya order who were members of the Barzinji family had held important positions in the court of the Emirate of Baban at least since the end of the eighteenth century.

3. Al-Bayati, *Shaykh Mahmud al-Hafidh*, 104; Wilson, *Loyalties: Mesopotamia, 1914–1917*, 86; Jwaideh, *The Kurdish National Movement*, 161–162.

4. Jwaideh, *The Kurdish National Movement*, 165–166.

5. Al-Bayati, *Shaykh Mahmud al-Hafidh*, 104–177; Tejel Gorgas, "Urban Mobilization," 539.

6. Ozoglu, *Kurdish Notables*, 105, 152; McDowall, *Modern History*, 128–129.

7. Klieman, *The Foundation of British Policy*.

8. Ibid., 111. On the British dilemmas and conduct regarding Kurdistan in the context of the shaping of Iraq after World War I from Gertrude Bell's viewpoint, see Lukitz, *A Quest in the Middle East*.

9. Olson, "Battle for Kurdistan."

10. Eskander, "Southern Kurdistan," 155–156.

11. Ibid., 157–160.

12. Olson, *The Kurdish Question*, 7; see also Olson, "Battle for Kurdistan," 35.

13. Jwaideh, *The Kurdish National Movement*, 129–130. For a biographical note on Sharif Pasha, see Ozoglu, *Kurdish Notables*, 110–113.

14. Arfa, *The Kurds*, 112.

15. McDowall, *Modern History*, 131.

16. Ozoglu, *Kurdish Notables*, 39–40.

17. Olson, *The Emergence of Kurdish Nationalism*, 36.

18. Ozoglu, *Kurdish Notables*, 83; see also Jwaideh, *The Kurdish National Movement*, 128; Eskander, "Southern Kurdistan," 157–160.

19. Olson, *The Emergence of Kurdish Nationalism*, 37.

20. Lukitz, *A Quest in the Middle East*, 156.

21. As mentioned earlier, even before the Treaty of Sèvres was signed in 1920, Major Noel toured eastern Anatolia with a view to encouraging Kurdish opposition to the Turkish nationalists. In fact, Britain provided limited assistance to Kurdish organizations in a number of towns in eastern Anatolia.

22. McDowall, *Modern History*, 160.

23. Olson, "Battle for Kurdistan," 36.

24. Eskander, "Southern Kurdistan," 169–170.

25. Initially, after he had recovered from his wounds, Shaykh Mahmoud was exiled to the Andaman Islands in the Indian Ocean. However, because the British had not yet given up the idea of using him for their own purposes, they transferred him to Kuwait, to be closer to Iraq.

26. Tejel Gorgas, "Urban Mobilization," 540–541.

27. Edmonds, *Kurds, Turks, and Arabs*, 19; Jwaideh, *The Kurdish National Movement*, 199.

28. Eskander, "Southern Kurdistan," 175.

29. Tejel Gorgas, "Urban Mobilization," 540.

30. Edmonds, *Kurds, Turks, and Arabs*, 337.

31. Tejel Gorgas, "Urban Mobilization," 541.

32. Ibid., 541–544.

33. Al-Bayati, *Shaykh Mahmud al-Hafidh*, 175–176.

34. Van Bruinessen, "Kurdish Paths to Nation," 36–37.

CONCLUSION: FROM DISTINCTIVENESS TO NATIONALISM— CONTINUING ISSUES OF KURDISH COLLECTIVE IDENTITY

1. In the Ararat (Agri Dag) revolt, which took place in eastern Turkey, on the Iranian border, between 1928 and 1931, a central role was played by the Khoybun nationalist movement, which was led by modern, educated Kurdish activists from Turkey who had orga-

nized it while in exile in Syria. The actual fighters, however, came from tribes in the Ararat area.

2. On the beginnings of the Kurdish national movement, see Wadie Jwaideh's pioneering research in *The Kurdish National Movement: Its Origins and Development*. See also the profound and detailed book by Robert Olson, *The Emergence of Kurdish Nationalism and the Shaykh Said Rebellion, 1880–1925*. For a comparative view of relations between the Kurds and the states, see Denise Natali, *The Kurds and the State*.

BIBLIOGRAPHY

Abu Manneh, Butrus A. "The Naqshbandiyya in Ottoman Lands in the Early 19th Century." *Die Welt des Islam*, vol. 22 (1984): 1–36.

———. *Studies in Islam and the Ottoman Empire in the 19th Century*. Istanbul: Isis Press, n.d.

Ahmad, Kamal Madhar. *Kurdistan during the First World War*. London: Saqi Books, 1994.

Ainsworth, William Francis. *Travels and Researches in Asia Minor, Mesopotamia, Chaldea, and Armenia*. 2 vols. London: John Parker, 1842.

Allen, William Edward David, and Paul Muratoff. *Caucasian Battlefields: A History of Wars on the Turco-Caucasian Border*. Cambridge: Cambridge University Press, 1953.

Amedroz, H. F. "The Marwanid Dynasty at Mayyafariqin in the Tenth and Eleventh Centuries AD." *Journal of the Royal Asiatic Society* (January 1903): 123–154.

Amin, Muhammad Zaki. *Khulasat ta'rikh al-kurd wa kurdistan min aqdam al-ʿusur hatta al-ʿan (Summary of the History of the Kurds and Kurdistan from the Most Ancient Times up to the Present)*. Cairo: Al-Saada Press, 1939 (Arabic).

Amitai-Preiss, Reuven. "The North Syrian Frontier between the Mamelukes and the Mongols." *Hamizrach Hehadash*, vol. 38 (1996): 17–25 (Hebrew).

Anderson, Benedict. *Imagined Communities*. London and New York, Verso, 1991.

Arfa, Hassan. *The Kurds: An Historical and Political Study*. London: Oxford University Press, 1966.

Asatrian, Garnik. "Prolegomena to the Study of Kurds." *Iran and Caucasus*, vol. 13 (2003): 1–58.

Aslan, Sulayman Azad. "Clashes of Agencies: Formation and Failure of Early Kurdish Nationalism, 1918–1922." PhD thesis, University of London, 2007.

Averianov, P. I. *Kurdi b voinakh Rossii k Persii i Turkei v techeniye 19 stoletia (The Kurds in the Russian Wars with Persia and Turkey in the Nineteenth Century)*. Tiflis (Tbilisi): Press of the General Command of the Caucasus Military Region, 1900 (Russian).

Badem, Candan. *The Ottoman Crimean War (1853–1856)*. Leiden and Boston: Brill, 2010.

Bajalan, Djene Rhys. "Sheref Khan's *Sharafnama*: Kurdish Ethno-Politics in the Early Modern World, Its Meaning, and Its Legacy." *Iran Studies*, vol. 45 (2012): 795–818.

———. "Between Conformism and Separatism: A Kurdish Students' Association in Istanbul, 1912–1914." *Middle Eastern Studies*, vol. 49 (2013): 805–823.

Al-Baladhuri, Ahmad Ibn Yahya Ibn Jabbar. *Futuh al-Buldan*. Beirut: Dar al-nashr lil-jamaʿiin, 1985.

Bani Ardalan, Emir Husraw ibn Muhammad. *Khronika—Istoriya Kniazhestva Bani Ardalan (Chronicles—History of the Princedom of Bani Ardalan)*. Translation from Persian to Russian and edited, with an introduction, by E. I. Vasileva. Moscow, 1984.

Barzani, Massoud. *Mustafa Barzani and the Kurdish Liberation Movement*. With an introduction by Ahmed Ferhadi. New York: Palgrave Macmillan, 2003.

Al-Bayati, ʿAbd al-Rahman Idris. *Shaykh Mahmud al-Hafidh wa-al-nufuz al-Britani fi Kurdistan al-ʿIraq hata ʿam 1925 (Shaykh Mahmud al-Hafidh and the British Influence in Iraqi Kurdistan until 1925)*. London: Dar al-Hikma, 2005 (Arabic).

Bedir Khan, Prince Sureya. "The Case of Kurdistan against Turkey 1928." Issued by the Kurdish Independence League, 1928. Reprinted in *International Journal of Kurdish Studies*, vol. 18 (2004): 113–154.

Bell, Gertrude Lowthian. *Amurath to Amurath*. London: Macmillan, 1924.

Al-Bidlisi, Sharaf Khan al-Din. *Sharafnama, Fi Ta'rikh al-Duwal wa-al-Imarat al-Kurdiyah*, 2 vols. Translation into Arabic by Muhammad ʿAli ʿUni, edited by Yahia al-Khashab. Damascus: Dar al-zaman liltibʿat wa-a-nashr wa-al-tawzʿi, 2006.

Bitlisi, Sharaf al-Din. *The Sharafnama, or, The History of the Kurdish Nation*. Book 1. Translation into English and commentaries by M. R. Izady. Costa Mesa, CA: Mazda, 2005.

Blau, Joyce. "Kurdish Written Literature." In *Kurdish Culture and Identity*, edited by Philip Kreyenbroek and Christine Allison, 20–28. London: Zed Books, 1996.

———. "Le Développement de la littérature kurde dans la cité." *Journal of Kurdish Studies*, vol. 3 (1998–2000): 85–91.

———. "Kurdish Language and Literature." Institut Kurde de Paris (n.d.). Available at: www.institutkurde.org/en/language/.

Blaum, Paul A. "From Steppe to Empire: The Turkmens in Iraq." *International Journal of Kurdish Studies*, vol. 21, nos. 1–2 (2007): 37–68.

Bozarslan, Hamit. "Remarques sur l'histoire des relations kurdo-arméniennes." *Journal of Kurdish Studies*, vol. 1 (1995): 55–69.

———. "Les Relations kurdo-arméniennes, 1894–1896." *Revue du Monde Arménien modern et contemporain*, vol. 4 (1998): 23–33.

Bruinessen, Martin van. "Kurdish Tribes and the State of Iran: The Case of the Simko Revolt." In *The Conflict and State in Iran and Afghanistan*, edited by Richard Tapper, 364–400. London and Canberra: Croom Helm; New York: St. Martin's Press, 1983.

———. *Agha, Shaikh, and State: The Social and Political Structures of Kurdistan*. London: Zed Books, 1992.

———. "Nationalisme kurde et ethnicités intra-kurdes" ("Kurdish Nationalism and Competing Ethnic Loyalties"). *Peuples Méditerranées* ("Les Kurdes et les États"), nos. 68–69 (1994): 15–37. Available at: http://bnk.institutkurde.org/images/pdf/5CR97JM6UK.pdf.

———. "Kurdistan in the 16th and 17th Centuries as Reflected in Evliya Celebi's *Seyahatname*." *Journal of Kurdish Studies*, vol. 3 (1998–2000).

———. *Mullas, Sufis, and Heretics: The Role of Religion in Kurdish Society*. Istanbul: Isis Press, 2000.

———. "The Qadiriyya and the Lineages of Qadiri Shaykhs in Kurdistan." In Martin van Bruinessen, *Mullas, Sufis, and Heretics: The Role of Religion in Kurdish Society*, 213–230. Istanbul: Isis Press, 2000.

———. "The Sadate Nehri or Gilanzade of Central Kurdistan." In *The Qadiriya Order*, a special issue of *Journal of History of Sufism*, vols. 1–2 (2000): 79–91.

———. "Ehmedi Khani's *Mem u Zin* and Its Role in the Emergence of Kurdish National Awareness." In *Essays on the Origins of Kurdish Nationalism*, edited by Abbas Vali. Costa Mesa, CA: Mazda, 2003.

———. "Kurdish Paths to Nation." In *The Kurds: Nationalism and Politics*, edited by Faleh A. Jabar and Hosham Dawod, 21–48. London, San Francisco, and Beirut: Saqi, 2006.

Bruinessen, Martin van, and Hendrik Boeschoten, eds. *Evliya Celebi in Diyarbekir*. Translation, with commentary and introduction, by the editors. Leiden and New York: E. J. Brill, 1988.

Çetinsaya, Gökhan. *Ottoman Administration of Iraq, 1890–1908*. London and New York: Routledge, 2006.

Ceylan, Ebubekir. *The Ottoman Origins of Modern Iraq*. London and New York: I. B. Tauris, 2011.

Al-Damaluji, Sadik. *Imarat Bahdinan al-Kurdiyya aw Imarat al-ʿAmadiya (The Kurdish Emirate of Bahdinan and the Emirate of ʿAmadiya)*. Irbil: Dar Aaras lil Tabaʿt wa al-Nashr, wizarat al-tarbiyya, 1999 (Arabic).

Dankoff, Robert, ed. *Evliya Celebi in Bitlis*. Translation, with commentary and an introduction, by the editor. Leiden and New York: E. J. Brill, 1990.

Driver, G. R. "Studies in Kurdish History." *Bulletin of the School of Oriental Studies*, vol. 2, no. 3 (1922): 491–511.

———. "The Name Kurd and Its Philological Connections." *Journal of the Royal Asiatic Society of Great Britain and Ireland*, vol. 55, no. 3 (July 1923): 393–403.

Eagleton, William. *The Kurdish Republic of 1946*. London: Oxford University Press, 1963.

Edmonds, C. J. *Kurds, Turks, and Arabs: Politics, Travel, and Research in Northern Iraq, 1919–1925*. London: Oxford University Press, 1957.

Eppel, Michael. "The Demise of the Kurdish Emirates: The Impact of Ottoman Reforms and International Relations on Kurdistan During the First Half of the Nineteenth Century." *Middle Eastern Studies*, vol. 44 (2008): 237–258.

Eskander, Saad. "Southern Kurdistan under Britain's Mesopotamian Mandate: From Separation to Incorporation, 1920–1923." *Middle Eastern Studies*, vol. 37, no. 2 (2001): 153–180.

Fraser, James Baillie. *Travels in Koordistan, Mesopotamia, and Including an Account of Parts of Those Countries Hitherto Unvisited by Europeans: With Sketches of the Character and Manners of the Koordish and Arab Tribes*. 2 vols. London: Richard Bentley, 1840.

Galleti, Mirella. "The Italian Contribution to Kurdology (13th to 20th Century)." *Journal of Kurdish Studies*, vol. 1 (1995): 97–112.

Gunter, Michael M. *Historical Dictionary of the Kurds*, 2nd ed. Lanham, MD: Scarecrow Press, 2011.

Hammer-Purgstall, Joseph von. *Histoire de l'Empire Ottoman*. Vol. 3, book III. Paris: Imprimerie de Béthune et Plon, 1844.

Hanioglu, Sukru. *The Young Turks in Opposition*. New York and Oxford: Oxford University Press, 1995.

Hassanpour, Amir. "Baradost." In *Encyclopaedia Iranica* (December 15, 1988). Available at: www.iranicaonline.org/articles/baradust-kurdish-bradost-name-of-kurdish-tribe-region-mountain-range-river-and-amirate.

———. *Nationalism and Language in Kurdistan, 1918–1985*. San Francisco: Mellen Research University Press, 1992.

———. "Dimdim." In *Encyclopaedia Iranica* (December 15, 1995; updated November 28, 2011). Available at: www.iranicaonline.org/articles/dimdim.

———. "The Making of Kurdish Identity: Pre-20th Century Historical and Literary Sources." In *Essays on the Origins of Kurdish Nationalism*, edited by Abbas Vali. Costa Mesa, CA: Mazda, 2003.

Hovanissian, Richard G. *Armenia on the Road to Independence, 1918*. Berkeley and Los Angeles: University of California Press, 1967.

Ibn al-Athir. *Al-Kamil fi al-Ta'rikh*. Vols. 6, 9, 10, 11. Beirut: Dar Beirut liltaba't wa-al-nashr, 1966.

———. *The Annals of the Saljuq Turks: Selections from al-Kamil fi al-Ta'rikh of 'Izz al-Din Ibn al-Athir*. Translation and annotations by D. S. Richards. London and New York: Routledge Curzon, 200).

———. *The Chronicle of Ibn al-Athir for the Crusading Period*, from *Al-Kamil fi al-Ta'rikh*, part 1, *The Years 491–541/1097–1146: The Coming of the Franks and the Muslim Response*. Translation by D. S. Richards. Aldershot and Burlington: Ashgate Publishing, 2006. Ibn Hawqal, Abi Al-Qasim al-Nusaibi. *Kitab surat al-ard*. Beirut: Manshurat dar maktabat al-Hayat, 1979.

Ibn Khaldun. *Ta'rikh al-'alamat*. Vol. 4. Beirut: Dar al-Katib al-Lubnani, 1958.

Izady, Mehrdad R. *The Kurds: A Concise History and Fact Book*. New York: Taylor & Francis, 1992.

———. "An Introduction to the *Sharafnama*." In Sharaf al-Din Bitlisi, *The Sharafnama, or The History of the Kurdish Nation*, book 1, translation into English and commentaries by M. R. Izady, xxvi–xxvii. Costa Mesa, CA: Mazda, 2005.

Jalil, Jalile. *Vosstaniye Kurdov 1880 goda* (*The Insurrection of the Kurds of the Year 1880*). Moscow: Nauka, 1966 (Russian).

———. *Kurdi osmanskoi imperii pervoy polovine 19 veka* (*The Kurds of the Ottoman Empire in the First Half of the Nineteenth Century*). Moscow: Nauka, 1970 (Russian).

——— (Jalilov, Jalil J.). *Kurdskij grodicheskij epos "Zlotorukij Khan."* Moscow: Nauka, 1967 (Russian).

James, Boris. "Uses and Values of the Term *Kurd* in the Arabic Medieval Literary Sources." Seminar at the American University of Beirut (AUB), Center for Arab and Middle Eastern Studies (CAMES), April 2006, Beirut. Available at: http://halshs/archives-ouvertesfr/halshs-00350119.

Joseph, John. *The Nestorians and Their Neighbors*. Princeton, NJ: Princeton University Press, 1961.

Jwaideh, Wadie. *The Kurdish National Movement: Its Origins and Development*. Syracuse, NY: Syracuse University Press, 2006.

Kerim, Mihemmedi Mela. "Mewlewi: A Great Poet and '*Alim* of Southern Kurdistan." Translation from Sorani by Homer Dizeyee and Michael L. Chyet. In *Islam des kurdes: Les annales de l'autre Islam*. Paris: INALCO-ERISM, no. 5, 1998.

Khalfin, H. A. *Borba za Kurdistan* (*Kurdskiy vopros v mezhdunarodnih otnosheniah xix beka*)(*The Struggle for Kurdistan* [*The Kurdish Question in International Relations of the Nineteenth Century*]). Moscow: Izdatestvo Vostochnei Literaturi, 1963 (Russian).

Khani, Ahmed. *Mam i Zin*, kriticeskiy tekst, pervod, predislovie, i ukazateli M. B. Rudenko. (Scientific edition of *Mam u Zin*, translation, introduction, commentaries, and notes by M. B. Rudenko). Moscow: Nauka, 1962 (Russian).

Kilic, Mehmet Firat. "Sheikh Ubeidallah's Movement." MA thesis, Bilkent University, Ankara, 2003.

Kinneir, John MacDonald. *A Geographical Memoir of the Persian Empire*. London: John Murray, 1813; reprint, New York: Arno Press, 1973.

Kirmanj, Sherko. *Identity and Nation in Iraq*. Boulder, CO: Lynne Rienner Publishers, 2013.

Klein, Janet. "Kurdish Nationalists and Non-nationalist Kurdists: Rethinking Minority

Nationalism and the Dissolution of the Ottoman Empire, 1908–1909." *Nations and Nationalism*, vol. 13, no. 1 (2007): 135–153.

———. "Conflict and Collaboration: Rethinking Kurdish-Armenian Relations in the Hamidian Period, 1876–1909." In *Identity and Identity Formation in the Ottoman World*, edited by Baki Tezcan and Karl K. Barbir, 153–166. Madison: University of Wisconsin Press, 2007.

———. *The Margins of Empire: Kurdish Militias in the Ottoman Tribal Zone.* Stanford, CA: Stanford University Press, 2011.

Klieman, Aaron S. *The Foundation of British Policy in the Arab World: The Cairo Conference of 1921.* Baltimore and London: Johns Hopkins University Press, 1970.

Kunt, I. Metin. *The Sultan's Servants: The Transformation of Ottoman Provincial Government, 1550–1650.* New York: Columbia University Press, 1983.

Kurdo, J. *Kurdistan: The Origins of Kurdish Civilization.* Stockholm: J. Rashid, 1988.

Layard, Austen Henry. *Popular Account of Discoveries at Nineveh.* London: John Murray, 1851.

———. *Discoveries in the Ruins of Nineveh and Babylon: With Travels in Armenia and Kurdistan, and the Desert.* New York: Harper & Bros., 1853.

———. *Nineveh and Its Remains.* Elibron Classics, 2005 (unabridged facsimile of the edition published by John Murray in 1854).

Lazarev, M. C. *Kurdistan i Kurdskaya Problema (90e godi 19 veka—1917) (Kurdistan and the Kurdish Problem [from the 1890s to 1917]).* Moscow: Izdatelstvo Nauka, 1964. [Russian].

Limbert, John. "Origins and Appearances of the Kurds in the Pre-Islamic Iran." *Iranian Studies*, vol. 1, no. 2 (Spring 1968): 41–51.

Longrigg, Stephen Hemsley. *Four Centuries of Modern Iraq.* Oxford: Clarendon Press, 1925.

Lukitz, Liora. *A Quest in the Middle East: Gertrude Bell and the Making of Modern Iraq.* London and New York: I. B. Tauris, 2006.

MacKenzie, D. N. "Origins of the Kurds." *Transactions of the Philological Society* (1961): 68–86.

Malcolm, John. *Sketches of Persia from the Journals of a Traveller in the East.* Vol. 2. London: John Murray, 1827.

Martin, Lawrence. *The Treaties of Peace 1919–1923.* New York: Carnegie Endowment for International Peace, 1924.

Al-Mas'udi, Abu al-Hasan 'Ali bin Husayn bin 'Ali. *Muruj al-Dhahab.* Vol. 3. Cairo: Dar al-fikr, 1937.

Maunsell, Francis Richard. "Kurdistan." *Geographical Journal*, vol. 3 (February 1894): 81–92. Available at: www.jstor.org/stable/1774022.

———. "Central Kurdistan." *Geographical Journal*, vol. 18 (August 1901): 121–141. Available at: www.jstor.org/stable/1775333.

McDowall, David. *A Modern History of the Kurds.* London and New York: I. B. Tauris, 2005.

Meiseles, Susan. *Kurdistan: In the Shadow of History.* Introduction by Martin van Bruinessen. Chicago: University of Chicago Press, 2008.

Minorsky, Vladimir. *Studies in Caucasian History.* London: Taylor's Foreign Press, 1953.

———. "Kurds." In *The Encyclopaedia of Islam*, vol. 4, *Iran-Kha*, edited by E. J. van Donzel. Leiden: E. J. Brill, 1998.

———. "Annazids." In *The Encyclopaedia of Islam*, vol. 1, edited by M. Th. Houtsma, T. W. Arnold, and R. Basset, 512–513. Leiden: E. J. Brill, 1913.

Mirawdeli, Kamal. *Love and Existence: An Analytical Study of Ahmadi Khani's Tragedy of Mem u Zin.* Bloomington, IN: Authorhouse, 2012.

Monshi, Eskander Beg. *History of Shah 'Abbas the Great (Taarik-e 'alamara-ye 'abbasi).* 2 vols. Translation by Roger M. Savory. Boulder, CO: Westview, 1978.

Monteith, William. *Kars and Erzeroum with the Campaigns of Prince Paskiewich.* London: Longmans, Brown, Green and Longmans, 1851.

Natali, Denise. *The Kurds and the State: Evolving National Identity in Iraq, Turkey, and Iran.* Syracuse, NY: Syracuse University Press, 2005.

Nieuwenhuis, Tom. *Politics and Society in Early Modern Iraq: Mamluk Pashas, Tribal Shayks, and Local Rule Between 1802–1831.* The Hague and Boston: M. Nijhoff, 1982.

Nikitine, Basile. "Les Kurdes racontés par eux-mêmes." *L'Asie Française* (1925): 148–157.

———. *Les Kurdes: Études sociologiques et historiques.* Paris: Éditions d'Aujourd'hui, 1956.

———. *Al-Kurd dirasat sosiologiya wa-taarikhiya.* Translation from French into Arabic by Nuri Talabani. London: Dar al-Saqi, 2001 (Arabic).

Nikitine, Basile, and C. E. Bosworth. "Rawwandiz." In *Encyclopedia of Islam*, 2nd ed. Available at: http://referenceworks.brillonline.com/entries/encyclopaedia-of-islam-2/rawandiz-COM_0914?s.num=0&s.rows=20&s.mode=DEFAULT&s.f.s2_parent=encyclopaedia-of-islam-2&s.start=0&s.q=rawandiz

Olson, Robert. *The Siege of Mosul and Ottoman-Persian Relations, 1718–1743.* Bloomington: Indiana University Press, 1975.

———. *The Emergence of Kurdish Nationalism and the Shaykh Said Rebellion, 1880–1925.* Austin: University of Texas Press, 1989.

———. "Battle for Kurdistan: The Churchill-Cox Correspondence Regarding the Creation of the State of Iraq, 1921–1923." *Kurdish Studies*, vol. 5 (1992): 29–34.

———. *The Kurdish Question and Turkish-Iranian Relations from World War I to 1998.* Costa Mesa, CA: Mazda, 1998.

O'Shea, Maria T. *Trapped between the Map and Reality: Geography and Perceptions of Kurdistan.* New York: Routledge, 2004.

Owen, Roger. *The Middle East in the World Economy.* London: Methuen, 1981.

Ozoglu, Hakan. "'Nationalism' and Kurdish Notables in the Late Ottoman–Early Republican Era." *International Journal of Middle Eastern Studies*, vol. 33 (2001): 343–409.

———. *Kurdish Notables and the Ottoman State: Evolving Identities, Competing Loyalties, and Shifting Boundaries.* Albany: State University of New York Press, 2004.

———. "The Impact of Islam on Kurdish Identity Formation in the Middle East." In *The Evolution of Kurdish Nationalism*, edited by Mohammad M. A. Ahmad and Michael Gunter. Costa Mesa, CA: Mazda, 2007.

Parvaneh, Pourshariati. *Decline and Fall of the Sassanian Empire: The Sassanian-Parthian Confederacy and the Arab Conquest of Iran.* London: I. B. Tauris, 2009.

Perry, John R. *Karim Khan Zand: A History of Iran, 1747–1779.* Chicago and London: University of Chicago Press, 1979.

Pirbal, Ferhad. "*Sharafnama*, the Book." *Kurdish Globe* (Erbil-Hewler), August 30, 2007.

Pistor-Hatam, Anja. "Sheikh 'Ubaidullah's Revolt and the Kurdish Invasion of Iran—Attempts at a New Assessment." *Journal of Kurdish Studies*, vol. 4 (2001–2002): 19–30.

Rawlinson, H. C. "Notes on a Journey from Tabriz, through Persian Kurdistan, to the Ruins of Takhti-Soleiman." *Journal of the Royal Geographical Society*, vol. 10 (1841): 1–64.

Reid, James J. "Rozhiki Revolt, 1065/1655." *Journal of Kurdish Studies*, vol. 3 (1998–2000): 13–40.

Reynolds, Michael A. "Abdurrezak Bedirhan: Ottoman Kurd and Russophile in the Twilight of Empire." *Kritika: Explorations in Russian and Eurasian History*, vol. 12, no. 2 (2011): 411–450.

Rich, Claudius J. *Narrative of a Residence in Koordistan*. 2 vols. London: James Duncan, 1836; reprint, Westmead, Farnborough, UK: Gregg International Publishers, 1972.

Rudenko, M. B. "Kurdskaya literatura XVII veka" ("Kurdish Literature of the Seventeenth Century"). *Narody Azii i Afriki*, no. 3 (1971): 93–105 (Russian).

Safrastian, Arshak. *Kurds and Kurdistan*. London: Harvill Press, 1948.

Salibi, Kamal, and Yusuf K. Khoury, eds. *The Missionary Herald: Reports from Northern Iraq 1833–1847*. Vol. 1. Amman: Royal Institute for Interfaith Studies, 2002.

Sandwith, Humphrey. *A Narrative: The Siege of Kars*. London: John Murray, 1856.

Sazonov, Serge. *Fateful Years 1909–1916*. London: Jonathan Cape, 1928; reprint, New York: Kraus, 1971.

Shakely, Farhad. *Kurdish Nationalism in MAM U ZIN of Ahmad-i Khani*. Brussels: Kurdish Institute of Brussels, 1992.

———. "The Naqshbandi Shaiks of Hawraman and the Heritage of Khalidiyya-Mujadidiyya in Kurdistan." *International Journal of Kurdish Studies*, vol. 19 (2005).

———. "Classical and Modern Kurdish Poetry." Part 1. *Kurdish Globe* (Erbil-Hewler), February 28, 2009.

———. "Classical and Modern Kurdish Poetry." Part 2. *Kurdish Globe* (Erbil-Hewler), March 13, 2009.

———. "Haji Qadir Koyi." *Kurdish Globe* (Erbil-Hewler), February 7, 2010.

Shedd, Mary Lewis. *A Measure of a Man: William A. Shedd of Persia: A Biography*. New York: George H. Doran Company, 1922.

Shiel, J. "Notes on a Journey from Tabriz, through Kurdistan, via Van, Bitlis, Se'ert, and Erbil to Sulaymaniah, in July and August, 1836." *Journal of the Royal Geographical Society*, vol. 8 (1838): 54–101.

Smith, Anthony. "The Nation: Invented, Imagined, Reconstructed?" *Millennium: Journal of International Studies*, vol. 20, no. 3 (1991): 353–368.

Soane, Ely Banister. *To Mesopotamia and Kurdistan in Disguise, with Historical Notices of the Kurdish Tribes and the Chaldeans of Kurdistan*. 2nd ed. London: John Murray, 1926.

Speer, Robert E. *The "Hakim Sabih," the Foreign Doctor: A Biography of Joseph Plumb Cochran, MD, of Persia*. New York: Fleming H. Revell, 1911.

Strabo. *The Geography of Strabo* [1930]. Vols. 5 and 7. Translation into English by Horace Leonard Jones. Reprint, London: William Heinemann, 1961.

Le Strange, Guy. *The Lands of the Eastern Caliphate Mesopotamia, Persia, and Central Asia from the Moslem Conquest to the Time of Timur* [1905]. Reprint, London: Frank Cass, 1966.

Strohmeier, Martin. *Crucial Images in the Presentation of Kurdish National Identity Heroes and Patriots, Traitors and Foes*. Leiden and Boston: Brill, 2003.

Al-Tabari (Abu Jaʿafar Muhammad bin Jarir al-Tabari). *History of Tabari (Taʾrikh al-rusul wa-al-muluk*), vol. 15, *The Crisis of the Early Caliphate.* Translation by R. Stephen Humphreys. Albany: State University of New York Press, 1990.

―――. *History of Tabari*, vol. 14, *The Conquest of Iran.* Translation by G. Rex Smith. Albany: State University of New York Press, 1994.

Tavernier, Jean-Baptiste. *Les Six voyages en turquie, en perse, et aux indes (Six Voyages to Turkey, Persia, and India).* Vol. 2. Paris: François Maspero, 1981.

Taylor, Gordon. *Fever and Thirst: Dr. Grant and the Christian Tribes of Kurdistan.* Chicago: Academy Chicago Publishers, 2005.

Tejel Gorgas, Jordi. "Urban Mobilization in Iraqi Kurdistan during the British Mandate: Sulaimaniya 1918–1930." *Middle Eastern Studies*, vol. 44, no. 4 (2008): 537–552.

Vali, Abbas, ed. *Essays on the Origins of Kurdish Nationalism.* Costa Mesa, CA: Mazda, 2003.

―――. *Kurds and the State in Iran: The Making of Kurdish Identity.* London: I. B. Tauris, 2011.

Valle, Pietro Della. *The Pilgrim: The Travels of Pietro Della Valle.* Translated and abridged, with an introduction, by George Bull. London, Sydney, Auckland, and Johannesburg: Hutchinson, 1989.

―――. *Rihlat Dillavalle ila al-ʿIraq (Matlaʿi al-kurn al-sabiʿi ʿashar) (The Journey of Della Valle to Iraq [Beginnings of the Seventeenth Century]).* Translation from Italian to Arabic, and commentaries, by Butrus Hadad. Beirut: al-dar al-Arabiyya lilmawsuʿat, 2006 (Arabic).

Vasileva, E. I. *Yugo-Vostochniy Kurdistan b 17—nachale 19 veki—ocharki istorii emiratov Ardalan i Baban (Southeastern Kurdistan from the Seventeenth Century to the Beginning of the Nineteenth Century—Chapters in the History of the Emirates of Ardalan and Baban).* Moscow: Academia Nauk USSR, Nauka, 1991 (Russian).

Villard, Ugo Monneret de. *Il Libro della peregrinazine nelle parti d'oriente di frate Ricoldo da Montecroce.* Romae Institutum Historicum ff. Praedicatorum, Romae ad S. Sabinae, 1948 (Italian).

Wigram, W. A., and Edgar T. A. Wigram. *The Cradle of Mankind: Life in Eastern Kurdistan.* London: Adam and Charles Black, 1914.

Wilson, Arnold Talbot. *Loyalties: Mesopotamia, 1914–1917: A Personal and Historical Record.* Vol. 1. London: Oxford University Press/Humphrey Milford, 1930; reissued 1936.

―――. *Mesopotamia, 1917–1920: A Personal and Historical Record.* Vol. 2. London: Oxford University Press, 1931.

Wilson, Samuel Graham. *Persian Life and Customs.* New York, Chicago, and Toronto: Fleming H. Revell, 1900; AMS edition, 1973.

Wood, Richard. *The Early Correspondence of Richard Wood, 1831–1841.* Edited by A. B. Cunningham. London: Royal Historical Society, 1966.

Woods, John E. *The Aqqoyunlu: Clan, Confederation, Empire.* Minneapolis and Chicago: Bibliotheca Islamica, 1976.

Xenophon. *Anabasis* [1922]. Translation by Carleton L. Brownson, revised by John Dilley. Revised, Cambridge, MA: Harvard University Press, 1998.

Zurcher, Erik Jan. *The Unionist Factor: The Role of the Committee of Union and Progress in the Turkish National Movement 1905–1926.* London and New York: I. B. Tauris, 2003.

―――. *Turkey: A Modern History.* London and New York: I. B. Tauris, 2003.

Page numbers in *italics* refer to illustrations.